The Platform Scripture of the Sixth Patriarch
- Deyi Edition
六祖法寶壇經 德異本

The Platform Scripture of the Sixth Patriarch - Deyi Edition
(六祖法寶壇經 德異本)

Author: Recorded by Disciple Fahai (門人 法海集)
Translated and Commented by: Jechang Kim, Ph.D. (김제창 옮김)
Publisher: 명상인문아카데미 AOMA (Academy of Meditative Arts)
Published by: AOMA
Original Publisher Registration Date: September 13, 2006
Current Publisher Registration Number: No. 2025-000071
Address: 1F, Unit 101, 104-6 Pilundae-ro, Jongno-gu, Seoul, Republic of Korea
Phone: +82-10-7202-2156
Email: aomameditation@gmail.com
Website: www.aomayoga.com / www.aomayoga.co.kr
Blog: https://blog.naver.com/aomayoga
YouTube: https://www.youtube.com/@aomameditation3497
Facebook: https://www.facebook.com/aomayoga
GemmaAi Companion: https://chatgpt.com/g/g-vtKw84IR8-gemma-gemmayerin
Printed by: Yesol Press
First Edition, First Printing: August 15, 2025
Price: ₩29,000 KRW
ISBN: 979-11-994015-0-1 (93150)
© AOMA 2025
All rights reserved. No part of this publication may be reproduced, distributed, or transmitted in any form or by any means without prior written permission from the translator, Jechang Kim.
Quotations for academic purposes are permitted with proper citation.

六祖法寶壇經 德異本
육조법보단경 덕이본

The Platform Scripture

of the Sixth Patriarch

- Deyi Edition

門人 法海集
문인 법해집

Recorded by Disciple Fahai

Translated by
Jechang Kim, PhD

김제창 옮김

Foreword	*S. E. Bhelke*	*7*
Translator's Preface		*17*
Introductory Commentary	*Jechang Kim*	*30*
Acknowledgements		*46*
Reader's Notes		*51*
독자 참고사항		*56*
The Platform Scripture		*61*

Foreword

to the Deyi Translation

by S. E. Bhelke

The human being, usually called a man, is actually a part of the indivisible cosmic consciousness appearing on the epistemic level for its comprehension through the faculties he has by his nature. The faculties are limited — limited to the forms of receiving and responding back to the cosmic consciousness and hence what are available are parts of the cosmic consciousness. At the epistemic level of humans the impressions are received through the channels of faculties and assume a presentable structure of parts of the cosmic consciousness. This is due to the inherent drive of the consciousness to realize its true, i.e., the original, nature. In this attempt, the first stage is receiving and collecting impressions which are further arranged in a definite order to give their true nature as well as to make them properly comprehensible to humans on the level humans live and interact as a part of presenting themselves outwardly to other human agents in particular, and to the whole of the cosmic consciousness in general. This is a permanent process of functioning of the consciousness through various faculties bestowed upon him by nature.

The most prominent level for this purpose, through which impressions are collected and organized systematically to create the world of human creation, is epistemic. We are basically concerned with this world of human creation which is epistemic at its core expressing its nature in a dynamic aspect of the consciousness, which is, in fact, the Becoming appearance of the Being. The dialectic of Becoming and Being is a dialogue between them focusing on inner as well as outer interactions between the individuated parts of consciousness and the indivisible whole of the cosmic consciousness, on the one hand, and amongst parts themselves, on the other.

The next stage of the epistemic level is, for us presently, more important. In this stage, the content of the impressions is conveyed in the form of a message. This is the level on which the becoming aspect of the consciousness becomes more approachable and tangible as it is a bridge between the onticity and epistemicity of the consciousness. This bridge is usually known to be a medium and in various realms of human life it assumes its presentable form or garb as required and is suitable to the realm to which it belongs.

In the present context of our deliberations, this medium is a verbal language capturing the glimpses of the consciousness which is to be grasped for epistemic and praxiotic purposes including axiotic aura of both. The content of the message ultimately aims to reveal the glimpses of the consciousness and presents them through the required medium, consistent with the context in which it operates effectively. There is a consistent and continuous flow of the process of conveying the content from one point to another through societies, cultures and traditions.

The content of the message is the same, though it appears and presents itself according to the specific parameters of each context. Although a man is the same everywhere in geographical areas and historical durations, his expressions of the contents of his experience of consciousness differ due to his positions determined by the geography and history of his being as an agent in the context of the dynamic process of the flow of life. All rivers flow, all rivers have their own pace, their own modes, their own styles and their own waves, but the water is the same. Similarly, while the man, the content and the consciousness are the same, their appearances, modes and styles of being are varied in shapes, speeds, rhythms and proportions.

This difference in each presentation makes each presentation unique and independent. When social, cultural, or historical interactions overlap and crisscross, the tone and tune of the medium change, no longer remaining identical. Although the content is accumulated and transitions between styles occur at a higher state, ensuring a smooth transition remains a significant challenge. A journey at this stage becomes an adventure to grasp the correct content presented through different media.

On the language level, it opens a door of translation. A translation is not a lexicographical exercise, but it is a way to catch the intended core of the message. The catching of the content depends on several factors, mainly on an interpretation through analysis. This is either a shift or a detour from one system of symbols to another. In this transitional stage, there are many pitfalls in understanding symbols in use and preserving their original spirit. The main obstacle in this task is of a lexicographical exercise which, at times, turns out to be misleading for grasping the correct and intended core of the content of the message.

The present work is one of the most adventurous attempts to put before us a differing version of the given text of the Buddhist tradition. The translator of this work, Dr. Jechang Kim, has politely taken the big and bold challenge to present a different understanding of the work — the Platform Scripture.

The work studied by Dr. Jechang Kim itself is a translation of a type of original Buddhist text written much earlier on the horizon of the Indian tradition and culture. The concepts were translated from the Sanskrit version to the Chinese version. Nevertheless, there is more than one translation and, hence, translations differing from one another, translations proposing, in a way, differing interpretations of the same text. It must be noted clearly with confidence that a version presented by Dr. Jechang Kim is worthy because it supports the authenticity of the original tradition of Buddhism as propounded in the classical Buddhism by great scholars and practitioners of Buddhist practices.

The original Pāli/Sanskrit concepts are the culmination of the highly specialized dialogue in the Indo-Chinese tradition between many stalwart scholars of different systems of Indian philosophy. Any new version of the content of the original text has to be consistent and coherent with it to be an authentic version of interpretation and understanding. Although any scholar of the subject carries a credit for his contribution, he does not shed off his identity of the thought tradition in which he has emerged, with his contributions showing as a novelty. This criterion of consistency and coherence does not strip away the creativity of the contribution; rather, it fortifies the authenticity of the author as belonging to the established tradition.

The present work has a great implication for human practices developing a yogic way of life and hence, from this point of view, an evaluation of the translation is solicited. As the author of this work has a main focus on the practicing aspect developing as a particular form of yoga, an evaluation of this work has to take heed of the practical employment of Buddhist philosophy as applied to yoga and its practices. The ultimate goal of yoga is to attain a state of realization. This is the philosophical level, and it is expected to build an unbroken continuum of (theoretical) knowledge and (practical) action working together without the help of each other.

The orientation of Dr. Kim's work is targeting the end culmination of yogic practices, and hence his contributions need to be evaluated based on success both in theory and in practice, or in knowledge and action, to attain the ultimate goal of life as realization. Here, realization refer to the realization of man as an agent of the cosmic consciousness, and the process of realization from the agent to his ultimate target, which is obtained by following a designated path. Thus it is a holistic way of philosophy, which is the true content of Buddhist philosophy, though it no longer remains restricted to and constrained within any particular system of philosophy, whether Indian, Western or non-Indian (ascetic), approach to philosophy on theoretical and practical levels simultaneously.

A philosophical approach is based on analysis of whatever data is available for understanding. It appears in specific styles of the content to be grasped and expressed through a medium. The approaches, and hence the styles of approaches, have their own face and mode. This is the basic reason for a multitude of approaches and their results. Each of these approaches is relative to its foundational principles.

The logical organization of these principles bestows us a science. Although all sciences have the same foundation and the same end of reaching the particularity of different sets of basic principles, they show a multiplicity amongst them. It must be noted that such a multiplicity does not presuppose or propose a diagonal opposition amongst them. At a higher level they are to be seen with their unity leading to oneness of the unitary whole. This is the spiritual level of functions of rational philosophical endeavors.

In spirituality, the indivisible wholeness is grasped. It transcends the mundane multiplicity. This cognitive state is transcends the operations of material levels of cognition. It gives a peep into the infinite absolute, which no epistemic means is capable of capturing it; and only consciousness which can grasp it. All human endeavors have this as their ultimate aim to be achieved for completion. A completion takes place by transcending plurality and multitude. Human endeavors take place in the realm of particularized and limited objects, but the ultimate human goal is to transcend this limitation and to realize the indivisible wholeness. All ways or paths aim at the same goal, and in the spiritual realm they are homogeneously united in one path; the royal path of spirituality. There is, and has to be, an ascendance from the philosophical to the spiritual, and it becomes possible with deliberate efforts to tune oneself to ascend as a spiritual agent in the higher domain of spirituality. We get insights into this attempt in Dr. Kim's present work, where he is translating one text to reach a better and more accurate understanding.

The significant point to be taken into consideration about Dr. Kim is that he holds specialty in philosophical approach to tackling an issue, with his actual experiential background of meditation. Here, as I understand, there is a richer understanding of meditation. Dr. Kim has not just compiled but has reconciled different traditions having the same goal to achieve through meditation. Realization is the goal, and meditation is a path to reach the goal. This is no dichotomy of means and end, where means belong to mundane level and the end to the transcendent level. What Dr. Kim is attempting to present before us is the unification of various means or methods to reach the unified end.

This work, in my opinion, is not just a translation in an ordinary sense, but is a richer revised version of the basic core of realization. A high-quality translation gives suggestions of insights to rise to a higher level of understanding the sought content, but Dr. Kim's work gives us a new revelation of the text in its depths on the one hand and light on the other. This makes a translation a creative enterprise which is beyond a mechanical exercise.

In fact, the original Buddhist text is an original contribution in the Buddhist tradition, and with the aid of other systems of philosophical approaches, Dr. Kim gives the text the status of an original, independent text in the widest tradition of meditational practices. He seems to be using this text not just as an academic exercise but for the upliftment of meditational practices on the actual experiential level.

Yoga schools are not gymnastics clubs. Yoga is a way of life where the entire life in all aspects is the ground or a laboratory for finding results leading to balance, peace, harmony and happiness.

On every station of the journey of Yoga we meet the Buddha in a garb or costume matching the texture of the station and, in every appearance the Buddha is the same, his message is the same, though the language codifying the message at every station may differ due to its occasional matching. The Pāli, the Sanskrit, the English and the Chinese versions carry the same Buddha with his same message. This is, for me, the gift offered to us by Dr. Kim.

I know Dr. Kim as a dedicated director for yogic practices of meditation and pray to God to increase his capabilities more and more for the richness of the human race. I praise him from the heart and express my best wishes to Dr. Kim with a concealed desire to see him in more advanced works in the future.

Dr. Subhashachandra Eknath Bhelke

Retired Professor of Philosophy, Savitribai Phule Pune University, Pune, Maharashtra, India

Ex-Director, Somaiya Centre for Jain Studies, Mumbai

Ex-Director for Buddhist Studies, Somaiya, Mumbai

Translator's Preface
for the Deyi Version Translation

by Jechang Kim

Personal Journey and Motivation

My journey toward this translation began in an unexpected field: Western music composition. As a student in the composition department at Seoul National University, I completed my B.A. and M.A. in Western music composition, starting in 1977. As my musical career progressed, however, I began to question the purpose and ultimate goal of both my music and my life. These philosophical inquiries led me, in 1989, to leave my career as a musician completely and to pursue a path toward inner enlightenment.

The path forward was challenging. I sought guidance from various teachers, each offering different approaches. Yet this exposure to diverse methods made maintaining mental and physical balance difficult. In August of 1996, I, alongside my wife, enrolled in the Hathayoga teacher training course of yoga college of Kaivalyadhama Yoga Institute, where I found a profound inspiration in Swami Kuvalayanandaji's scientific approach to spiritual practices such as yoga and meditation. Recognizing that my own inclination toward philosophical inquiry could contribute meaningfully to a scientific understanding of meditation, I entered the philosophy department at Pune University in 1997, dedicating myself to the study and research of meditation techniques.

Initially, my M.Phil. research focused on the concept of Self-realization in Zen Buddhism, specifically through Huineng's teachings as presented in the Dunhuang version of the Platform Scripture, under the guidance of Dr. S. E. Bhelke. This study laid the groundwork for my Ph.D. research, which expanded into a comparative analysis of Zen and Vipassana meditation, focusing closely on the Platform Scripture and the Mahāsatipaṭṭhāna Sutta. By the conclusion of my Ph.D. dissertation in 2008, I observed that the essence of Zen meditation as conveyed in the Platform Scripture aligns remarkably with the principles of Vipassana as outlined in the Mahāsatipaṭṭhāna Sutta, suggesting a common origin between these two practices.

Despite these insights, I was hesitant to publish my findings because of the differing metaphysical assumptions embedded in the enlightenment verses between the Dunhuang version and the anātman (non-self) theory in the Mahāsatipaṭṭhāna Sutta. This uncertainty shifted, however, in 2021 when I encountered the Deyi 德異 version of the Platform Scripture. In this version, Huineng's enlightenment verse aligns more closely with the concept of anātman found in early Buddhism, alleviating my concerns. The Deyi version's assertion of "inherent emptiness" 本來無一物 provides a metaphysical foundation that harmonizes with the teachings of anātman, as explained in the MahāsatipaṭṭhānaSutta.

To clarify this pivotal difference, here is a brief comparison of the enlightenment verses in the Dunhuang and the Deyi versions, which I explore further in the Introductory Commentary below.

The enlightenment verse in the Dunhuang version reads,

菩提本無樹,　　Bodhi has no tree;
明鏡亦無臺.　　The bright mirror has no stand.
佛性常清淨,　　Buddha-nature is forever clear and pure.
何處有塵埃?　　Where could dust be accumulated?

while the one in the Deyi version goes,

菩提本無樹,　　Bodhi has no tree;
明鏡亦非臺.　　The bright mirror has no stand.
本來無一物,　　Fundamentally, there is not a single thing.
何處惹塵埃?　　Where could dust be accumulated?

As seen, the third line of each version differs fundamentally.

(Dunhuang)
Buddha-nature is forever clear and pure.

(Deyi)
Fundamentally, there is not a single thing.

Preface 19

This contrast reflects divergent metaphysical orientations: the Dunhuang version resonates more with the ātman (self) theory of Indian philosophy, while the Deyi version aligns more with the anātman (non-self) theory central to the early Buddhism.

I understood that this seemingly fundamental difference could cause significant discord for Zen practitioners, prompting me to contemplate deeply on how to reconcile these perspectives. Ultimately, this led me to translate the Deyi version as a foundational resource and to consider revising my Ph.D. dissertation to integrate insights from this version.

This discovery underscored the need for a precise and accessible translation that could support meditation practitioners. Without such clarity, practitioners might experience confusion or develop misguided practices. Although demanding, the translation of the Deyi version was felt essential to offer a renewed and reliable text to guide meditators on their journey.

As mentioned above, my Ph.D. research concluded that the Chinese Zen according to the Dunhuang version of the Platform Scripture, as taught by Huineng, and Vipassana meditation as expounded in the Mahāsatipaṭṭhāna Sutta share a common origin and closely aligned principles, despite their seemingly distinct metaphysical assumptions. In the Dunhuang version, the verse emphasizes ātman, resonating with the traditional Indian philosophy, while the Deyi version highlights anātman, aligning with the early Buddhist teachings. This congruence between the Deyi version's enlightenment verse and the anātman principle in the Mahāsatipaṭṭhāna Sutta offered invaluable clarity for my own practice, profoundly informing this translation. This realization not only motivated the translation but also provided an essential link between my academic studies and personal meditative path, helping me to harmonize both traditions in my own journey without conflict.

Furthermore, I intended for this translation to extend beyond academic precision by incorporating insights from lived practice. Previous English translations, while valuable, often lacked the experiential depth derived from dedicated meditation practice. My aim for this translation is to bridge that gap, grounding the work in both scholarly research and direct practice. Following this translation, I plan to revisit the Dunhuang version and publish my Ph.D. dissertation, now further enriched with insights from the Deyi version's alignment with the principles of the early Buddhism.

Translation Challenges and Methodology

The English translation of the Platform Scripture posed several significant challenges:

Expertise in Chinese characters Although I extensively studied the original Chinese text to deepen my Zen meditation practice, I lack formal training in classical Chinese. This limitation made deciphering certain nuances and grammatical structures challenging, particularly when a precise language was essential for conveying Huineng's teachings accurately.

Potential errors in the original text Certain sections of the original Chinese text appear to contain transcription errors. Recognizing possible mistakes in a historical text is challenging, as irregularities may stem from errors or deliberate stylistic choices by the original scribes.

Philosophical variations between the Dunhuang and the Deyi versions Although both versions of the Platform Scripture are attributed to Huineng, the Sixth Patriarch of Chinese Zen Buddhism, they exhibit philosophical differences. Since Huineng was illiterate, his teachings were recorded by his disciples, potentially leading to variations that alter the underlying message. Translating these variations required not only linguistic accuracy but also a comparative philosophical analysis to address doctrinal discrepancies.

Complexity of key terms Not a few Chinese characters, such as xiang 相, se 色, and xing 性 etc., carry multiple meanings. Translating them into English required careful consideration, as prioritizing character accuracy could obscure the intended meaning, while focusing solely on meaning risked inconsistencies.

Personal physical and mental strain   Having dedicated over 27 years to this work since 1997, the physical and mental fatigue, especially during the final stages, was substantial.

The Process of the Deyi Version Translation

The English translation of the Deyi version began in early 2023, shortly after OpenAI's release of ChatGPT in November 2022. Initially, I attempted the translation independently, but as the work progressed, I found collaborating with ChatGPT beneficial. I shared my drafts and engaged in an iterative process to refine the translation through thorough discussion, especially where the meanings of Chinese characters remained unclear. With meticulous verification of each character and reference to His Reverence Muil Uhak's Korean translation, I aimed for the most accurate English rendering.

By August 2023, while staying at Amma Ji's ashram in Kerala, India, I completed an initial draft. However, the subsequent proofreading and revision process extended beyond a year due to ongoing adjustments.

By June 2024, a polished manuscript was prepared, yet I still felt it required further refinement, particularly in nuanced choices for specific Chinese terms. I recognized that subtle shifts in meaning could occur depending on how the phrasing of the original classical Chinese text was interpreted, highlighting the need for a classical Chinese expert's insight.

To further refine the translation, I sought assistance from Mr. Sejoong Kim, an expert in Chinese Classics, through Mr. Jaesun Kim, the president of Yesol Publishing. Mr. Sejoong Kim meticulously reviewed the phrasing and subtle variations in meaning within the original text, greatly enhancing the overall precision and depth of the translation. His careful work culminated in the first finalized draft on October 22, 2024, at which point I began preparing this preface as we transitioned into the editing and typesetting stages.

Continuous Meditation Practice in Zen and Vipassana

My most significant methodology, however, was integrating my personal meditation practice and teachings. My journey toward enlightenment began in 1989 and, since then, I have explored Zen and Vipassana meditation with numerous masters, embedding these experiential insights into my translation work:

April through December 1989   Engaged in a 28-day fasting practice followed by a 90-day intensive meditation period in Daegu, South Korea. During the summer, I participated in a three-month summer meditation retreat, haan-geo 夏安居, at the laymen's Zen center in

Wondangam 願堂庵 within the Haein Temple 海印寺. Afterward, I returned to Daegu, continuing a rigorous, self-directed meditation routine, often staying in Gyeongju for additional fasting and meditation. This intense period of repeated fasting and deep meditation ultimately took a significant toll on my health.

January through November 1990 Participated in dongsaseop 同事攝, "shared life practice", a form of group counselling rooted in Buddhist principles and meditation, held at Baekjangam 百丈庵 in Namwon. Through this practice, I was able to regain a measure of balance in mind and body, recovering from the significant strain my health had suffered previously.

1990 through 1991 Practiced Vipassana meditation under the guidance of His Reverence Geohae at the Daeheung Temple 大興寺 in Haenam.

1992 through 1995 Engaged in intensive study and practice of gongan 公案 (or seon mundap 禪問答), a unique form of Zen meditation involving profound questions and responses, under the guidance of a renowned Zen master.

1996 through 1997 Completed the Hatha Yoga Instructor Course at Kaivalyadhama Yoga College in Lonavla, India, earning a Diploma in Yoga Education.

1997 through 2017   Dedicated myself with my wife to the Vipassana tradition as taught by S. N. Goenka, completing over twenty sessions of the 10-day course, one 20-day, and two 30-day courses. Alongside my wife, I played a key role in establishing the 10-day Vipassana meditation courses of this tradition in South Korea.

December 2014 through February 2015   Practiced intensive Vipassana meditation at the Mahasi Tradition Vipassana Center in Myanmar, under the guidance of Panditarama Sayadaw.

December 2017 through January 2018   Studied the two-hour immobile sitting technique at the Sunlun Vipassana Center, guided by U Wara Sayadaw in Myanmar.

November 2019   Presented an article including a scientific Vipassana meditation formula drawn from a comparative philosophical analysis of seven major meditation texts, at a conference hosted by the Korean Association for Body, Mind and Spirit Science.

May 2020 up to the present   Founded an online meditation center at the onset of the COVID-19 pandemic, conducting repeated 100-day meditation programs via Zoom. As of November 6, 2024, we are in our 13th program, currently on day 48.

This long-term practice allowed me to reexamine and deepen my understanding of the Deyi version's teachings. The conclusion reached in my Ph.D. research — that Zen meditation according to Huineng and Vipassana share a common origin as essentially the same meditation practice — played a crucial role in both my personal meditation journey and the translation process. This realization provided a foundational clarity that enabled me to integrate Zen and Vipassana seamlessly in my practice, fostering a balanced approach to both traditions. The experiential insights gained from this integrated practice allowed me to refine the translation with an authenticity rooted in lived experience, ensuring that the text can serve as a reliable guide for practitioners.

Future Goals and Personal Hopes

A clear guide for English-speaking Zen practitioners This translation aspires to serve as a practical and reliable guide for Zen practitioners, helping them access and interpret Huineng's teachings in a way that deepens their understanding and practice. By bridging the language barrier, I hope this work encourages a more accurate and insightful engagement with the Platform Scripture.

Laying the foundation for scientific studies in meditation This translation also seeks to contribute to future scientific studies on meditation, especially those exploring the empirical aspects of Zen as seen through Huineng's approach. By creating a bridge between ancient practices and contemporary research, this work aims to support future interdisciplinary studies that integrate the spiritual insight with the empirical observation.

Clarifying philosophical differences in core texts Given the philosophical variations between the Dunhuang and the Deyi versions of the Platform Scripture, this translation highlights these nuances to support a balanced understanding for both practitioners and scholars. By distinguishing between these versions, I hope to prevent misunderstandings and misinterpretations that may arise in Zen practice, offering a clear foundation for meaningful dialogue and insight.

Publishing the Dunhuang version translation Following this work, I plan to publish my translation of the Dunhuang version, originally developed for my M.Phil. thesis at Pune University. Presenting these two versions side-by-side will provide readers with a unique opportunity to appreciate the distinctive insights each version offers while considering their shared teachings.

Revising and expanding the Ph.D. Research Building on this translation, I aim to revise and publish my Ph.D. research on the Dunhuang version of the Platform Scripture. With the added insights from the Deyi version, I hope this work will benefit both English and Korean readers, enriching both academic and practical understanding within the Zen community.

Harmonizing Zen and Vipassana: A guiding resource for practitioners I hope that this translation will serve as a guiding resource for practitioners of both Zen and Vipassana, helping them to navigate potential conflicts and confusions. By offering clear insights and practical guidance, I hope this work will support practitioners in reconciling the shared essence of both approaches, enabling them to progress confidently on their meditation journey. It is my sincere wish that this translation, informed by my research, will allow readers and practitioners alike to understand the underlying unity between the two practices, thus fostering a stable, harmonious path in their spiritual pursuits.

Advancing comparative philosophical analyses Lastly, I intend to deepen this exploration through a comparative philosophical analysis of the Deyi and the Dunhuang versions. This study will aim to reveal the distinct philosophical foundations of each text, providing a clearer framework for both academic inquiry and spiritual interpretation, supporting a nuanced appreciation of Zen's diversity and depth.

In these ways, I hope this translation will contribute meaningfully to the academic, spiritual, and practitioners' communities, advancing not only the knowledge but also the sincere practice and realization of the complete freedom from all the sufferings.

Introductory Commentary

by Jechang Kim

The Unique Importance of the Deyi Version of the Platform Scripture

The Platform Scripture of the Sixth Patriarch, Huineng 慧能 (638-713), occupies a uniquely influential place in Zen Buddhism, often regarded as the only "Scripture" attributed to a Chinese-born Buddhist master. Unlike most Zen texts, which primarily record dialogues and teachings of various masters, the Platform Scripture is treated with a scriptural authority traditionally reserved for the words of an enlightened Buddha himself. It presents transformative Zen principles, such as that afflictions are themselves enlightenment 煩惱即菩提, that every ordinary being is Buddha 衆生即佛, and seeing-nature 見性 through sudden enlightenment and sudden purification 頓悟頓修. Other essential teachings include paññā observation 般若觀照 內外明徹, constant samādhi 一行三昧 and the integration of samādhi and wisdom 定慧等持, as well as the foundational principles of no-thought 無念, no-form 無相 and no-abiding 無住. Together, these concepts form a comprehensive guide to understanding the nature of the mind and the core of Zen practice.

This Introductory Commentary seeks to illuminate the historical, philosophical and practical significances of the Platform Scripture, with a particular focus on the nuanced differences between its two primary versions: from Dunhuang and by Deyi 德異 (1231-ca.1308). Each version offers a distinct perspective on the enlightenment and Self-nature, revealing subtle but profound variations that influence the interpretation and application of Huineng's teachings.

As outlined in the Preface, my comparative research into Zen and Vipassana meditation led to the conclusion that both traditions share a fundamentally similar structure of practice rooted in early Buddhist methods. However, the differing philosophical assumptions in the enlightenment verses of the Dunhuang and the Deyi versions present challenges for Zen practitioners. Recognizing these differences, I undertook a new translation of the Deyi version, which aligns more closely with the early Buddhist principles. This translation project has also motivated me to revise my Ph.D. dissertation to integrate the insights derived from the Deyi version. Furthermore, I aim to conduct a comprehensive philosophical analysis to clarify these textual and doctrinal distinctions, providing practitioners and scholars with a deeper understanding of Huineng's intent and the original foundation of Zen practice.

Historical Significance of the Platform Scripture and Huineng's Teachings

Zen Buddhism in China traces its roots to Bodhidharmā, the twenty-eighth patriarch in the Indian lineage and revered as the First Patriarch of Chinese Zen. Bodhidharmā emphasized direct insight into one's Self-nature with the teaching of "the method of observing the mind encompasses all practices" 觀心一法總攝諸行. This teaching established the core of Zen practice as an experiential approach, in contrast to reliance on intellectual study or scriptural learning.

Huineng, the Sixth Patriarch, significantly advanced this direct approach by advocating for seeing-nature through the doctrine of sudden enlightenment and sudden purification and teaching that afflictions are themselves bodhi, as well as the integration of samādhi and wisdom. These teachings marked a decisive shift away from the gradual cultivation of previous traditions, offering practitioners an immediate path to awakening.

Huineng's radical perspective defined the enlightenment not as something separate from afflictions, the very source of suffering, but as something realized directly within them. His teaching that afflictions themselves are bodhi offers practitioners a pathway to liberation from suffering in an instant, without dependence on rituals, scriptures or gradual steps. This experiential, non-dualistic approach, as recorded in the Platform Scripture, established Zen as a school of immediate awakening within Chinese Buddhism.

Huineng's teachings provided a philosophical foundation for Zen, and the Platform Scripture laid the groundwork for Zen's transmission to Korea, Japan and beyond, where it continued to shape and influence Zen practice across different cultural contexts.

Metaphysical Differences in the Dunhuang and the Deyi Versions' Enlightenment Verses

A pivotal point of divergence between the Dunhuang and the Deyi versions is found in the third line of Huineng's enlightenment verse.

(Dunhuang)

佛性常清淨

"Buddha-nature is always clear and pure."

(Deyi)

本來無一物

"Fundamentally, there is not a single thing."

The Dunhuang version suggests an intrinsic, pure Buddha-nature within all beings, which may be interpreted as an unchanging essence, resembling the concept of ātman (self): a kind of eternal, self-like entity in Indian philosophy. This interpretation risks suggesting a permanent essence at the core of enlightenment, potentially conflicting with the Buddhist teaching of anātman (non-self). In contrast, the Deyi version's phrase that "Fundamentally, there is not a single thing" aligns closely with the early Buddhist doctrines of anātman and śūnyatā (emptiness), reinforcing the view that the enlightenment is about perceiving the impermanence, emptiness, and interdependent nature of all phenomena, rather than uncovering a pure, unchanging essence.

For practitioners, this philosophical difference has profound implications. The Dunhuang version could lead practitioners to perceive Buddha-nature as a distinct, unchanging entity, while the Deyi version directs them to recognize the impermanence and emptiness of the body-mind phenomena. These distinct approaches highlight the importance of critically evaluating each version's metaphysical orientation to ensure a logically coherent approach to Zen practice.

The Significance of Translating the Deyi Version in Upholding Huineng's Core Teachings

My English translation of the Deyi version of the Platform Scripture is crucial for both contemporary Zen practitioners and those seeking a deeper understanding of Huineng's teachings. The Deyi version distinctly aligns with the principles of anātman in early Buddhism and śūnyatā in Mahāyāna Buddhism, preserving the logical coherence of Huineng's transformative insights. The phrase "Fundamentally, there is not a single thing" in the Deyi version's enlightenment verse reinforces an understanding of enlightenment as impermanent, non-substantial, and free from any enduring entity, standing in stark contrast to the Dunhuang version, which presents Buddha-nature as "always clear and pure."

The language of the Deyi version challenges interpretations of Buddha-nature of the Dunhuang version as an eternal or unchanging essence, similar to ātman or puruṣa in Indian philosophy. This distinction is essential for Zen practice, as interpreting Buddha-nature as an eternal entity could inadvertently transform the practice into a search for an immutable inner Self. Such an approach would not only diverge from both the early and Mahāyāna Buddhist principles but also misalign with Huineng's teachings on "seeing-nature through sudden enlightenment and sudden purification," that "afflictions are bodhi," and "paññā observation." Instead, the Deyi version directs practitioners to realize that there is "not a single thing" to cling to: no inherent essence or Self, encouraging an alignment with the doctrines of anātman and śūnyatā.

In contrast, the Dunhuang version's phrase "Buddha-nature is always clear and pure" can be interpreted as suggesting an unchanging essence, similar to ātman. While this perspective may appeal to those seeking spiritual continuity or permanence, it introduces significant challenges for Zen practitioners by fostering attachment to an eternal Self-concept. Such an orientation diverges from Zen's emphasis on the empty, interdependent nature of all phenomena, a fundamental insight for the true liberation.

Prioritizing the translation of the Deyi version provides a corrective to potential misinterpretations that may arise from the Dunhuang version. It encourages practitioners to fully engage with Huineng's insights into the empty nature of reality, fostering a non-dual experience free from conceptual fixations. In this way, the Deyi version clarifies Huineng's original intent: not to guide practitioners toward the discovery of an eternal Self, but rather to cultivate a direct awareness of impermanence, non-self and emptiness.

My translation of the Deyi version thus fulfills a dual role: it preserves the authenticity and logical coherence of Huineng's teachings within the Zen tradition on the one hand, and provides contemporary practitioners with a framework for pursuing enlightenment free from conceptual entanglements, on the other. This work ensures that essential practices like "paññā observation," "sudden enlightenment and sudden purification" and "seeing-nature" remain aligned with Huineng's original teaching, supporting a Zen practice that is faithful to its origins and accessible to practitioners today.

The Essential Role of "Fundamentally Not a Single Thing" in Zen Practice

The phrase "Fundamentally, there is not a single thing" in the Deyi version represents far more than a metaphysical concept: it acts as a guiding principle and a logical formula for Zen practice. In Huineng's teachings, this phrase encourages practitioners to approach each moment with the realization that there is "not a single thing" to cling to, freeing their minds from attachment to any inherent essence or fixed purity. As a dynamic and practical guide, "not a single thing" roots the meditator in the direct observation of the impermanence, resonating with the early Buddhist teachings on anātman and Mahāyāna's principle of śūnyatā.

This insight shapes the practice of paññā in the Platform Scripture, where paññā observation is described as "the constant cultivation of wisdom in every situation and moment, without ignorance in every thought." Here, ignorance signifies any fixed concept, belief or notion that distorts a direct perception. Thus, "Fundamentally, not a single thing" provides a foundation for paññā observation, enabling practitioners to experience the unfiltered reality of each moment. In this direct seeing, practitioners can realize seeing-nature through sudden enlightenment and sudden purification, which Huineng presents as an immediate path to liberation from suffering.

The Logical and Practical Challenge of "Buddha-Nature Is Always Clear and Pure" in Zen Practice

In contrast, the Dunhuang version's phrase "Buddha-nature is always clear and pure" presents a fixed notion that may lead practitioners to view Buddha-nature as a static, unchanging essence — akin to concepts such as ātman or puruṣa in Indian philosophy, where the eternal essence is central. If understood as a metaphysical ideal, this phrase risks steering practitioners toward seeking an inner, immutable Self. Such an orientation runs counter to Huineng's teachings, which emphasize liberation from attachment to thought, form and abiding through the principles of no-thought, no-form and no-abiding. "Buddha-nature is always clear and pure" could therefore serve as a conceptual obstacle, as it constitutes a thought, an idealized form and a potential object of clinging.

This conflict is not purely metaphysical but also introduces a serious logical inconsistency in Zen practice. The Platform Scripture, in both its Dunhuang and the Deyi versions, defines paññā as "the constant cultivation of wisdom in every situation and moment, without ignorance in every thought." This statement implies that wisdom requires an active, ongoing observation, free from fixed ideas or preconceptions. Practicing with a pre-established notion such as that "Buddha-nature is always clear and pure" imposes a mental framework that disrupts the direct, moment-to-moment observation essential to Zen. Instead of observing reality as it unfolds, practitioners may become preoccupied with upholding this idealized notion of purity, which compromises the adaptability and open receptivity vital to Zen meditation.

The core issue lies in practical application: if "Buddha-nature is always clear and pure" is embraced as a guiding ideal, it inevitably becomes the formula through which meditation is conducted. This attachment disrupts the practitioner's ability to engage authentically with Huineng's core practices — paññā observation, no-thought, no-form and no-abiding. The concept obstructs the direct perception of change and non-substantiality, which are fundamental to liberation in Theravada, Mahāyāna and Zen Buddhisms alike. By adopting "Buddha-nature is always clear and pure" as a central ideal, practitioners' risk becoming attached to the notion of a permanent Self, creating not only a logical but also a practical barrier to the realization of the impermanent, interdependent nature of all phenomena.

The Need for a Comparative Philosophical Analysis of the Deyi and the Dunhuang Versions

The contrasting phrase in the Deyi version, "Fundamentally, there is not a single thing," provides a more practical foundation for Zen practice. Grounding meditation in the absence of inherent essence, this phrase frees practitioners from attachment to conceptual ideals and encourages the observation of each moment as inherently empty, fluid, and interdependent. Such an approach aligns with Huineng's original intent, fostering a Zen practice that is deeply engaged with non-self, impermanence and emptiness, rather than with the pursuit of imagined purity or permanence.

In contrast, the phrase "Buddha-nature is always clear and

pure" in the Dunhuang version introduces a concept that can lead to attachment, potentially drawing practitioners toward the idea of an eternal, unchanging essence. Not only does this phrase conflict with the doctrines of anātman and śūnyatā, but it also disrupts the inner coherence of Huineng's teachings, which emphasize the rejection of fixed notions in favor of paññā observation with the help of no-thought, no-form and no-abiding. By focusing on "Fundamentally, there is not a single thing," the Deyi version better supports a Zen practice true to the Platform Scripture's original intent, facilitating a path toward enlightenment that remains free from conceptual fixations on purity, Self or permanence.

As a practitioner and philosopher myself, I see this discord between the two versions as a critical issue. The conflict between their metaphysical orientations can create serious challenges for dedicated Zen practitioners, potentially leading them to confusion and even existential crisis, as I described in the preface from my own experience in the early stages of my practice. This discord risks causing practitioners to wander in search of an idealized essence, diverting them from the immediate realization Huineng intended.

Therefore, I propose a comparative philosophical analysis of the Deyi and the Dunhuang versions as the next step in my research, aiming to resolve this discord in a way that supports a coherent and effective approach to Zen practice.

Before concluding this commentary, I would like to highlight two further issues identified in the Deyi version that warrant an in-depth study.

First, the possible weakening of sati (mindfulness) in Zen practice of the Platform Scripture, potentially contributing to the rise of kanhua/ganhwa 看話 Zen, especially as systematized by Zen Master Dahui Zonggao 大慧宗杲 (1089-1163).

Second, the introduction of "permanence, bliss, Self and purity" 常樂我淨 in the eighth chapter of the Deyi version, which seems to contradict the foundational doctrine of "Fundamentally not a single thing" and the early Buddhist principles of anātman and śūnyatā in Mahāyāna Buddhism.

A Hypothesis on the Weakening of Sati and the Rise of Kanhua Zen

The Platform Scripture emphasizes no-thought, no-form and no-abiding, which may have inadvertently led to a diminishing role, or even a loss for sati — a critical aspect of the early Buddhist Vipassana practice. In Vipassana, sati is essential for cultivating an ongoing awareness that directly fosters liberation by observing each moment's arising and passing without forgetting.

I hypothesize that this potential decrease in sati within the Platform Scripture's framework contributed indirectly to the emergence of kanhua Zen as a skill-based method for maintaining mindfulness in later Zen practice. Initially referred to in the seventh chapter of the Deyi version and later expanded by Dahui Zonggao, kanhua Zen became a central practice in Korean Buddhist community. In my assessment, it does not align with the prescribed meditation formula of the Platform Scripture, because the formula of the Platform Scripture is paññā observation based on "Fundamentally not a single thing."

However, it seems that huatou/hwadu 話頭 was eventually considered as a primary meditative formula rather than a supplementary skill. As seen in the teachings of the prominent Korean Zen Master Seongcheol 性徹 (1912-1993), who advocated adherence to the Platform Scripture, while also emphasizing the importance of huatou.

This shift represents a potential departure from the Platform Scripture's original meditation formula "paññā observation" based on "Fundamentally not a single thing" to realize seeing-nature, which is more aligned with the formula of ātāpi sampajāno satimā ("consistent mindfulness rooted in a profound understanding of impermanence to realize nibbāna according to Mahāsatipaṭṭhāna Sutta of the early Buddhism. I believe this misidentification may introduce a confusion for dedicated practitioners.

Therefore, I suggest that further research is warranted to clarify whether the original emphasis on wisdom observation based on "Fundamentally not a single thing" in Huineng's teachings as a meditation formula has been overshadowed, and whether kanhua Zen was introduced as a substitute to address the absence of sati in the

Platform Scripture. I hope this further research will aid practitioners and scholars in distinguishing between essential meditative formulas, which are crucial for realizing enlightenment, and supportive skills like sati.

Why "Permanence, Bliss, Self and Purity," Which Seems Contradictory to "Fundamentally Not a Single Thing," Appears in the Deyi Version

Another critical issue is the presence of "permanence, bliss, Self, and purity" in the eighth chapter of the Deyi version, likely drawn from the Nibbāna Sutta. This doctrine introduces a complex and potentially conflicting layer to the Deyi version when juxtaposed with "Fundamentally not a single thing" and with anātman and śūnyatā.

The doctrine of "permanence, bliss, Self and purity" associated with the later Mahāyāna teachings offers an optimistic vision of nibbāna, but risks reintroducing substantial qualities like ātman in Indian philosophy, implying permanence and Self-like attributes that run contrary to both early Buddhist doctrines and Huineng's teaching of "Fundamentally not a single thing." This tension invites questions about the doctrinal layers within the Deyi version, suggesting that the later Mahāyāna influences may have obscured Huineng's original intention.

Therefore, I propose one more comparative philosophical

analysis to clarify the implications of "permanence, bliss, Self and purity" within the Deyi version. Such research could reveal whether "permanence, bliss, Self and purity" should be interpreted metaphorically or as a later addition reflecting evolving Mahāyāna thought rather than Huineng's foundational teachings. This inquiry may help interpret "permanence, bliss, Self and purity" in a way that aligns with "Fundamentally not a single thing" and sustains Huineng's emphasis on non-duality and non-substantiality. Such clarification could enrich both scholarly understanding and practical application, offering Zen practitioners a coherent foundation grounded in Huineng's original vision.

Conclusion

In this commentary, I have sought to address the significant challenges and issues encountered in translating the Deyi version. By highlighting the issues such as the inconsistency between the Deyi and the Dunhuang versions, I hope to open a pathway for scholars and practitioners to engage deeply with the Platform Scripture and to develop a more nuanced understanding of Zen practice.

While translating, I encountered additional passages in the Deyi version that warrant further philosophical inquiries. These topics represent valuable insights gained through this translation work, underscoring the need for future study.

Personally, I am very gratified to have completed one of my most important long-term projects, which I have pursued with dedication for 27 years since 1997. My hope is that this translation, along with the questions it raises, will serve as a catalyst for renewed study of Zen meditation grounded in the authentic framework of the Platform Scripture. I appreciate the readers' thoughtful consideration of this work.

Seoul, November 2024

Acknowledgments

This work stands on the foundation of countless individuals and institutions whose support, guidance, and inspiration have been invaluable. My heartfelt gratitude extends to:

Personal mentors

Dr. S. E. Bhelke   My Ph.D. advisor, whose mentorship in the philosophical study of meditation techniques has been a guiding light throughout this journey. His profound insights and unwavering support made this work, including the translation of the Deyi version, possible.

Sunlun Sayadaw (1878-1952) and U Wara Sayadaw (1945-2021)
I offer my deepest gratitude to these revered meditation teachers for imparting the transformative two-hour sitting meditation technique. Designed by Sunlun Sayadaw, a fully enlightened Arahant, this practice facilitates direct realization of enlightenment. I learned this invaluable technique from U Wara Sayadaw, the third generation dis-

ciple of Sunlun Sayadaw, who passed away three years ago, which I deeply mourn. Their teachings have profoundly shaped my practice and the guidance I offer at AOMA.

U Panditarama Sayadaw (1921–2016) My wife and I participated in a two-month intensive Vipassana retreat with him from December 2014 to January 2015. At the remarkable age of 93, his daily discourses, filled with wisdom and compassion, left an indelible mark on our understanding and practice.

S. N. Goenka (1924–2013) On the centennial of his birth, I honor S. N. Goenka and the Vipassana tradition for their profound influence on my understanding of meditation, the MahāsatipaṭṭhānaSutta and the Platform Scripture. My wife and I studied this tradition deeply from 1997 to 2017, and its teachings continue to enrich our lives.

The Late Swami Maheshananda (?–2021) As the spiritual leader of Kaivalyadhama, Swami Maheshananda extended great personal affection and guidance during my time at the institute in 1996–1997. His kindness and mentorship remain cherished memories.

The Late Professor Sungjae Lee (1924–2009) Commemorating the centennial of his birth, I honor Prof. Sungjae Lee for his wisdom and virtue, which profoundly influenced my life. Meeting him at the age of 16 in 1974 was a pivotal moment for me, and his mentorship inspired me for over fifty years.

Institutions

Philosophy Department, Pune University, India For providing the academic foundation and nurturing environment that supported my research into the philosophical underpinnings of meditation practices.

Kaivalyadhama Yoga Institute (celebrating centennial) For sparking my interest in the scientific study of meditation and inspiring a rigorous and integrative approach to its practice and understanding.

Department of Composition, Seoul National University For initiating me into the depths of artistic and creative exploration. Although my journey later shifted toward spirituality, the teachings I received here remain a treasured part of my life.

Chuncheon Senior High School (celebrating centennial) My alma mater, whose guiding principle of jeongdo 正道 (right path) resonates deeply with the meditative path I have pursued. On the occasion of its centennial, I express my heartfelt gratitude for the formative values it instilled in me.

Collaborators and supporters
Mr. Sejoong Kim and Mr. Jaesun Kim My sincere thanks to Mr. Sejoong Kim for his expertise in classical Chinese and his invaluable

contributions to the translation process through meticulous proofreading and editing. I am also grateful to Mr. Jaesun Kim for introducing me to Mr. Sejoong Kim and providing practical guidance throughout the publication process.

Meditation community

Practitioners and volunteers of AOMA To the dedicated meditators and volunteers at AOMA, whose unwavering commitment to intense practice and selfless service continues to inspire me. I am especially grateful to Ms. Jeonghee Lee, who, at the age of 86, has been practicing diligently for over four years, exemplifying remarkable dedication.

Family

The Late Mr. Jeyul Kim (1946-2022) In loving memory of my elder brother, whose steadfast encouragement and belief in me remain a source of strength. His spirit lives on in this work.

My family To my extended family — both my own and my wife's — for their boundless love, patience and encouragement, which have supported me throughout this journey.

My wife Lastly but most profoundly, to Soonjong Kim, my wife and lifelong meditation partner. Her unwavering devotion, companionship, and support have been my greatest strength. This work is as much hers as it is mine.

Reader's Notes

This translation of the Platform Scripture has been prepared with meticulous attention, balancing fidelity to the Deyi version with accessibility for modern readers. The following notes aim to guide readers in navigating this work and engaging deeply with Huineng's teachings.

Terminology and translation choices

Consistency in key terms Technical terms central to the Platform Scripture have been translated consistently to maintain coherence throughout the text. Even when certain terms may seem awkward in English, such as "seeing-nature" for "見性," simplicity and uniformity have been prioritized.

    (Further examples)
    自性 Self-nature
    無念, 無相, 無住 no-thought, no-form, no-abiding
    頓悟頓修 sudden enlightenment and sudden purification

Exceptional uses of Japanese transliterations for Zen and related terms   While the Chinese/Korean pronunciations of terms like chan/seon 禪 and zuochan/jwaseon 坐禪 ("sitting meditation") more accurately reflect their original context, this translation adopts two of the widely recognized Japanese transliterations, Zen and Zazen. These terms, popularized by Japanese scholars like Dr. Suzuki Daisetz, are familiar to global English-speaking audiences. This decision ensures accessibility and continuity with existing discourse.

Preservation of original nuances in Pāli and Sanskrit terms   For terms transliterated into Chinese from Pāli or Sanskrit, the original Pāli or Sanskrit is used without English translation wherever possible, preserving their nuanced meanings.

> 般若   paññā
> 三昧, 定   samādhi
> 菩提   bodhi

Contextual adaptation of ambiguous terms   Some Chinese characters carry multiple meanings depending on their context. While maintaining consistency, their translations have been adapted to align with the specific usage within the text.

> 相   usually as "form," but also as "appearance" or "object" in certain contexts

色 as "matter" (or materiality), "body" (physical form) or "color", depending on contexts

性 as "nature" (e.g., "Self-nature" 自性) or "characteristic" (personality traits)

Layout and translation process

Layout The Chinese original text appears above the English translation, offering clarity and ease of reference for bilingual readers.

Korean pronunciation Korean pronunciations of Chinese characters are provided to enhance accessibility for Korean readers.

Philological editing The Chinese text underwent meticulous editing by Mr. Sejoong Kim, who refined punctuation and spacing to improve readability.

Translation process The initial drafts were developed using OpenAI's ChatGPT, but all the final decisions reflect deliberate philosophical and linguistic judgment by the translator.

Historical context and philosophical distinctions

The Platform Scripture exists in several versions, notably the Dunhuang and the Deyi versions, which diverge significantly in their philosophical orientations. As noted in the Preface and the Introductory Commentary, this translation emphasizes the Deyi version's alignment with the early Buddhist principles such as non-self (anātman) and emptiness (śūnyatā).

Readers are encouraged to approach the text with an open mind, reflecting on the historical and doctrinal contexts that shape the unique insights of the Deyi version.

Simplified formatting

To enhance readability, the use of capitalization, italicization, and other formatting has been minimized. This approach prioritizes simplicity and ensures a seamless reading experience.

Usage of Pāli and Sanskrit

For scriptural references, Roman transliterations of original Pāli terms with diacritical marks have been prioritized. When Pāli terms are unavailable, Sanskrit terms are used, each marked with an additional [s] on the right shoulder.

No annotations and Glossary

Detailed annotations and a glossary were intentionally omitted to maintain focus on the main text. This decision reflects the translator's commitment to allowing the teachings to speak directly, without extensive commentary.

Suggestions for reading

The Platform Scripture is not merely a text for intellectual engagement but a guide for meditative practice. Its teachings are best absorbed through contemplative reflection. The translator suggests:

- Read slowly, pausing to reflect on Huineng's words, and
- take time between sections to meditate on key insights.
- Each chapter has been translated to balance readability with depth for meditative reflection.
- This translation seeks to support both casual readers and dedicated practitioners in engaging authentically with Zen teachings.

The Reader's Notes aim to guide readers in their exploration of the Platform Scripture. May it serve as a bridge to understanding and practicing the profound teachings of Huineng.

독자 참고사항

이 『육조단경』 번역본은 덕이본(德異本)의 원문에 충실하면서도, 현대 독자들이 쉽게 접근할 수 있도록 정성을 다해 준비하였습니다. 아래의 독자 참고사항은 독자들이 본 번역본을 탐구하며 혜능 대사의 가르침을 깊이 이해하는 데 도움이 되도록 작성되었습니다.

용어 및 번역 선택

핵심 기술 용어의 일관성 유지 『육조단경』의 주요 기술(記述) 용어는 번역의 통일성을 유지하기 위해 신중하게 선택되었습니다. 일부 용어는 영어로 번역될 때 다소 어색하게 느껴질 수도 있으나, 단순성과 일관성을 우선하여 사용하였습니다.

(예시)
견성(見性): Seeing-nature
자성(自性): Self-nature
무념(無念), 무상(無相), 무주(無住): no-thought, no-form, no-abiding
돈오돈수(頓悟頓修): sudden enlightenment and sudden purification

선(禪) 관련 용어의 일본식 음역 사용 선(禪), 좌선(坐禪)과 같은 용어는 한국어 발음 "(jwa)seon" 또는 중국어 병음 "(zuo)chan"이 원문 맥락을 더 정확하게 반영합니다. 그러나 본 번역에서는 영어권 독자들에게 더 익숙한 일본식 음역 "Zen, Zazen"을 사용하였습니다. 이는 스즈키 다이세쓰(鈴木大拙) 박사와 같은 일본 학자들이 널리 보급한 용어로, 국제적인 영어 독자들에게 친숙한 표현을 반영한 것입니다.

빨리어 및 산스크리트어 원어 보존 빨리(Pāli)어나 산스끄리뜨(Sanskrit)어에서 유래하여 중국어로 음역(音譯)된 용어들은, 가능하면 영어 번역 없이 원어 음역을 유지하여 원래의 의미를 보존하였습니다.

- 般若: paññā (반야, 지혜)
- 三昧, 定: samādhi (삼매)
- 菩提: bodhi (보리, 깨달음)

맥락에 따른 모호한 용어의 번역 일부 한자는 맥락에 따라 다양한 의미를 가질 수 있습니다. 번역의 일관성을 유지하면서, 문맥에 맞게 의미를 조정하였습니다.

- 상(相): 일반적으로 "form"으로 번역했지만, 맥락에 따라 "appearance" 또는 "object"로 번역함.
- 색(色): 물질(materiality)을 의미할 때는 "matter", 신체를 지칭할 때는 "body", 색상을 뜻할 때는 "color"로 번역함.
- 성(性): "nature"(보기: 자성自性, Self-nature)로 번역했지만, 성격을 지칭할 때는 "characteristic"으로 번역함.

구성과 번역 과정

구성   중국어 원문을 영어 번역 위에 배치하여, 이중언어 독자들이 쉽게 비교할 수 있도록 하였습니다.

한글 독음   한문 원문의 한글 독음을 함께 제공하여, 한국 독자들이 보다 쉽게 접근하도록 하였습니다.

원문 편집   김세중 선생의 도움으로 한문 원문에 현대식 구두점을 추가하여 가독성을 높였습니다.

번역 과정   초안은 OpenAI의 ChatGPT를 활용하여 작성되었으나, 최종 번역은 역자의 철학적·언어적 판단을 바탕으로 신중하게 수정되었습니다.

역사적 맥락과 철학적 차이점

『육조단경』은 돈황본(燉煌本)과 덕이본 등 여러 판본이 존재하며, 철학적 해석에서 큰 차이를 보입니다.

본 번역본은 서문과 해설에서도 언급했듯이, 덕이본이 초기 불교의 무아(無我, anātman)와 공(空, śūnyatā) 원칙에 더 부합한다고 강조합니다.

독자 여러분께서는 이러한 역사적·철학적 맥락을 염두에 두고, 덕이본의 독특한 통찰에 열린 마음으로 접근하시기를 권장합니다.

간소화된 서식

가독성을 높이기 위해 대문자, 이탤릭체, 기타 서식 요소의 사용을 최소화하였습니다. 이러한 접근은 텍스트의 단순성과 명료성을 우선하여 독자 경험을 향상시키고자 합니다.

빨리어와 산스끄리뜨어 사용

경전의 제목에는 가능한 한 원래의 빨리어를 로마자로 음역한 용어를 사용하며, 디아크리틱(diacritical marks)을 포함하여 표기하였습니다. 빨리어 사용이 불가능할 경우, 산스끄리뜨어를 사용하고 매번 위첨자 [S]를 덧붙였습니다.

주석과 용어 해설 생략

독자들이 본문에 집중할 수 있도록, 주석과 용어 해설은 의도적으로 생략하였습니다.

이는 독자들이 교리와 가르침 자체에 직접 몰입할 수 있도록 하기 위한 번역자의 의도를 반영합니다.

읽는 방법

『육조단경』은 단순한 지적 탐구를 위한 텍스트가 아니라, 수행과 실천을 위한 지침서입니다.

ㄱ 가르침은 명상적 성찰을 통해 가장 깊이 이해될 수 있습니다.

읽는 방법 안내:

- 천천히 읽고, 혜능 대사의 말씀을 깊이 숙고한 후 수행에 적용해 보십시오.
- 각 단락을 읽은 후, 시간을 두고 명상하며 핵심 구절을 숙고해 보십시오.
- 각 장은 읽기 쉬우면서도 깊은 명상을 할 수 있도록 번역되었습니다.
- 이 번역본은 일반 독자와 수행자를 모두 지원하며, 선(禪)의 가르침에 진정성 있게 접근할 수 있는 길잡이가 되고자 합니다.

이 독자 참고사항은 독자들이 『육조단경』을 깊이 탐구하고 이해하며, 수행으로 이어지는 여정에 도움을 주기 위해 작성되었습니다. 혜능 대사의 심오한 가르침을 온전히 이해하고 실천하는 데 이 번역본이 든든한 가교(架橋)가 되기를 바랍니다.

The Platform Scripture of the Sixth Patriarch
- Deyi Edition
六祖法寶壇經 德異本

六祖法寶壇經原序　　육조법보단경 원서　　65

六祖大師法寶壇經略序　육조대사법보단경 약서　71

　　　　　第一 行由品　　제일 행유품　　83
　　　　　第二 般若品　　제이 반야품　　119
　　　　　第三 疑問品　　제삼 의문품　　147
　　　　　第四 定慧品　　제사 정혜품　　163
　　　　　第五 坐禪品　　제오 좌선품　　173
　　　　　第六 懺悔品　　제육 참회품　　177
　　　　　第七 機緣品　　제칠 기연품　　201
　　　　　第八 頓漸品　　제팔 돈점품　　261
　　　　　第九 宣詔品　　제구 선조품　　287
　　　　　第十 付囑品　　제십 부촉품　　295
　　　　　　　附錄　　　　　부록　　　　333

Original Preface 65

Brief Preface 71

Chapter One. Of the Origin 83
Chapter Two. Of Paññā (Wisdom) 119
Chapter Three. Of Enquiry 147
Chapter Four. Of Samādhi and Paññā 163
Chapter Five. Of Zazen 173
Chapter Six. Of Repentance and Penitence 177
Chapter Seven. Of Disciples 201
Chapter Eight. Of the Sudden and the Gradual 261
Chapter Nine. Of Reception 287
Chapter Ten. Of Entrustment 295

Appendix 333

六祖法寶壇經原序

육조법보단경 원서

古筠比丘 德異 撰

고균비구 덕이 찬

妙道虛玄, 不可思議. 忘言得旨, 端可悟明.

묘도허현, 불가사의. 망언득지, 단가오명.

故世尊分座於多子搭前, 拈花於靈山會上, 似火與火, 以心印心.

고세존분좌어다자탑전, 염화어영산회상, 사화여화, 이심인심.

The Original Preface
to the Dhamma Treasure Platform Scripture of the Sixth Patriarch

compiled by Monk Deyi of Gujun

The subtle path is mysterious and beyond comprehension. Only by forgetting the words and attaining the essence can one awaken and attain clarity.

Thus, the World-Honored-One shared his seat with Mahākāśyapa before the stupa, and held up a flower at Vulture Peak. This was an instance of transmitting mind to mind, like fire passing from one torch to another.

> 西傳四七, 至菩提達摩東來此土, 直指人心, 見性成佛.
> 서전사칠, 지보리달마동래차토, 직지인심, 견성성불.
>
> 有可大師者首於言下悟入, 末上三拜得髓, 受衣紹祖, 開闡正宗.
> 유가대사자수어언하오입, 말상삼배득수, 수의소조, 개천정종.
>
> 三傳而至黃梅, 會中高僧七百, 惟負舂居士一偈傳依, 爲六代祖.
> 삼전이지황매, 회중고승칠백, 유부용거사일게전의, 위육대조.
>
> 南遯十餘年, 一旦以非風幡動之機觸開印宗正眼.
> 남둔십여년, 일단이비풍번동지기촉개인종정안.

After it was transmitted through twenty-eight generations in the West, Bodhidharmā[S] came eastward to this land and taught directly pointing to the human mind, realizing seeing-nature and becoming Buddha.

The Great Master Huike first attained enlightenment under the words and grasped the essence after three bows, became the successor of the patriarchal lineage by receiving the robe, and opened up the True Doctrine.

When it was transmitted through three generations and reached Huangmei, there were seven hundred renowned monks in the assembly, but only the layman pounding rice was transmitted the robe with a single verse and became the Sixth Patriarch.

After he fled to the south for over ten years, one day he prompted Yinzong to open the true eyes of the dhamma with the statement "Neither the wind, nor the flag, that moves."

> 居士由是祝髮登壇, 應跋陀羅懸記開東山法門.
> 거사유시축발등단, 응발타라현기개동산법문.
>
> 韋使君命海禪者錄其語, 目之曰『法寶壇經』.
> 위사군명해선자록기어, 목지왈『법보단경』.
>
> 大師始於五羊, 終至曹溪, 説法三十七年. 霑甘露味, 入聖超凡者
> 대사시어오양, 종지조계, 설법삼십칠년, 점감로미, 입성초범자
>
> 莫記其數. 悟佛心宗, 行解相應, 爲大知識者名載『傳燈』.
> 막기기수. 오불심종, 행해상응, 위대지식자명재『전등』.

Thus the layman had his hair shaved and ascended the platform, fulfilling the prophecy of Guṇabhadra, and established the East Mountain Dhamma School.

Prefect Wei instructed Zen practitioner Fahai to record the Master's words, and titled it the Dhamma Treasure Platform Scripture.

The Great Master began in Wuyang and ended in Caoqi, teaching for thirty-seven years. Nourished by the taste of the nectar, countless people transcended the mundane to enter the sages' stage. Those who realized the Buddha's mind's doctrine, with actions matching their comprehension, and became great enlightened knowers had their names recorded in the Transmitting Lamplights.

> 惟南嶽・青原執侍最久, 盡得無巴鼻. 故出馬祖・石頭, 機智圓明,
> 유남악・청원집시최구, 진득무파비. 고출마조・석두, 기지원명,
>
> 玄風大振. 乃有臨濟・潙仰・曹洞・雲門・法眼諸公巍然而出, 道德歷
> 현풍대진. 내유임제・위앙・조동・운문・법안제공외연이출, 도덕역
>
> 群, 門庭險峻, 啓迪英靈衲子, 奪志衝關, 一門深入.
> 군, 문정험준, 계적영령납자, 탈지충관, 일문심입.
>
> 五派同源, 歷遍爐錘, 規模廣大, 原其五家網要盡出『壇經』.
> 오파동원, 역편노추, 규모광대, 원기오가강요진출『단경』.
>
> 夫『壇經』者, 言簡義豊, 理明事備, 具足諸佛無量法門, 一一法門
> 부『단경』자, 언간의풍, 이명사비, 구족제불무량법문, 일일법문

Among them, Nanyue and Qingyuan served the Master the longest, fully grasping his teachings of non-obtaining. Hence emerged Mazu and Shitou, whose wisdoms were bright and clear, greatly invigorated the profound path. Succeedingly, masters like Linji, Guiyang, Caodong, Yunmen and Fayan flourished and widely spread the teaching. Their virtue and ethics excelled others and their schools were rigorous and demanding, so they inspired and guided numerable exceptional monks to overcome obstacles with determined will, delving deeply into one path.

Those Five Schools share the same origin and refined it meticulously and expanded themselves, and the essences of all the Five Schools' teachings originates from the Platform Scripture.

The Platform Scripture, though concise in words, is rich in meaning, clear in principles and comprehensive in practices.

具足無量妙義, 一一妙義發揮諸佛無量妙理, 即彌勒樓閣中, 即普
구족무량묘의, 일일묘의발휘제불무량묘리, 즉미륵누각중, 즉보

賢毛孔中. 善入者即同善財, 於一念間圓滿功德, 與普賢等, 與諸
현모공중. 선입자즉동선재, 어일념간원만공덕, 여보현등, 여제

佛等.
불등.

惜乎! 『壇經』爲後人節略太多, 不見六祖大全之旨. 德異幼年嘗見
석호! 『단경』위후인절략태다, 불현육조대전지지. 덕이유년상견

古本, 自後遍求三十餘載, 近得通上人尋到全文, 遂刊於吳中休休
고본, 자후편구삼십여재, 근득통상인심도전문, 수간어오중휴휴

禪庵與諸勝士同一受用.
선암여제승사동일수용.

It encompasses the countless dhamma gates of all Buddhas, each dhamma gate containing infinite subtle meanings, each in turn revealing the limitless profound principles of all Buddhas. It is like the inner side of Maitreya's palace as well as of Samantabhadra's[S] pores. Those who are introduced well are to be like Sudhana[S], achieving complete virtues in a single thought, to become equal to Samantabhadra, equal to all Buddhas.

Alas! The Platform Scripture has been excessively abbreviated by later generations, losing much of the Sixth Patriarch's complete intent. I, Deyi, when young, once saw an ancient edition and, after searching for over thirty years, recently obtained the complete text from His Venerability Tong, and was able to publish and share it together with the virtuous scholars at the Xiuxiu Zen Center in Wuzhong.

> 惟願開卷擧目, 直入大願覺海, 續佛祖慧命無窮, 斯余志願滿矣.
> 유원개권거목, 직입대원각해, 속불조혜명무궁, 사여지원만의.
>
> 至元二十七年庚寅歲仲春 日 叙
> 지원이십칠년경인세중춘 일 서

It is my wish that those who open and look upon this Scripture directly enter the vast ocean of awakening and carry on the endless wisdom life of Buddhas and Patriarchs. Then my aspiration and desire would be fulfilled.

April, the twenty-seventh year, gengyin, of the Zhiyuan era.

六祖大師法寶壇經略序

육조대사법보단경 약서

門人 法海 撰
문인 법해 찬

大師名惠能. 父盧氏, 諱行瑫.
대사명혜능. 부노씨, 휘행도.

母李氏誕師於唐貞觀十二年戊戌二月八日子時. 時毫光騰空, 異香 滿室.
모이씨탄사어당정관십이년무술이월팔일자시. 시호광등공, 이향 만실.

A Brief Preface

to the Dhamma Treasure Platform Scripture of the Sixth Patriarch

by Disciple Fahai

The Great Master's name was Huineng. His father was from the Lu family, named Xingtao.

The Master's mother, from the Li family, gave birth to him at midnight on the eighth day of February, in the twelfth year, wuxu, of the Zhenguan era of the Tang Dynasty. At that time, a brilliant light rose into the sky and the room was filled with a strange fragrance.

黎明, 有二異僧造謁, 謂師之父曰:"夜來生兒, 專爲安名. 可上惠, 下能也."
여명, 유이이승조알, 위사지부왈:"야래생아, 전위안명. 가상혜, 하능야."

父曰:"何名惠能?"
부왈:"하명혜능?"

僧曰:"惠者, 以法惠施衆生; 能者, 能作佛事."
승왈:"혜자, 이법혜시중생; 능자, 능작불사."

言畢而出, 不知所之.
언필이출, 부지소지.

師不飮乳, 遇夜神人灌以甘露.
사불음유, 우야신인관이감로.

At dawn, two strange monks visited and said to the Master's father, "Last night, a child was born. What if we give him the name: Hui followed by Neng?"

The father asked, "Why the name Huineng?"

The monks replied, "Hui, to give benefit to all sentient beings with the dhamma; Neng, to accomplish Buddha's enterprise."

After speaking, they left, and no one knew where they had gone.

The Master did not drink breast milk, and a divine being fed nectar for him at nights.

> 既長, 年二十有四, 聞經悟道, 往黃梅求印可. 五祖器之, 付衣法,
> 기장, 연이십유사, 문경오도, 왕황매구인가. 오조기지, 부의법,
>
> 令嗣祖位. 時龍朔元年辛酉歲也.
> 영사조위. 시용삭원년신유세야.
>
> 南歸隱遯一十六年, 至儀鳳元年丙子正月八日會印宗法師. 宗悟契
> 남귀은둔일십육년, 지의봉원년병자정월팔일회인종법사. 종오계
>
> 師旨, 是月十五日普會四衆, 爲師薙髮. 二月八日集諸名德, 授具足戒.
> 사지, 시월십오일보회사중, 위사체발. 이월팔일집제명덕, 수구족계.

Having reached the age of twenty-four, the Master heard the Scripture and attained enlightenment, so he went to Huangmei to seek confirmation. The Fifth Patriarch recognized his potential and transmitted to him the robe and the dhamma, designating him as his successor. It was in the first year, xinyou, of the Longshuo era.

After returning to the south and hiding for sixteen years, on the eighth day of January, the first year, bingzi, of the Yifeng era, the Master met with Dhamma Master Yinzong. He understood the Master's teaching very well, so he gathered the assembly and shaved the Master's hair on the fifteenth day of that month. Further, on the eighth day of February, he gathered all the virtuous masters together and conferred the Master an Upasampadā.

Brief Preface

> 西京智光律師爲授戒師, 蘇州慧靜律師爲羯磨, 荊州通應律
> 서경지광율사위수계사, 소주혜정율사위갈마, 형주통응율
>
> 師爲教授, 中天耆多羅律師爲説戒, 西國密多三藏爲證戒.
> 사위교수, 중천기다라율사위설계, 서국밀다삼장위증계.
>
> 其戒檀乃宋朝求那跋陀羅三藏創建, 立碑曰:"後當有肉身菩薩於
> 기계단내송조구나발타라삼장창건. 입비왈: "후당유육신보살어
>
> 此受戒."
> 차수계."
>
> 又梁天監元年智藥三藏自西竺國航海而來, 將彼土菩提樹一株植此檀畔,
> 우양천감원년지약삼장자서축국항해이래, 장피토보리수일주식차단반,

Disciplinary Master Zhiguang from the Western Capital was the preceptor for bestowing the precepts; Disciplinary Master Huijing from Suzhou was the karmaṇācārya(S)(ritual master); Disciplinary Master Tongying from Jingzhou was the instructor of the dhamma; Disciplinary Master Kṣitigarbha(S) from Zhongtian(Central India) was the preceptor for expounding the precepts; and Disciplinary Master Mitrasaṃgha(S) from Xiguo(India) was the certifying master for the precepts.

The ceremonial platform had first been established during the Song Dynasty by Guṇabhadra, who erected a stele, stating, "In the future, a living Bodhisattva(S) shall receive Upasampadā here."

Again, in the first year of the Tianjian era, Tripiṭaka(S) Master Zhiyue sailed from India with a bodhi tree and planted it beside the platform,

亦預誌曰:"後一百七十年有肉身菩薩於此樹下開演上乘, 度
역예지왈: "후일백칠십년유육신보살어차수하개연상승, 도
無量衆, 眞傳佛心印之法主也."
무량중, 진전불심인지법주야."

師至是祝髮受戒, 及與四衆開示單傳之法旨, 一與昔識.
사지시축발수계, 급여사중개시단전지법지, 일여석참.

次年春, 師辭衆, 歸寶林. 印宗與緇白送者千餘人. 直至曹溪, 時
차년춘, 사사중, 귀보림. 인종여치백송자천여인. 직지조계, 시
荊州通應律師與學者數百人依師而住.
형주통응율사여학자수백인의사이주.

and also predicted, "After some one hundred and seventy years, a living Bodhisattva[S] shall expound the supreme teachings under this tree and save innumerable sentient beings, becoming the true Master of transmitting the dhamma of the Buddha's mind seal."

Now that the Master had his hair shaved, received Upasampadā and revealed the essential points of the solely transmitted dhamma, it was all in accordance with the prophecies of the past.

In the following spring, the Master bid farewell to the assembly and returned to the Baolin. More than a thousand, including Yinzong as well as the monks and lay followers, saw him off. The Master proceeded directly to Caoqi, where Disciplinary Master Tongying from Jingzhou and several hundred disciples resided under his guidance.

BRIEF PREFACE

> 師至曹溪寶林, 覩堂宇湫隘, 不足容衆, 欲廣之. 遂謁里人陳亞仙,
> 사지조계보림, 도당우초애, 부족용중, 욕광지. 수알이인진아선,
>
> 曰: "老僧欲就檀越, 求坐具地. 得不?"
> 왈: :노승욕취단월, 구좌구지, 득불?"
>
> 仙曰: "和尚坐具幾許闊?"
> 선왈: "화상좌구기허활?"
>
> 祖出坐具, 示之. 亞仙唯然. 祖以坐具一展, 盡罩曹溪四境,
> 조출좌구, 시지. 아선유연. 조이좌구일전, 진소조계사경,
>
> 四天王現身, 坐鎭四方. 今寺境有天王嶺因玆而名.
> 사천왕현신, 좌진사방. 금사경유천왕령인자이명.

The Master arrived at the Baolin in Caoqi and found the hall too narrow to hold the assembly. He wanted to enlarge it, so he visited a local resident Chen Yaxian and asked, "The old monk wants to seek a piece of land to spread his seat upon. Is it available?"

Yaxian asked back, "How wide is Your Reverence's seat?"

The Master displayed his seat to him. Yaxian said yes. When the Master unfolded the seat, it covered the entire Caoqi region, and the Four Devas appeared and sat to press the four corners of the seat. The Tianwangling Pass near the temple was named after this occasion.

仙曰:"知和尚法力廣大. 但吾高祖墳墓竝在此地, 他日造塔, 幸望
선왈: "지화상법력광대. 단오고조분묘병재차지, 타일조탑, 행망

存留. 餘願盡捨, 永爲寶坊. 然此地乃生龍・白象來脈, 只可平天,
존류. 여원진사, 영위보방. 연차지내생룡・백상래맥, 지가평천,

不可平地."
불가평지."

寺後營建一依其言.
사후영건일의기언.

師遊境內山水勝處, 輒憩止, 遂成蘭若一十三所, 今曰花果院, 隷
사유경내산수승처, 첩게지, 수성난야일십삼소, 금왈화과원, 예

籍寺門.
적사문.

Yaxian said, "Now I see that Your Reverence's spiritual power is immense. However, as my great-great-grandparents' tombs are all located here, I hope they will be preserved when you build stupa in the future. I am willing to donate all the rest. May it be a treasured site for ever. However, since here beneath this land flows a vein of a living dragon and a white elephant, you may well respect the lay of the land and should not level it flat."

His words were thoroughly observed when they constructed the temple buildings afterwards.

The Master walked through picturesque hills and streams within the temple site and would stop and rest from time to time. He established thirteen serene retreats, now known as the Flowers and Fruits Garden.

> 茲寶林道場亦先是西國智藥三藏自南海經曹溪口, 掬水而飲, 香美
> 자보림도량역선시서국지약삼장자남해경조계구, 국수이음, 향미
>
> 異之, 謂其徒曰:"此水與西天之水無別. 溪源上必有勝地, 堪爲蘭
> 이지, 위기도왈:"차수여서천지수무별. 계원상필유승지, 감위난
>
> 若."
> 야."
>
> 隨流至源上, 四顧山水回環, 峯巒奇秀, 歎曰:"宛如西天寶林山
> 수류지원상, 사고산수회환, 봉만기수, 탄왈:"완여서천보림산
>
> 也."
> 야."

The records are kept in the temple.

This Baolin site was also previously visited by Tripiṭaka[S] Master Zhiyue from India. He arrived from the South Sea at the mouth of Caoqi. He drank a sip of water from the stream and found it extraordinarily fragrant. So he said to his followers, "The water is no different from that of India. Upstream, there must be a supreme land, suitable for a monastery."

As Zhiyue followed the stream to reach above the fountain and looked around the surrounding mountains and streams, he found that the peaks and valleys were extraordinarily fine, and exclaimed, "It's completely like the Treasure Forest Mountain in India!"

> 乃謂曹侯村居民曰:"可於此山建一梵刹. 一百七十年後, 當有無上
> 내위조후촌거민왈: "가어차산건일범찰. 일백칠십년후, 당유무상
> 法寶於此演化, 得道者如林, 宜號寶林."
> 법보어차연화, 득도자여림, 의호보림."
> 時韶州牧侯敬中以其言具表聞奏. 上可其請, 賜寶林爲額, 遂成梵
> 시소주목후경중이기언구표문진. 상가기청, 사보림위액, 수성범
> 宮, 落成於梁天監三年.
> 궁, 낙성어양천감삼년.
>
> 寺殿前有潭一所, 龍常出沒其間, 觸橈林木. 一日現形甚巨, 波浪
> 사전전유담일소, 용상출몰기간, 촉뇨임목. 일일현형심거, 파랑
> 洶涌, 雲霧陰翳. 徒衆皆懼.
> 흉용, 운무음예. 도중개구.

So he told the residents of Caohou Village, "A temple may be built on this mountain. In one hundred and seventy years, the Supreme Dhamma Treasure will flourish here, and those who attain enlightenment will be as countless as the trees in the forest. Thus the temple shall be named Baolin, 'Treasure Forest.'"

Then Hou Jingzhong, the prefect of Shaozhou, submitted a report on such words to the Emperor. The Emperor approved the request and bestowed the name Baolin for its signboard. The temple was completed, and the inauguration ceremony task place in the third year of the Tianjian era, during the Liang Dynasty.

In front of the temple's hall was a pond, where a dragon often appeared, touching and brushing against the trees in the forest. One day, it emerged in an enormous, ominous form, stirring up violent waves, while dense clouds and mist shrouded the entire area. The entire assembly was overcome with fear.

> 師叱之曰："爾只能現大身, 不能現小身. 若爲神龍, 當能變化, 以
> 사질지왈: "이지능현대신, 불능현소신. 약위신룡, 당능변화, 이
>
> 小小現大, 以大現小也."
> 소소현대, 이대현소야."
>
> 其龍忽沒, 俄頃復現小身, 躍出潭面. 師展鉢試之, 曰："爾且不敢
> 기룡홀몰, 아경부현소신, 약출담면. 사전발시지, 왈: "이차불감
>
> 入老僧鉢盂裏."
> 입노승발우리."
>
> 龍乃游揚至前, 師以鉢舀之, 龍不能動.
> 용내유양지전, 사이발요지, 용불능동.

The Master scolded the dragon, saying, "You can only manifest yourself in a large body, not in a small one. If you're a divine dragon, you must be able to transform yourself from small to large and large to small."

The dragon suddenly disappeared, and reappeared after a while in its small body, leaping out of the pond. The Master held out his alms bowl to test it, saying, "I doubt you would even dare to enter the old monk's alms bowl."

As the dragon swam near the Master, he swiftly scooped it up with his alms bowl, rendering it motionless.

師持鉢上堂, 與龍説法. 龍遂蛻骨而去. 其骨長可七寸, 首尾·角足
사지발상당, 여룡설법. 용수태골이거. 기골장가칠촌, 수미·각족

皆具, 留傳寺門. 師後以土石堙其潭. 今殿前左側有鐵塔鎭處是也.
개구, 유전사문. 사후이토석인기담. 금전전좌측유철탑진처시야.

The Master carried alms bowl into the hall and delivered a sermon to the dragon. Finally, the dragon shed its physical form and departed. The bones measured nearly seven inches in length, with the head, tail, horns and feet intact. They were preserved and passed down within the temple. Later the Master filled the pond with soil and rocks. Today, on the left side of the main hall an iron pagoda stands at the very spot to supress it.

第一 行由品
제일 행유품

時大師至寶林. 韶州韋刺史與官僚入山, 請師於大梵寺講堂, 爲衆
시대사지보림. 소주위자사여관료입산, 청사어대범사강당, 위중

開緣, 説摩訶般若波羅密法.
개연, 설마하반야바라밀법.

師升座次. 刺史·官僚三十餘人, 儒宗學士三十餘人, 僧尼·道俗一
사승좌차. 자사·관료삼십여인, 유종학사삼십여인, 승니·도속일

千餘人同時作禮, 願聞法要.
천여인동시작례, 원문법요.

Chapter One

Of the Origin

At that time, the Master arrived at Baolin in Shaozhou. Prefect Wei and his officials entered the mountain, and invited the Master to the lecture hall of Dafan Temple, requesting him to expound the teaching of Mahāpaññāpāramitā, establishing a karmic connection with the public.

The Master ascended the platform. The prefect along with over thirty officials, more than thirty Confucian scholars, and over a thousand monks, nuns, and lay followers, all paid their respects and sincerely requested to hear the essential teaching of the dhamma.

大師告衆曰:
대사고중왈:

"善知識, 菩提自性本來淸淨. 但用此心, 直了成佛.
"선지식, 보리자성본래청정. 단용차심, 직료성불.

善知識, 且聽惠能行由·得法事意.
선지식, 차청혜능행유·득법사의.

能嚴父, 本貫范陽. 左降, 流于嶺南, 作新州百姓. 此身不幸, 父又
능엄부, 본관범양. 좌강, 유우영남, 작신주백성. 차신불행, 부우

早亡. 老母·孤遺後來南海, 艱辛貧乏, 於市賣柴.
조망. 노모·고유후래남해, 간신빈핍, 어시매시.

The Master told the assembly,

"Good learned friends, Self-nature of bodhi is originally clear and pure. Use this mind only, and then you shall directly accomplish Buddhahood.

Good learned friends, listen to my personal history and how I came to attain the dhamma, and its meaning.

My father was from Fanyang. Degraded and exiled to Lingnan, he became a commoner at Xinzhou. Unfortunately for me, he passed away early. The elderly mother and the orphan later moved to Nanhai, where we suffered from poverty and hardship, selling firewood in the market.

時有一客買柴, 使令送至客店. 客收去, 能得錢, 却出門外, 見一
시유일객매시, 사령송지객점. 객수거, 능득전, 각출문외, 견일

客誦經. 能一聞經云'應無所住而生其心', 心即開悟.
객송경. 능일문경운'응무소주이생기심', 심즉개오.

遂問: '客誦何經?'
수문: '객송하경?'

客曰: '『金剛經』.'
객왈: '『금강경』.'

復問: '從何所來持此經典?'
부문: '종하소래지차경전?'

客云: '我從蘄州黃梅懸東禪寺來. 其寺是五祖忍大師在彼主
객운: '아종기주황매현동선사래. 기사시오조인대사재피주
化, 門人一千有餘.
화, 문인일천유여.

One day, a customer purchased some firewood, requesting it to be delivered to the inn. After delivering the firewood and receiving payment, I was about to leave out through the gate, when I encountered another traveler who was reciting a Scripture. As soon as I heard the phrase 'Produce the mind that has nowhere to abide in,' my mind was immediately opened up and enlightened.

So I asked him, 'What Scripture is it that you are reciting, Sir?'

He replied, 'It's the Diamond Scripture.'

I asked again, 'Where did you obtain that Scripture?'

He replied, 'I come from the Dongchan Temple of Huangmei County in Qizhou. The temple is led by Master Hongren, the Fifth Patriarch, and there are over a thousand followers.

> 我到彼中禮拜, 聽受此經. 大師常勸僧俗: 但持『金剛
> 아도피중예배, 청수차경. 대사상권승속: 단지『금강
>
> 經』, 即自見性, 直了成佛.'
> 경』, 즉자견성, 직료성불.'
>
> 能聞說, 宿昔有緣, 乃蒙一客取銀十兩與能, 令充老母衣糧, 教便
> 능문설, 숙석유연, 내몽일객취은십량여능, 영충노모의량, 교변
>
> 往黃梅, 禮拜五祖.
> 왕황매, 예배오조.
>
> 能安置母, 畢即便辭親, 不經三十餘日便至黃梅禮拜.
> 능안치모, 필즉변사친, 불경삼십여일변지황매예배.

I went there, paid my respects, and listened to this Scripture. The Master always encourages both monks and lay followers, saying, 'Just hold onto the Diamond Scripture, and you shall see your Self-nature and directly accomplish Buddhahood.'

Upon hearing these words, as if there had been a karmic connection from the past, another kind traveler gave me ten liangs of silver, urging me to provide my elderly mother with clothing and food, and to travel to Huangmei to pay respects to the Fifth Patriarch.

After serving my elderly mother's livelihood, I bid farewell to her and set out, reaching Huangmei in just over thirty days, and paying my respects.

> 五祖問曰:'汝何方人? 欲求何物?'
> 오조문왈: '여하방인? 욕구하물?'
>
> 能對曰:'弟子是嶺南新州百姓. 遠來禮師, 惟求作佛, 不求餘物.'
> 능대왈: '제자시영남신주백성. 원래예사, 유구작불, 불구여물.'
>
> 祖言:'汝是嶺南人, 又是獦獠, 若爲堪作佛?'
> 조언: '여시영남인, 우시갈료, 약위감작불?'
>
> 能曰:'人雖有南北, 佛性本無南北. 獦獠身與和尚不同, 佛性有何 差別?'
> 능왈: '인수유남북, 불성본무남북. 갈료신여화상부동, 불성유하 차별?'

The Fifth Patriarch asked me, 'Where are you from, and what do you seek?'

I replied, 'I am a commoner from Xinzhou, Lingnan. I have come from far away and to pay my respects, seeking only to become Buddha and nothing else.'

The Patriarch said, 'You are from Lingnan, and you are a barbarian. How could you possibly become a Buddha?'

I replied, 'Even though people from the north and from the south may be different, there is no such distinction in Buddha-nature. Although I may have a barbarian's body which differs from that of Your Reverence, how can there be any difference in Buddha-nature?'

祖更欲與語, 且見徒衆總在左右, 乃令隨衆作務.
조갱욕여어, 차견도중총재좌우, 내령수중작무.
惠能曰: '啓, 和尙, 弟子自心, 常生智慧, 不離自性, 卽是福田.
혜능왈: '계, 화상, 제자자심, 상생지혜, 불리자성, 즉시복전.
未審和尙敎作何務?'
미심화상교작하무?'
祖云: '這獦獠根性大利. 汝更勿言, 著槽廠去.'
조운: '저갈료근성대리. 여갱물언, 착조창거.'
能退, 至後院, 有一行者差能破柴踏碓, 經八月餘.
능퇴, 지후원. 유일행자차능파시답대, 경팔월여.
祖一日忽見能曰: '吾思汝之見可用, 恐有惡人害汝, 遂不與汝言.
조일일홀견능왈: '오사여지견가용, 공유악인해여, 수불여여언.
汝知之否?'
여지지부?'

The Patriarch wished to continue the conversation, but seeing that his disciples were constantly surrounding him, he instructed me to attend to the followers' affairs.

I then said to the Patriarch, 'Please, Your Reverence, in my mind, if one always gives rise to wisdom and is never separate from his Self-nature, there is the field of merit in him. I do not yet know what task Your Reverence wishes to assign me.'

The Patriarch said, 'This barbarian has a keen disposition. Say no more, go to work in the granary.'

I retired to the backyard, where a practitioner instructed me to break firewood and operate the millstone for more than eight months.

One day the Patriarch suddenly visited me, saying, 'I recognized that your views can be of use, but I was afraid that someone wicked might harm you, so I did not speak to you. Did you know?'

> 能曰: '弟子亦知師意, 不敢行至堂前, 令人不覺.'
> 능왈: '제자역지사의, 불감행지당전, 영인불각.'
>
> 祖一日喚諸門人總來.
> 조일일환제문인총래.
>
> '吾向汝說. 世人生死事大. 汝等終日只求福田, 不求出離生死苦海.
> '오향여설. 세인생사사대. 여등종일지구복전, 불구출리생사고해.
>
> 自性若迷, 福何可救? 汝等各去, 自看智慧, 取自本心般若之性,
> 자성약미, 복하가구? 여등각거, 자간지혜, 취자본심반야지성,
>
> 各作一偈, 來吾呈看.
> 각작일게, 내오정간.

I replied, 'I also understood your intention and I have not been near the main hall, so that no one would notice.'

One day, the Patriarch summoned all the disciples and said,

'Listen carefully. The matter of birth and death is of great importance to worldly people. However, you all seek only blessings and merit, but do not seek to liberate yourselves from the painful sea of birth and death. If you are ignorant of your Self-nature, how can blessings save you? Go, each of you, examine your own wisdom, take your own nature of paññā and, each of you, compose a verse and come show it to me.

若悟大意, 付汝衣法, 爲第六代祖. 火急速
약오대의, 부여의법, 위제육대조. 화급속

去, 不得遲滯. 思量即不中用, 見性之人言下須見. 若如此者, 輪
거, 부득지체. 사량즉부중용, 견성지인언하수견. 약여차자, 윤

刀上陣, 亦得見之.'
도상진, 역득견지.'

衆得處分, 退而遞相謂曰: '我等衆人不須澄心用意. 作偈將呈和
중득처분, 퇴이체상위왈: '아등중인불수징심용의. 작계장정화

尚, 有何所益? 神秀上座現爲教授師, 必是他得. 我輩謾作偈頌,
상, 유하소익? 신수상좌현위교수사, 필시타득. 아배만작계송,

枉用心力?'
왕용심력?'

Should there be anyone that understands the main point, I will give him the robe and the dhamma and he shall become the Sixth Patriarch. Hurry up, leave without delay. Thinking about it won't do any good. He who has realized seeing-nature must see it in a word. Such a man can see it, even amid a battle of swords.'

Now that the disciples received their assignments and left, they discussed among themselves, saying, 'We ordinary disciples don't have to clear our minds and pay attention. Even if we compose our verses and present them to His Reverence, what benefit is there? As the senior disciple Shenxiu is now our instructor and is expected to receive the transmission, there is no need for the rest of us to waste our efforts composing verses.'

餘人聞語, 總皆息心, 咸言：'我等已後依止秀師, 何煩作偈?'
여인문어, 총개식심, 함언：'아등이후의지수사, 하번작게?'

神秀思惟：'諸人不呈偈者, 爲我與他爲教授師. 我須作偈, 將呈和
신수사유：'제인부정게자, 위아여타위교수사. 아수작게, 장정화

尚. 若不呈偈, 和尚如何知我心中見解深淺? 我呈偈意, 求法即善,
상. 약불정게, 화상여하지아심중견해심천? 아정게의, 구법즉선,

覓祖即惡, 却同凡心奪其聖位奚別? 若不呈偈, 終不得法. 大難大難.'
멱조즉악, 각동범심탈기성위해별? 약부정게, 종부득법. 대난대난.'

Upon hearing this, the rest of the disciples calmed their minds, saying, 'Since we will hence forth rely on Shenxiu as our instructor, there is no need to bother ourselves composing verses.'

Shenxiu thought to himself, 'It is because the other disciples consider me their instructor that they do not compose and present their verses to His Reverence. I should compose one and present it to His Reverence. If I don't, how could he know the depth of my understanding? If my intention in presenting a verse is to seek the dhamma, it is good; if it is to seek the position of patriarch, it is bad, as it is no different from the ordinary mind that seeks to claim the position of a saint. If I don't present a verse, however, I will never attain the dhamma. Very difficult, very difficult!'

> 五祖堂前有步廊三間, 擬請供奉盧珍畫『楞伽經』變相及五祖血脈
> 오조당전유보랑삼간, 의청공봉노진화『능가경』변상급오조혈맥
>
> 圖, 流傳供養.
> 도, 유전공양.
>
> 神秀作偈成已, 數度欲呈, 行至堂前, 心中恍惚, 遍身汗流, 擬呈
> 신수작게성이, 수도욕정, 행지당전, 심중황홀, 변신한류, 의정
>
> 不得. 前後經四日一十三度, 呈偈不得.
> 부득. 전후경사일일십삼도, 정게부득.
>
> 秀乃思惟: '不如向廊下書着, 從他和尚看見, 忽若道好, 即出禮拜,
> 수내사유: '불여향낭하서착, 종타화상간견, 홀약도호, 즉출예배,

In front of the Fifth Patriarch's chamber, there was a three-span corridor. The Patriarch was to invite the painter Luzhen to create a painting depicting the Laṅkāvatāra Sutta and a genealogy chart of the five Patriarchs, which would be passed down and offered for worship.

Shenxiu had already finished composing his verse. He intended to present it to the Fifth Patriarch several times, but every time he walked to his chamber, he suddenly felt confused and began to sweat all over his body, so he couldn't bring himself to present the verse. He tried thirteen times for four days, but failed to do so.

> 云是秀作；若道不堪, 枉向山中數年, 受人禮拜, 更修何道？'
> 운시수작; 약도불감, 왕향산중수년, 수인예배, 갱수하도?'
> 是夜三更, 不使人知, 自執燈, 書偈於南廊壁間, 呈心所見.
> 시야삼경, 불사인지, 자집등, 서게어남랑벽간, 정심소견.
> 偈曰:
> 게왈:
> '身是菩提樹, 心如明鏡臺.
> '신시보리수, 심여명경대.
> 時時勤拂拭, 勿使惹塵埃.'
> 시시근불식, 물사야진애.'

He thought again, 'It would be better to write the verse on the corridor wall so that His Reverence can see it. If he were to see it and praise it, then I would immediately come forward to pay my respects and say that I had composed it; if he says it is not enough, what is the use of vainly practicing in this mountain for years receiving others' respect?'

That midnight, without letting anyone know, Shenxiu took a lamp and wrote a verse on the wall of the southern corridor, expressing what was in his mind.

The verse goes,

'The body is the tree of bodhi;
And the mind is like a mirror's stand.
At all times diligently polish it,
Lest it should gain any dust.'

> 秀書偈了, 便却歸房. 人總不知.
> 수서게료, 변각귀방. 인총부지.
>
> 秀復思惟: '五祖明日見偈歡喜, 即我與法有緣; 若言不堪, 自是我
> 수부사유: '오조명일견게환희, 즉아여법유연; 약언불감, 자시아
>
> 迷, 宿業障重, 不合得法. 聖意難測.'
> 미, 숙업장중, 불합득법. 성의난측.'
>
> 房中思想, 坐臥不安, 直至五更.
> 방중사상, 좌와불안, 직지오경.

After Shenxiu finished writing the verse, he went back to his room, without anyone knowing.

Again Shenxiu reflected on the matter. 'The next day, if the Patriarch sees the verse and is delighted, I have a connection with the dhamma; but if he says it is not enough, I am not qualified to attain the dhamma, just because I myself am deluded and my karmic obstacles are great. How difficult it is to fathom his intention!'

Shenxiu was lost in thought in his room, unable to sit or lie down comfortably. This continued until dawn.

> 祖已知神秀入門未得, 不見自性.
> 조이지신수입문미득, 불견자성.
>
> 天明, 祖喚盧供奉來, 向南廊壁間繪畫圖相. 忽見其偈, 報言供奉:
> 천명, 조환노공봉래, 향남랑벽간회화도상. 홀견기게, 보언공봉:
>
> '却不用畫, 勞爾遠來. 經云: 凡所有相皆是虛妄. 但留此偈, 與人
> '각불용화, 노이원래. 경운: 범소유상개시허망. 단류차게, 여인
>
> 誦持. 依此偈修, 免墮惡道, 依此偈修, 有大利益.'
> 송지. 의차게수, 면타악도, 의차게수, 유대이익.'
>
> 令門人炷香禮敬, 盡誦此偈, 即得見性. 門人誦偈, 皆歎: '善哉!'
> 영문인주향예경, 진송차게, 즉득견성. 문인송게, 개탄: '선재!'

The Patriarch already knew that Shenxiu had not yet entered the gate and didn't see his Self-nature.

At dawn, the Patriarch summoned the painter Luzhen to paint on the wall of the southern corridor. Suddenly he saw Shenxiu's verse, and said to the painter, 'You don't need to paint anymore. You made the effort to come from afar in vain. The Scripture says, All phenomena are illusory and empty. Let's just retain this verse, for people to recite. Practicing according to it can prevent you from falling into the path of suffering; by practicing according to this verse, great benefits can be gained.'

The Patriarch ordered the followers to burn incense and pay their respects while reciting the verse. Through this, they would immediately realize seeing-nature. All the followers recited the verse and praised it, 'Excellent!'

I. Of the Origin

> 祖三更喚秀入堂, 問曰: '偈是汝作否?'
> 조삼경환수입당, 문왈: '게시여작부?'
>
> 秀言: '實是秀作, 不敢妄求祖位. 望和尚慈悲看. 弟子有少智慧否?'
> 수언: '실시수작, 불감망구조위. 망화상자비간. 제자유소지혜부?'
>
> 祖曰: '汝作此偈, 未見本性. 只到門外, 未入門內. 如此見解, 覓
> 조왈: '여작차게, 미견본성. 지도문외, 미입문내. 여차견해, 멱
>
> 無上菩提, 了不可得. 無上菩提, 須得言下. 識自本心, 見自本性
> 무상보리, 요불가득. 무상보리, 수득언하. 식자본심, 견자본성
>
> 不生不滅.
> 불생불멸.

At midnight, the Patriarch summoned Shenxiu to come in to his chamber and asked him, 'You composed this verse, didn't you?'

Shenxiu replied, 'Yes, I did compose it, but I dare not recklessly seek the patriarchate. Please have mercy, Your Reverence: Does your pupil have even a little bit of wisdom?'

The Patriarch said, 'The verse you composed does not show that you have seen your original nature. You have only arrived at the gate, not entering yet. With such understanding, seeking the unsurpassable bodhi, it is ultimately impossible to attain. One must realize the unsurpassable bodhi the moment words are spoken. Therefore know your original mind and see your original nature, which is neither born nor destroyed.

> 於一切時中, 念念自見萬法無滯. 一眞一切眞, 萬境自
> 어일체시중, 염념자견만법무체. 일진일체진, 만경자
>
> 如如. 如如之心, 即是眞實. 若如是見, 即是無上菩提之自性也.
> 여여. 여여지심, 즉시진실. 약여시견, 즉시무상보리지자성야.
>
> 汝且去, 一兩日思惟, 更作一偈, 將來吾看. 汝偈若入得門, 付汝
> 여차거, 일량일사유, 갱작일게, 장래오간. 여게약입득문, 부여
>
> 衣法.'
> 의법.'
>
> 神秀作禮而出. 又經數日, 作偈不成. 心中恍惚, 神思不安, 猶如
> 신수작례이출. 우경수일, 작게불성. 심중황홀, 신사불안, 유여
>
> 夢中, 行坐不樂.
> 몽중, 행좌불락.

Throughout all times, constantly see that all phenomena are unobstructed. When one is true, then everything is true. All environments, all things are as they are and the mind just as it is, which is the true reality. If you can see things in this way, then it is the Self-nature of unsurpassable bodhi. Go and contemplate for a couple of days, compose another verse, and bring it to me for inspection. If your verse shows that you have entered the gate, I will transmit to you the robe and the dhamma.'

Shenxiu paid his respects and withdrew, but within several days he was unable to compose a verse. His mind was scattered and restless as if in a dream, and was uncomfortable while walking or sitting.

> 復兩日, 有一童子於碓坊過, 唱誦其偈. 能一聞便知此偈未見本性.
> 부량일, 유일동자어대방과, 창송기게. 능일문변지차게미견본성.
>
> 雖未蒙教授, 早識大意.
> 수미몽교수, 조식대의.
>
> 遂問童子曰: '誦者何偈?'
> 수문동자왈: '송자하게?'
>
> 童子言: '爾這獦獠不知? 大師言: 世人生死事大. 欲得傳付衣法,
> 동자언: '이저갈료부지? 대사언: 세인생사사대. 욕득전부의법,
>
> 令門人作偈來看. 若悟大意, 即付衣法, 爲第六祖.
> 영문인작게래간. 약오대의, 즉부의법, 위제육조.

Again a couple of days later, an acolyte passed by the mill, reciting Shenxiu's verse. As soon as I heard it, I knew that the author had not yet seen his original nature. For I understood the essence, even though I had not received any teaching.

So I asked the boy, 'What is the verse that you are reciting?'

The boy replied, Don't you barbarian know? The Master said, The matter of birth and death is of great importance to worldly people. He wished to transmit the robe and the dhamma to him who truly comprehends the dhamma, so that he can instruct his disciples. Whoever writes a verse and comes to show him, if he has understood the great meaning, he shall be transmitted the robe and the dhamma and become the Sixth Patriarch.

> 神秀上座於南廊壁上書無相偈.
> 신수상좌어남랑벽상서무상게.
>
> 大師令人皆誦此偈. 依此偈修, 免墮惡道, 依此
> 대사령인개송차게. 의차게수, 면타악도, 의차
>
> 偈修, 有大利益.'
> 게수, 유대이익.'
>
> 惠能曰:'上人, 我此踏碓八箇餘月, 未曾行到堂前. 望上人慈悲指
> 혜능왈:'상인, 아차답대팔개여월, 미증행도당전. 망상인자비지
>
> 示, 引至偈前禮拜.'
> 시, 인지게전예배.'
>
> 童子引至偈前. 作禮, 能曰:'能不識字, 請上人爲讀.'
> 동자인지게전. 작례, 능왈:'능불식자, 청상인위독.'

Then Shenxiu the elder monk wrote a verse of no-form on the wall of the southern corridor, and the Master ordered everyone to recite it. Practicing according to it can prevent one from falling into the path of suffering; by practicing according to this verse, great benefits can be gained.'

So I said to him, 'Please, Your Venerability, I have been treading the mill for over eight months and have never been in front of the hall. Please, Elder, take compassion on me and guide me to the verse, so that I can pay my respects.'

The boy led me to the verse. I paid my respects, and told the boy, 'I cannot read, so I beg Your Venerability to read it for me.'

時有江州別駕, 姓張, 名一用, 便高聲讀. 惠能聞已, 遂言: '亦有一偈. 望別駕爲書.'
시유강주별가, 성장, 명일용, 변고성독. 혜능문이, 수언: '역유일게. 망별가위서.'

別駕言: '獦獠汝亦作偈, 其事希有!'
별가언: '갈료여역작게, 기사희유!'

能啓別駕言: '欲學無上菩提, 不得輕於初學. 下下人有上上智, 上上人有沒意智. 若輕人, 卽有無量無邊罪.'
능계별가언: '욕학무상보리, 부득경어초학. 하하인유상상지, 상상인유몰의지. 약경인, 즉유무량무변죄.'

別駕言: '汝但誦偈, 吾爲汝書. 汝若得法, 先須度吾. 勿忘此言.'
별가언: '여단송게, 오위여서. 여약득법, 선수도오. 물망차언.'

At that time, a provincial official from Jiangzhou, named Zhang Yiyong was reciting the verse aloud. Upon hearing it, I said to him, 'I also have composed a verse. Please, write it down for me.'

The official replied, 'You barbarian also composed a verse! How extraordinary!'

But I insisted, saying, 'If you are to learn the unsurpassable bodhi, you should not take the beginners lightly. Even the lowest people can have the highest wisdom, and the highest people can lack intelligence. If you take someone lightly, you are committing immeasurable and boundless sins.'

The official said, 'You just recite the verse. I will write it down for you. If you attain the dhamma, you should first guide me. Do not forget my words.'

> 能偈曰:
> 능게왈:
>
> '菩提本無樹, 明鏡亦非臺.
> '보리본무수, 명경역비대.
>
> 本來無一物, 何處惹塵埃?'
> 본래무일물, 하처야진애?'
>
> 書此偈已, 徒衆總驚, 無不嗟訝, 各相謂言: '奇哉! 不得以貌取人.
> 서차게이, 도중총경, 무불차아, 각상위언: '기재! 부득이모취인.
>
> 何得多時使他肉身菩薩?'
> 하득다시사타육신보살?'

Huineng then recited the following verse.

'Bodhi has no tree;

The bright mirror has no stand.

Fundamentally, there is not a single thing,

Where could dust be accumulated?'

After he wrote down my verse, all the disciples were amazed and impressed, saying to one another, 'Amazing! You should not judge another by his appearance. For how could we have been in the presence of such a living Bodhisattva[s] for so long!'

祖見衆人驚怪, 恐人損害, 遂將鞋擦了偈, 云:'亦未見性.'衆人疑
조견중인경괴, 공인손해, 수장혜찰료게, 운:'역미견성.'중인의
息.
식.
次日祖潛至碓坊, 見能腰石舂米, 語曰:'求道之人爲法忘軀, 當如
차일조잠지대방, 견능요석용미, 어왈:'구도지인위법망구, 당여
是乎!'
시호!'
即問曰:'米熟也未?'
즉문왈:'미숙야미?'
能曰:'米熟久矣, 猶欠篩在.'
능왈:'미숙구의, 유흠사재.'

The Patriarch saw the assembly's surprise and wonder. Afraid that someone should harm me, he wiped away the verse with his shoe, saying, 'He has not yet realized seeing-nature.' No one doubted.

The next day, the Patriarch secretly visited the mill and saw me pounding rice with a stone tied around my waist. He said, 'He who seeks the path should forget his body for the sake of dhamma just like that!'

Then he asked me, 'Is the rice husked yet?'

I replied, 'It was husked long before, but has not yet been winnowed.'

> 祖以杖擊碓三下而去. 能即會祖意. 三鼓入室. 祖以袈裟遮圍, 不
> 조이장격대삼하이거. 능즉회조의. 삼고입실. 조이가사차위, 불
>
> 令人見, 爲說『金剛經』. 至'應無所住而生其心', 能言下大悟一切
> 령인견, 위설『금강경』. 지'응무소주이생기심', 능언하대오일체
>
> 萬法不離自性. 遂啓祖言:
> 만법불리자성. 수계조언:
>
> '何期自性本自淸淨?
> '하기자성본자청정?
>
> 何期自性本不生滅?
> 하기자성본불생멸?

The Patriarch hit the mortar three times with his stick and left. I immediately understood his intention. After three drumbeats, I entered the Patriarch's chamber. He covered the surroundings with his robe, not allowing others to see. Then he preached the Diamond Scripture to me. Upon reaching the phrase, 'Produce the mind that has nowhere to abide in,' I had a great enlightenment, realizing that all phenomena are inseparable from their Self-nature.

I then spoke to the Patriarch:

'Who would have thought that Self-nature is originally clear and pure?

Who would have thought that Self-nature is neither born nor destroyed?

> 何期自性本自具足?
> 하기자성본자구족?
>
> 何期自性本無動搖?
> 하기자성본무동요?
>
> 何期自性能生萬法?'
> 하기자성능생만법?'
>
> 祖知悟本性, 謂惠能曰:'不識本心, 學法無益. 若識自本心, 見自
> 조지오본성, 위혜능왈: 불식본심, 학법무익. 약식자본심, 견자
>
> 本性, 卽名丈夫, 天人師佛.'
> 본성, 즉명장부, 천인사불.'

Who would have thought that Self-nature is inherently complete?

Who would have thought that Self-nature is unshakable?

Who would have thought that Self-nature can create all phenomena?'

The Patriarch, recognizing my enlightenment to my original nature, said, 'If you do not know your original mind, studying the dhamma is of no benefit. If you know your original mind and see your original nature, you can be called a true hero, whom the heavenly beings serve as Buddha.'

> 三更受法, 人盡不知. 便傳頓敎及衣鉢, 云:'汝爲第六代祖. 善自
> 삼경수법, 인진부지. 변전돈교급의발, 운:'여위제육대조. 선자
>
> 護念, 廣度有情, 流布將來, 無令斷絶. 聽吾偈.' 曰:
> 호념, 광도유정, 유포장래, 무령단절. 청오게.' 왈:
>
> '有情來下種, 因地果還生.
> '유정래하종, 인지과환생.
>
> 無情旣無種, 無性亦無生.'
> 무정기무종, 무성역무생.'

At midnight I received the dhamma. No one else noticed it.

Now that the Patriarch had transmitted the sudden teaching as well as the robe and the bowl to me, he said, 'I declare you as the Sixth Patriarch. Take good care of yourself, and widely save sentient beings. Spread the teachings far into the future and never let the teaching die out. Listen to my verse.'

It goes,

'Sentient beings come to sow seeds.
According to the ground, the fruits are produced.
Insentient beings do not sow seeds,
For there is no nature, nor production.'

> 祖復曰: '昔達摩大師初來此土, 人未之信. 故傳此衣, 以爲信體,
> 조부왈: '석달마대사초래차토, 인미지신. 고전차의, 이위신체,
>
> 代代相承. 法卽以心傳心, 皆令自悟自解. 自故佛佛惟傳本體,
> 대대상승. 법즉이심전심, 개령자오자해. 자고불불유전본체,
>
> 師師密付本心. 衣爲爭端, 止汝勿傳. 若傳此衣, 命如懸絲.
> 사사밀부본심. 의위쟁단, 지여물전. 약전차의, 명여현사.
>
> 汝須速去, 恐人害汝.'
> 여수속거, 공인해여.'
>
> 能曰: '向甚處去?'　　　祖云: '逢懷卽止, 遇會卽藏.'
> 능왈: '향심처거?'　　　조운: '봉회즉지, 우회즉장.'

The Patriarch continued, 'In the past, when the Great Master Bodhidharma[S] first came to this land, people did not believe in him. Therefore, he transmitted this robe as a symbol of faith, which was to be passed down from generation to generation. The dhamma is transmitted from mind to mind, allowing each person only to enlighten and realize it for themselves. Since ancient times, each Buddha has transmitted His essence, and each master has secretly passed on his original mind. The robe will be a source of contention, so from now on, do not hand it down. If you transmit this robe, your life will become as dangerous as if hanging by a thread. You must leave quickly, lest others should harm you.'

I asked, 'Where should I go?'

The Patriarch replied, 'Stop when you encounter huai, hide at hui.'

> 惠能三更領得衣鉢, 云: '能本是南中人, 久不知此山路. 如何出得
> 혜능삼경영득의발, 운: '능본시남중인, 구부지차산로. 여하출득
> 江口?'
> 강구?'
>
> 五祖言: '汝不須憂. 吾自送汝.'
> 오조언: '여불수우. 오자송여.'
>
> 祖相送, 直至九江驛邊. 有一隻船子, 祖令惠能上船. 五祖把艣自
> 조상송, 직지구강역변. 유일척선자, 조령혜능상선. 오조파로자
> 搖.
> 요.
>
> 惠能言: '請和尚坐. 弟子合搖艣.'
> 혜능언: '청화상좌. 제자합요로.'

At midnight I was given the robe and the bowl. I asked, 'I am originally from the south, not familiar with the roads of this mountain for long. How can I reach the mouth of the river?'

The Patriarch replied, 'Do not worry. I will send you off myself.'

The Patriarch accompanied me all the way to the edge of the Jiujiang Station, where there was a boat. The Patriarch told me to board, and he took the oars himself and started rowing.

I said, 'Please, Your Reverence, take a seat. Let your disciple row.'

> 五祖云: '合是吾渡汝.'
> 오조운: '합시오도여.'
>
> 能云: '迷時師度, 悟了自度. 度名雖一, 用處不同. 惠能生在邊方,
> 능운: '미시사도, 오료자도. 도명수일, 용처부동. 혜능생재변방,
>
> 語音不正, 蒙師傳法, 今已得悟. 只合自性自度.'
> 어음부정, 몽사전법, 금이득오. 지합자성자도.'
>
> 祖云: '如是如是. 以後佛法由汝大行. 汝去三年, 吾方逝世. 汝今
> 조운: '여시여시. 이후불법유여대행. 여거삼년, 오방서세. 여금
>
> 好去, 努力向南. 不宜速説, 佛法難起.'
> 호거, 노력향남. 불의속설, 불법난기.'

The Patriarch replied, 'It is appropriate that I ferry you across.'

I said, 'When I was deluded, my Master guided me, but now that I have become enlightened, I can guide myself. Although the word to guide is one and the same, the way it functions is different. I was born in a borderland, and my speech is not refined. Yet, thanks to my Master's transmission of the dhamma, I have now attained enlightenment. I should rely on my Self-nature to guide myself.'

The Patriarch said, 'That's right, that's right. From now on, Buddha's teachings will flourish greatly through you. After three years, I will pass away. Now, go well. Make an effort to head south. Do not preach too early, for the Buddha-dhamma is difficult to spread.'

能辭違祖已, 發足南行. 兩月中間至大庾嶺.
능사위조이, 발족남행. 양월중간지대유령.

逐後數百人來, 欲奪衣鉢. 一僧, 俗姓陳, 名惠明, 先是四品將軍,
축후수백인래, 욕탈의발. 일승, 속성진, 명혜명, 선시사품장군,

性行麤慥, 極意參尋, 爲衆人先, 趁及於能.
성행추조, 극의참심, 위중인선, 진급어능.

惠能擲下衣鉢於石上, 云: '此衣表信, 可力爭耶?' 能隱草莽中.
혜능척하의발어석상, 운: '차의표신, 가력쟁야?' 능은초망중.

I bid farewell to the Patriarch and started southward. In about two months, I reached the Dayuling Pass.

Meanwhile, hundreds of people were running after me, seeking to seize the robe and the bowl. One of them, a monk named Huiming, who was from the Chen family and previously a general of the fourth rank, known for his coarse and rough personality and behavior, was extremely eager to seek the robe. He led a group of people and nearly caught up with me.

I threw the robe and bowl onto a rock, saying to myself, 'This robe represents faith. How could one fight over it?' Then, I hid myself in the tall grass.

I. Of the Origin   109

> 惠明至, 提掇不動. 乃喚云: '行者行者, 我爲法來, 不爲衣來.'
> 혜명지, 제철부동. 내환운: '행자행자, 아위법래, 불위의래.'
>
> 能遂出, 坐盤石上.
> 능수출, 좌반석상.
>
> 惠明作禮, 云: '望行者爲我説法.'
> 혜명작례, 운: '망행자위아설법.'
>
> 能云: '汝既爲法而來, 可屏息諸緣. 勿生一念. 吾爲汝説.'
> 능운: '여기위법이래, 가병식제연. 물생일념. 오위여설.'
>
> 良久, 謂明曰: '不思善, 不思惡. 正與麼時, 那箇是明上座本來面目?'
> 양구, 위명왈: '불사선, 불사악. 정여마시, 나개시명상좌본래면목?'

Huiming reached the robe and bowl but was unable to pick them up. He then called out, 'Lay brother, lay brother, I have come for the dhamma, not for the robe.'

I then came out and sat on a flat rock.

Huiming paid his respects and said, 'I beseech you, lay brother, teach me the dhamma.'

I replied, 'Since you have come for the dhamma, you should put aside all worldly concerns and do not produce even a single thought. I will then speak to you about it.'

After a good while, I said to Huiming, 'At that very moment when you are thinking of neither good nor evil, what is the original face of Your Venerability Huiming?'

> 惠明言下大悟, 復問云:'上來密語·密意外, 還更有密意否?'
> 혜명언하대오, 부문운: '상래밀어·밀의외, 환갱유밀의부?'
>
> 能云:'與汝説者, 即非密也. 汝若返照, 密在汝邊.'
> 능운: '여여설자, 즉비밀야. 여약반조, 밀재여변.'
>
> 明曰:'惠明雖在黃梅, 實未省自己面目. 今蒙指示, 如人飲水, 冷
> 명왈: '혜명수재황매, 실미성자기면목. 금몽지시, 여인음수, 냉
>
> 暖自知. 今行者即惠明師也.'
> 난자지. 금행자즉혜명사야.'
>
> 能曰:'汝若如是, 吾與汝同師黃梅, 善自護持.'
> 능왈: '여약여시, 오여여동사황매, 선자호지.'

Upon hearing this, Huiming had a great enlightenment, and further asked, 'Apart from the secret instructions and secret intentions you gave, is there another deeper secret meaning?'

I replied, 'What I have told you is not a secret. If you turn your attention inward, the secret is within you.'

Huiming said, 'Although I, Huiming, was at Huangmei, I never truly realized my own original face. Now, thanks to your guidance, it is like drinking water and knowing whether it is cold or warm. From now on, you, lay brother, are my Master.'

I said, 'If you truly understand this, let's take good care of the teaching, since you and I both have the same Master in Huangmei.'

明又問:'惠明今後向甚處去?'
명우문: '혜명금후향심처거?'

能曰:'逢袁即止,遇蒙即居.'
능왈: '봉원즉지, 우몽즉거.'

明禮辭.
명례사.

能後至曹溪, 又被惡人尋逐, 乃於四會縣避難獵人隊中, 凡經一十
능후지조계, 우피악인심축, 내어사회현피난엽인대중, 범경일십

五載. 時與獵人隨宜説法. 獵人常令守網, 每見生命, 盡放之. 每
오재. 시여엽인수의설법. 엽인상령수망, 매견생명, 진방지. 매

至飯時, 以菜寄煮肉鍋. 或問則對曰:'但喫肉邊菜.'
지반시, 이채기자육과. 혹문즉대왈: '단끽육변채'

Huiming further asked, 'Where should I go from now on?'

I replied, 'Stop when you encounter yuan, stay at meng.'

Huiming paid his respects and bid farewell.

Later, I arrived at Caoqi, at times chased by malicious people. To avoid trouble, I hid myself among a group of hunters in Sihui for fifteen years. During that time, I occasionally shared the dhamma with the hunters as situations allowed. They usually ordered me to watch the nets, and whenever I saw living creatures, I tried my best to set them free. When it was time for meals, I would cook vegetables in the same pot as the meat. When someone asked about it, I would say, 'I just take the vegetables next to the meat.'

> 一日思惟: '時當弘法, 不可終遯.'
> 일일사유: '시당홍법, 불가종둔.'
>
> 遂出, 至廣州法性寺. 值印宗法師講『涅槃經』. 時有風吹幡動. 一
> 수출, 지광주법성사. 치인종법사강『열반경』. 시유풍취번동. 일
>
> 僧云風動, 一僧云幡動, 議論不已.
> 승운풍동, 일승운번동, 의론불이.
>
> 能進曰: '不是風動, 不是幡動, 仁者心動.' 一衆駭然.
> 능진왈: '불시풍동, 불시번동, 인자심동.' 일중해연.
>
> 印宗延至上席, 徵詰奧義, 見能言簡理當, 不由文字.
> 인종연지상석, 징힐오의, 견능언간리당, 불유문자.

One day, I thought, 'It is time to spread the dhamma, hiding no longer.'

So I left and arrived at the Faxing Temple in Guangzhou. At that time, the Dhamma Master Yinzong was lecturing on NibbānaSutta. A gust of wind was blowing, causing a flag to flutter. One monk said, 'The wind is moving,' while another said, 'The flag is moving.' They debated back and forth, unable to reach an agreement.

I stepped forward and said, 'It's neither the wind, nor the flag, that moves. It is your minds that move.' The assembly was astonished.

Yinzong invited me to sit on the high seat and inquired about the profound meanings behind my words. He recognized that my understanding was direct and appropriate, not relying on written words.

> 宗云: '行者定非常人. 久聞黃梅衣法南來, 莫是行者否?'
> 종운: '행자정비상인. 구문황매의법남래, 막시행자부?'
>
> 能曰: '不敢.'
> 능왈: '불감.'
>
> 宗於是執弟子禮, 告請傳來衣鉢出示大衆.
> 종어시집제자례, 고청전래의발출시대중.
>
> 宗復問曰: '黃梅付囑, 如何指授?'
> 종부문왈: '황매부촉, 여하지수?'
>
> 能曰: '指授即無. 唯論見性, 不論禪定解脱.'
> 능왈: '지수즉무. 유론견성, 불론선정해탈.'

He asked me, 'Lay brother, you are not an ordinary person. I have long heard that the robe and the dhamma of Huangmei was transmitted to someone, who went to the south. You are the one, aren't you?'

Huineng replied, 'I dare not deny it.'

Yinzong then performed the ritual of becoming a pupil and asked me to show the transmitted robe and the bowl to the assembly.

Yinzong further asked, 'What instructions did you receive from Huangmei?'

I replied, 'There were no specific instructions. They only discuss seeing-nature, not about jhānasamādhi, nor liberation.'

> 宗曰:'何不論禪定解脱?'
> 종왈:'하불론선정해탈?'
> 謂曰:'爲是二法, 不是佛法. 佛法是不二之法.'
> 위왈:'위시이법, 불시불법. 불법시불이지법.'
> 宗又問:'如何是佛法不二之法?'
> 종우문:'여하시불법불이지법?'
> 能曰:'法師講『涅槃經』, 明見佛性是佛法不二之法.
> 능왈:'법사강『열반경』, 명견불성시불법불이지법.
> 如『涅槃經』, 高貴德王菩薩白佛言: 犯四重禁, 作五逆罪及一闡提
> 여『열반경』, 고귀덕왕보살백불언: 범사중금, 작오역죄급일천제
> 等, 當斷善根佛性否?
> 등, 당단선근불성부?

Yinzong asked again, 'Why not discuss jhānasamādhi and liberation?'

I replied, 'Because those are dualistic concepts, not the true Buddha-dhamma. The true Buddha-dhamma is a non-dualistic teaching.'

Yinzong further inquired, 'What does it mean that the Buddha-dhamma is a non-dualistic teaching?'

I replied, 'As you lecture on Nibbāna Sutta, you would brightly see that Buddha-nature is the non-dualistic teaching of Buddha-dhamma.'

In Nibbāna Sutta, Suvikrāntavikramin[S] asks Buddha, For those who have committed the four grave offenses, the five heinous crimes, or icchantikas[S] and so forth, will their wholesome roots of Buddha-nature be severed?

> 佛言: 善根有二, 一者常, 二者無常. 佛性非常非無常, 是故不斷,
> 불언: 선근유이, 일자상, 이자무상. 불성비상비무상, 시고부단,
>
> 名爲不二. 一者善, 二者不善. 佛性非善非不善, 是名不二.
> 명위불이. 일자선, 이자불선. 불성비선비불선, 시명불이.
>
> 蘊之與界, 凡夫見二, 智者了達其性無二. 無二之性, 即是佛性.'
> 온지여계, 범부견이, 지자요달기성무이. 무이지성, 즉시불성.'
>
> 印宗聞説, 歡喜合掌言: '某甲講經猶如瓦礫, 仁者論義猶如眞金.'
> 인종문설, 환희합장언: '모갑강경유여와력, 인자논의유여진금.'

Buddha replies, 'There are two types of wholesome roots: one is permanent, and the other, impermanent. Buddha-nature is neither permanent nor impermanent; hence not severed. Therefore it is also called not-two. One aspect is wholesome, and the other, unwholesome. Buddha-nature is neither wholesome nor unwholesome, hence called not-two.

Regarding the five aggregates and the universe, ordinary people see duality, but the wise see their natures as non-dual. The non-dual nature itself is Buddha-nature.'

Upon hearing this, Yinzong joyfully clasped his hands and said, 'My lectures on the Scripture have been like broken tiles, while Your Reverence's discussion of the principle is like pure gold.'

> 於是爲能剃髮, 願事爲師. 能遂於菩提樹下開東山法門.
> 어시위능체발, 원사위사. 능수어보리수하개동산법문.
>
> 能於東山得法, 辛苦受盡, 命似懸絲. 今日得與使君官僚・僧尼道俗
> 능어동산득법, 신고수진, 명사현사. 금일득여사군관료・승니도속
>
> 同此一會, 莫非累劫之緣, 亦是過去生中供養諸佛同種善根.
> 동차일회, 막비누겁지연, 역시과거생중공양제불동종선근.
>
> 方始得聞如上頓敎得法之因. 敎是先聖所傳, 不是惠能自智.
> 방시득문여상돈교득법지인. 교시선성소전, 불시혜능자지.

Henceforth, Yinzong shaved my head and wanted to follow me as his master. I then established the East Mountain Dhamma School under the bodhi tree.

Since I obtained the dhamma at East Mountain, I have endured countless hardships and faced situations where my life was hung by a thread. Today, Your Honourable Prefect and officials, monks, nuns and lay followers have met altogether in this assembly, which must be the result of countless kalpas of karmic connections. This is also due to our past lives when we made offerings to innumerable Buddhas and cultivated wholesome roots together.

Now you have heard the teachings of sudden enlightenment and how to attain the dhamma. The teachings have been transmitted from earlier sages, not my own wisdom.

> 願聞 先聖敎者, 各令淨心聞了, 各自除疑, 如先代聖人無別."
> 원문 선성교자, 각령정심문료, 각자제의, 여선대성인무별."
>
>
> 一衆聞法, 歡喜作禮而退.
> 일중문법, 환희작례이퇴.

May those who desire to hear the teachings of earlier sages purify their minds and listen; if you have listened, remove any doubts. Then there shall be no distinction between you and the sages of previous generations."

Upon hearing the teachings, the assembly rejoiced, paid their respects and withdrew.

第二　般若品

제이 반야품

次日韋使君請益.
차일위사군청익.

師陞座, 告大衆曰: "總淨心念摩訶般若波羅密多."
사승좌, 고대중왈: "총정심념마하반야바라밀다."

復云:
부운:

"善知識, 菩提般若之智, 本自有之. 只緣心迷, 不能自悟,
"선지식, 보리반야지지, 본자유지. 지연심미, 불능자오,

Chapter Two

Of Paññā (Wisdom)

The next day, Prefect Wei begged further teachings.

The Master ascended the platform, and addressed the assembly, saying, "Everyone, purify your mind and recite in mind Mahāpaññāpāramitā."

The Master continued,

"Good learned friends, the wisdom of Bodhipaññā is inherent within you. It is only because your mind is deluded that you are unable to enlighten yourself.

須假大善知識示導見性. 當知愚人・智人, 佛性本無差別,
수가대선지식시도견성. 당지우인・지인, 불성본무차별,

只緣迷悟不同,
지연미오부동,

所以有愚・有智. 吾今爲說摩訶般若波羅密法, 使汝等各得智慧. 志
소이유우・유지. 오금위설마하반야바라밀법, 사여등각득지혜. 지

心諦聽, 吾爲汝說.
심제청, 오위여설.

善知識, 世人終日口念般若, 不識自性般若. 猶如說食不飽, 口但
선지식, 세인종일구념반야, 불식자성반야. 유여설식불포, 구단

說空, 萬劫不得見性, 終無有益.
설공, 만겁부득견성, 종무유익.

So you need the guidance of greater good learned teachers to help you realize seeing-nature. You should understand that there is no distinction in Buddha-nature between the deluded and the wise. The only difference lies in whether you are deluded or enlightened. This is why some are deluded, while the others are wise. Now I will explain the dhamma of Mahāpaññāpāramitā so that each one of you attain wisdom. Listen carefully with focused minds. I will speak for you.

Good learned friends, worldly people recite paññā all day long, yet they don't recognize paññā of their Self-nature. If you just talk about emptiness just as talking about eating without ever feeling full, you will never realize seeing-nature, however many eons pass, and ultimately there shall be no benefit at all.

> 善知識, 摩訶般若波羅密是梵語. 此言:'大智慧到彼岸.'
> 선지식, 마하반야바라밀시범어. 차언: '대지혜도피안.'
>
> 此須心行, 不在口念. 口念心不行, 如幻如化, 如露如電; 口念心
> 차수심행, 부재구념. 구념심불행, 여환여화, 여로여전; 구념심
>
> 行, 則心口相應. 本性是佛, 離性無別佛.
> 행, 즉심구상응. 본성시불, 이성무별불.
>
> 何名摩訶? 摩訶是大. 心量廣大, 猶如虛空, 無有邊畔, 亦無方圓·
> 하명마하? 마하시대, 심량광대, 유여허공, 무유변반, 역무방원
>
> 大小, 亦非靑·黃·赤·白, 亦無上下·長短, 亦無瞋無喜, 無是無非,
> 대소, 역비청·황·적·백, 역무상하·장단, 역무진무희, 무시무비,

Good learned friends, 'Mahāpaññāpāramitā' is a Pāli term. It means 'Great Wisdom that can help to reach to the other shore.' This requires practice of mind, not mere verbal recitation. Recitation without practice in mind is like illusion, like change, like dew and like lightning; only when the recitation is accompanied by the practice of the mind, then are the mind and the mouth in harmony. The original nature itself is Buddha. There is no Buddha apart from the nature.

What does 'mahā' mean? Mahā means great. The mind is broad and vast: It is like the vast expanse of space, it has no boundaries, no concepts of square or round, nor big or small, no colors like blue, yellow, red or white, no concepts of up or down, nor long or short; it is also free from anger or joy, nor right or wrong, nor good or evil; it has neither beginning nor end.

> 無善無惡, 無有頭尾. 諸佛刹土, 盡同虛空. 世人妙性本空, 無有
> 무선무악, 무유두미. 제불찰토, 진동허공. 세인묘성본공, 무유
>
> 一法可得. 自性眞空, 亦復如是.
> 일법가득. 자성진공, 역부여시.
>
> 善知識, 莫聞吾說空, 便即着空. 第一莫着空. 若空心靜坐, 即着
> 선지식, 막문오설공, 변즉착공. 제일막착공. 약공심정좌, 즉착
>
> 無記空.
> 무기공.
>
> 善知識, 世界虛空能含萬物色像. 日月星宿·山河大地·泉源溪澗·
> 선지식, 세계허공능함만물색상. 일월성수·산하대지·천원계간·
>
> 草木叢林·惡人善人·惡法善法·天堂地獄·一切大海·須彌諸山總在空中.
> 초목총림·악인선인·악법선법·천당지옥·일체대해·수미제산총재공중.

All Buddhas' lands are as vast as empty space. The subtle nature of worldly people is originally empty, and there is no dhamma to obtain. Self-nature is true emptiness just like that.

Good learned friends, don't attach to emptiness after listening to my talking about emptiness. First of all, do not attach to emptiness. If you sit in meditation with an empty mind, it is the attachment to the concept of emptiness, which lacks any capacity for cognizance.

Good learned friends, the empty space of the world can contain myriad forms and images: the sun, the moon, the stars and constellations; mountains, rivers and the great earth; springs and streams; grasses, trees and forests; good people and the wicked; good dhammas and bad ones; heaven and hell; all the great oceans; and all the mountains like Sumeru. All are within emptiness.

世人性空, 亦復如是.
세인성공, 역부여시.

善知識, 自性能含萬法, 是大. 萬法在諸人性中. 若見一切人惡之
선지식, 자성능함만법, 시대. 만법재제인성중. 약견일체인악지

與善盡皆不取不捨, 亦不染着, 心如虛空, 名之爲大. 故曰摩訶.
여선진개불취불사, 역불염착, 심여허공, 명지위대. 고왈마하.

善知識, 迷人口說, 智者心行. 又有迷人, 空心靜坐, 百無所思,
선지식, 미인구설, 지자심행. 우유미인, 공심정좌, 백무소사,

自稱爲大.
자칭위대.

The nature of the worldly people is also empty just like that.

Good learned friends, Self-nature is capable of encompassing all dhammas, hence great. All phenomena exist within the nature of each individual. When you observe all the evil with the good in people, neither grasp nor discard them, also remain unstained and unattached, and your mind shall be like empty space, which is called great. Hence mahā.

Good learned friends, deluded people merely talk about it with their mouths, while wise people practice it with their minds. There are also deluded individuals who engage in silent sitting meditation with an empty mind, not thinking any thoughts, and proudly claim themselves to be great.

> 此一輩人不可與語, 爲邪見故.
> 차일배인불가여어, 위사견고.
>
> 善知識, 心量廣大, 遍周法界. 用即了了分明, 應用便知一切. 一
> 선지식, 심량광대, 변주법계. 용즉요료분명, 응용변지일체. 일
>
> 切即一, 一即一切. 去來自由, 心體無滯, 即是般若.
> 체즉일, 일즉일체. 거래자유, 심체무체, 즉시반야.
>
> 善知識, 一切般若智皆從自性而生, 不從外入. 莫錯用意, 名爲眞
> 선지식, 일체반야지개종자성이생, 부종외입. 막착용의, 명위진
>
> 性自用. 一眞一切眞. 心量大事. 不行小道, 口莫終日說空.
> 성자용. 일진일체진. 심량대사. 불행소도, 구막종일설공.

Due to their attachment to deviant views, we cannot engage in meaningful conversation with such people.

Good learned friends, the capacity of the mind is vast and expansive. It pervades the entire realm of phenomena. Its function is extremely clear and distinct: once it functions, it comprehends all situations and phenomena, All is one, and one is all. It freely comes and goes, there being no obstruction in the body of mind. That's the very paññā.

Good learned friends, all wisdom of paññā arises from your own Self-nature, not from outside. Not misusing your intention is called the self-application of your true nature. When one is true, then everything is true. Do not spend the whole day speaking about emptiness while you're contemplating only grand matters in your mind without practicing even the smallest things.

> 心中不修此行, 恰似凡人自稱國王, 終不可得, 非吾弟子.
> 심중불수차행, 흡사범인자칭국왕, 종불가득, 비오제자.
>
> 善知識, 何名般若?
> 선지식, 하명반야?
>
> 般若者, 唐言智慧也. 一切處所, 一切時中, 念念不愚, 常行智慧,
> 반야자, 당언지혜야. 일체처소, 일체시중, 염념불우, 상행지혜,
>
> 即是般若行. 一念愚即般若絶, 一念智即般若生. 世人愚迷, 不見
> 즉시반야행. 일념우즉반야절, 일념지즉반야생. 세인우미, 불견
>
> 般若, 口說般若, 心中常愚, 常自言'我修般若', 念念說空, 不識眞空.
> 반야, 구설반야, 심중상우, 상자언'아수반야', 염념설공, 불식진공.

If you do not follow this path in your mind, you are just like an ordinary person who self-claims to be a king but will never attain the position. Such a person is not my disciple.

Good learned friends, what is called paññā?

Paññā translates into wisdom in Chinese. The constant cultivation of wisdom in every situation and moment, without ignorance in every thought is the practice of paññā. If one thought is deluded, paññā is lost; if a single thought is wise, paññā arises. Worldly people are deluded and fail to perceive paññā. Although they may speak of paññā, their minds remain deluded, so they continue to assert, 'I practice paññā,' and discuss emptiness without comprehending the true emptiness.

> 般若無形象, 智慧心即是. 若作如是解, 即名般若智.
> 반야무형상, 지혜심즉시. 약작여시해, 즉명반야지.
> 何名波羅密? 此是西國語, 唐言到彼岸, 解義離生滅. 著境生滅起,
> 하명바라밀? 차시서국어, 당언도피안, 해의이생멸. 착경생멸기,
> 如水有波浪, 即名爲此岸; 離境無生滅, 如水相通流, 即名爲彼岸.
> 여수유파랑, 즉명위차안; 이경무생멸, 여수상통류, 즉명위피안.
> 故號波羅密.
> 고호바라밀.
> 善知識, 迷人口念, 當念之時, 有妄有非. 念念若行, 是名眞性. 悟
> 선지식, 미인구념, 당념지시, 유망유비. 염념약행, 시명진성. 오
> 此法者是般若法, 修此行者是般若行.
> 차법자시반야법, 수차행자시반야행.

Paññā is formless; it is the wise mind. Comprehending it in this way is called the wisdom of paññā.

What is called pāramitā? It is a Western term, meaning 'reaching the other shore' in Chinese, which signifies transcending the cycle of birth and death. When you cling to objects, the cycle of birth and death arises, like waves on water: this is referred to 'this shore.' When detached from objects, there is no cycle of birth and death, like the uninterrupted flow of water: this is referred to 'the other shore.' Thus, it is named pāramitā.

Good learned friends, deluded people merely recite with their mouths and have thoughts prone to falsehoods and errors. To practice mindfulness with each thought, this is named the true nature. He who comprehends this dhamma is practicing the dhamma of paññā. He who engages in this practice is following the path of paññā.

不修即凡. 一念修行, 自身等佛.
불수즉범. 일념수행, 자신등불.

善知識, 凡夫即佛, 煩惱即菩提. 前念迷即凡夫, 後念悟即佛. 前
선지식, 범부즉불, 번뇌즉보리. 전념미즉범부, 후념오즉불. 전

念着境即煩惱, 後念離境即菩提.
념착경즉번뇌, 후념리경즉보리.

善知識, 摩訶般若波羅密, 最尊·最上·最第一. 無住·無往亦無來,
선지식, 마하반야바라밀, 최존·최상·최제일. 무주·무왕역무래,

Without practice, you remain an ordinary man. But with the practice of continuous mindfulness, you are the same as Buddha.

Good learned friends, an ordinary man is already Buddha, and afflictions themselves are bodhi. If the preceding thoughts are deluded, you are an ordinary man; if the subsequent thoughts are awakened, you are Buddha. When the previous thoughts attach to objects, they result in affliction; when the subsequent thoughts detach from objects, they result in bodhi.

Good learned friends, Mahāpaññāpāramitā is the most honorable, the highest, and the very first. It neither abides nor goes, nor does it come from anywhere.

> 三世諸佛皆從中出. 當用大智慧, 打破五蘊煩惱塵勞. 如此修行,
> 삼세제불개종중출. 당용대지혜, 타파오온번뇌진로. 여차수행,
> 定成佛道, 變三毒爲戒·定·慧.
> 정성불도, 변삼독위계·정·혜.
> 善知識, 我此法門從一般若生八萬四千智慧. 何以故?
> 선지식, 아차법문종일반야생팔만사천지혜. 하이고?
> 爲世人有八萬四千塵勞. 若無塵勞, 智慧常現, 不離自性. 悟此法
> 위세인유팔만사천진로. 약무진로, 지혜상현, 불리자성. 오차법
> 者, 卽是無念·無憶·無着, 不起誑妄. 用自眞如性, 以智慧觀照,
> 자, 즉시무념·무억·무착, 불기광망. 용자진여성, 이지혜관조,
> 於一切法不取不捨, 卽是見性成佛道.
> 어일체법불취불사, 즉시견성성불도.

All Buddhas of the three ages emerge from it. You should use great wisdom to shatter the five aggregates of afflictions and troubles. By practicing this way, you shall indeed attain the path to Buddhahood, transforming the three poisons into sīla, samādhi and paññā.

Good learned friends, this dhamma gate of mine gives rise to eighty-four thousand wisdoms through a single paññā. Why is this so?

It's because worldly people have eighty-four thousand afflictions. If there were no afflictions, wisdom would always be present and would not depart from Self-nature. He who understands this dhamma will attain no-thought, no-memory and no-attachment, and will not give rise to any mad delusions. Use your own True-thusness, observe yourself with wisdom, and do neither grasp nor reject among all dhammas. This is the attainment of Buddha's path through seeing-nature.

> 善知識, 若欲入甚深法界及般若三昧者, 須修般若行. 持誦『金剛般
> 선지식, 약욕입심심법계급반야삼매자, 수수반야행. 지송『금강반
>
> 若經』, 即得見性. 當知此功德無量無邊. 經中分明讚嘆, 莫能具
> 야경』, 즉득견성. 당지차공덕무량무변. 경중분명찬탄, 막능구
>
> 説.
> 설.
>
> 此法門是最上乘, 爲大智人説, 爲上根人説. 小根・小智人聞, 心生
> 차법문시최상승, 위대지인설, 위상근인설. 소근・소지인문, 심생
>
> 不信. 何以故?
> 불신. 하이고?

Good learned friends, if you aspire to enter the profound realm of the dhamma and paññā samādhi, you must practice the method of paññā. Always recite the Vajracchedikā Prajñāpāramitā Sūtra[S], and you can realize seeing-nature. Understand this properly: its merits are immeasurable and boundless. They are clearly praised in the Scripture, yet cannot be fully expressed.

This dhamma gate is indeed the highest vehicle, spoken for those of great wisdom and superior capacity. However, those of limited capacity and lesser wisdom, even though they hear it, might disbelieve in their minds. Why is this so?

> 譬如大龍下雨於閻浮提, 城邑·聚落悉皆漂流如漂棗葉; 若雨大海,
> 비여대룡하우어염부제, 성읍·취락실개표류여표조엽; 약우대해,
> 不增不減.
> 부증불감.
> 若大乘人, 若最上乘人, 聞說『金剛經』, 心開悟解. 故知本性自有
> 약대승인, 약최상승인, 문설『금강경』, 심개오해. 고지본성자유
> 般若之智. 自用智慧, 常觀照, 故不假文字.
> 반야지지. 자용지혜, 상관조, 고불가문자.
> 譬如雨水不從天有, 元是龍能興致, 令一切衆生·一切草木·有情無
> 비여우수부종천유, 원시용능흥치, 영일체중생·일체초목·유정무
> 情悉皆蒙潤, 百川衆流却入大海, 合爲一體.
> 정실개몽윤, 백천중류각입대해, 합위일체.

It's like when a great dragon pours rains upon Jambudvipa, towns and villages are all washed away like floating jujube leaves; yet, when it pours upon great ocean, there is neither increase nor decrease.

If one is of the great vehicle or of the supreme vehicle, upon hearing the teaching of the Diamond Scripture, his mind will open, become enlightened and gain understanding. Therefore, understand that your original-nature inherently possesses the wisdom of paññā. Use this wisdom by yourself and be constantly engaged in insightful observation, and you need not rely on written words.

It's like that the rainwater does not come from the sky but originates from the ability of a dragon, and it allows all beings, all the grass and trees, sentient and non-sentient to receive its nourishment, and all rivers and streams ultimately flow into great ocean to unite into one.

> 衆生本性·般若之智亦復如是.
> 중생본성·반야지지역부여시.
>
> 善知識, 小根之人聞此頓教, 猶如草木根性小者, 若被大雨, 悉皆
> 선지식, 소근지인문차돈교, 유여초목근성소자, 약피대우, 실개
>
> 自到, 不能增長. 小根之人亦復如是. 元有般若之智, 與大智人更
> 자도, 불능증장. 소근지인역부여시. 원유반야지지, 여대지인갱
>
> 無差別. 因何聞法, 不自開悟? 緣邪見障重, 煩惱根深. 猶如大雲
> 무차별. 인하문법, 부자개오? 연사견장중, 번뇌근심. 유여대운
>
> 覆蓋於日, 不得風吹, 日光不現.
> 부개어일, 부득풍취, 일광불현.

The original-nature and the wisdom of paññā of all beings are also like this.

Good learned friends, those of small capacity hearing this sudden teaching are like plants with shallow roots. If they are subjected to heavy rain, they are altogether turned over and cannot thrive and grow. People of small capacity are also like this. They inherently possess the wisdom of paññā, and there is no difference compared to those of great wisdom. But why can't they awaken themselves upon hearing the dhamma? It is due to the heavy obstruction of their erroneous views and deep-rooted afflictions. It's like if a thick cloud covers the sun and there is no wind to disperse it, the sunlight does not appear.

> 般若之智亦無大小, 爲一切衆生, 自心迷悟不同. 迷心外見, 修行
> 반야지지역무대소, 위일체중생, 자심미오부동. 미심외견, 수행
>
> 覓佛, 未悟自性, 即是小根. 若開悟頓教, 不執外修, 但於自心常
> 멱불, 미오자성, 즉시소근. 약개오돈교, 부집외수, 단어자심상
>
> 起正見, 煩惱·塵勞常不能染, 即是見性.
> 기정견, 번뇌·진로상불능염, 즉시견성.
>
> 善知識, 內外不住, 去來自由, 能除執心, 通達無碍. 能修此行, 與
> 선지식, 내외부주, 거래자유, 능제집심, 통달무애. 능수차행, 여
>
> 『般若經』本無差別.
> 『반야경』본무차별.

The wisdom of paññā is also neither great nor small. The difference among all beings lies in whether one's mind is deluded or awakened. The deluded mind sees only outward, and though he practices and seeks Buddha, he is never awakened to their own Self-nature. He is one of limited capacity. If you are awakened to the sudden teaching and does not cling to external practices, and constantly cultivates right views within your own mind, afflictions and worldly troubles cannot defile you. This is the realization of seeing-nature.

Good learned friends, don't abide in either the internal or the external, come and go freely, and you shall be able to eliminate attachment and attain unobstructed state. If you can practice in this way, there shall be no difference from the PaññāSutta.

> 善知識, 一切修多羅及諸文字, 大小二乘・十二部經皆因人置, 因智
> 선지식, 일체수다라급제문자, 대소이승・십이부경개인인치, 인지
> 慧性方能建立. 若無世人, 一切萬法本自不有. 故知萬法本自人興,
> 혜성방능건립. 약무세인, 일체만법본자불유. 고지만법본자인흥,
> 一切經書因人說有. 緣其人中有愚・有智. 愚爲小人, 智爲大人. 愚
> 일체경서인인설유. 연기인중유우・유지. 우위소인, 지위대인. 우
> 者問於智人, 智者與愚人說法. 愚人忽然悟解心開, 即與智人無別.
> 자문어지인, 지자여우인설법. 우인홀연오해심개, 즉여지인무별.

Good learned friends, all the various suttas and written texts, be it from Mahāyāna or Hīnayāna traditions, and the twelve divisions of Scriptures, are created by humans and established based on the nature of wisdom. Without worldly beings, all the myriad dhammas do not exist from the beginning. Therefore, understand this: all the dhammas arise from human beings, and all the Scriptures exist because they are based on human speaking. Among human beings, there are the ignorant and the wise. The ignorant are of small capacity, while the wise are of great capacity. The ignorant seek guidance from the wise, and the wise teach the dhamma to the ignorant. When the ignorant suddenly awaken and open their minds, they are no different from the wise.

> 善知識, 不悟即佛是眾生. 一念悟時, 眾生是佛. 故知萬法盡在自
> 선지식, 불오즉불시중생. 일념오시, 중생시불. 고지만법진재자
> 心. 何不從自心中頓見眞如本性?
> 심. 하부종자심중돈견진여본성?
>
> 『菩薩戒經』云: '我本元自性淸淨.' 若識自心見性, 皆成佛道.
> 『보살계경』운: '아본원자성청정.' 약식자심견성, 개성불도.
>
> 『淨名經』云: '即是豁然, 還得本心.'
> 『정명경』운: '즉시활연, 환득본심.'
>
> 善知識, 我於忍和尚處一聞言下便悟, 頓見眞如本性.
> 선지식, 아어인화상처일문언하변오, 돈견진여본성.

Good learned friends, if you are not awakened, then Buddhas themselves are ordinary beings; if once awakened, however, in a single moment, ordinary beings become Buddhas. Therefore, understand this: all the dhammas have been present entirely within your own mind. Why not suddenly see the original-nature of True-thusness within your own mind?

The Bodhisattvabhūmi Sūtra[S] states: 'My original-nature is inherently clear and pure.' If you recognize your own mind and realize seeing-nature, you shall all attain Buddha's path.

The Vimalakīrti Nirdeśa Sūtra[S] says: 'Be immediately enlightened and regain your original mind.'

Good learned friends, when I was under His Reverence Hongren, I gained immediate enlightenment and suddenly saw the True-thusness' original nature.

> 是以將此教法流行, 令學道者頓悟菩提, 各自觀心, 自見本性.
> 시이장차교법유행, 영학도자돈오보리, 각자관심, 자견본성.
>
> 若自不悟, 須令得見性. 一切善法因善知識能發起故.
> 약자불오, 수영득견성. 일체선법인선지식능발기고.
>
> 覓大善知識解最上乘法者直示正路. 是善知識有大因緣. 所謂化導
> 멱대선지식해최상승법자직시정로. 시선지식유대인연. 소위화도
>
> 三世諸佛·十二部經在人性中本自具有. 不能自悟, 須求善知識指
> 삼세제불·십이부경재인성중본자구유. 불능자오, 수구선지식지
>
> 示方見; 若自悟者, 不假外求.
> 시방견; 약자오자, 불가외구.

Hence, I am spreading this teaching enabling those who study the path to achieve sudden enlightenment of bodhi, each observing his own mind and seeing his original nature. However, if you do not awaken by yourself, you should seek greater good learned teachers to explain to you the supreme vehicle and directly point out the right path, as you have great karmic connections with those good learned friends. It is so-called the process of transformation and guidance allowing the realization of seeing-nature. For all the beneficial teachings become possible through the presence of good learned friends.

All the Buddhas of the three ages and the twelve divisions of Scriptures are inherent to human nature: each man has all of them from the beginning. If you cannot awaken by yourself, seek good learned friends for guidance, and you shall see. He who can awaken by himself need not seek externally.

> 若一向執, 謂'須要他善知識望得解脫'者, 無有是處. 何以故?
> 약일향집, 위'수요타선지식망득해탈'자, 무유시처. 하이고?
>
> 自心內有智識自悟. 若起邪迷, 妄念顚倒, 外善知識雖有教授, 救
> 자심내유지식자오. 약기사미, 망념전도, 외선지식수유교수, 구
>
> 不可得. 若起正眞般若觀照, 一刹那間妄念俱滅. 若識自性一悟,
> 불가득. 약기정진반야관조, 일찰나간망념구멸. 약식자성일오,
>
> 卽至佛地.
> 즉지불지.

If you stubbornly insists that you must rely on good learned friends to teach you to attain liberation, there is no such thing.

Why is it so?

Within your own mind, there is wisdom that can awaken by itself. If you generate evil and deluded thoughts and are overturned with delusion, you cannot be saved even by the help of good learned friends who teach you externally. However, if you generate correct and true paññā observation, all deluded thoughts will be completely extinguished in a single moment. If you know how to enlighten your own Self-nature and awaken all at once, you shall reach the land of Buddhas.

> 善知識, 智慧觀照, 內外明徹, 識自本心. 若識本心, 即本解脫.
> 선지식, 지혜관조, 내외명철. 식자본심. 약식본심, 즉본해탈.
> 若得解脫, 即是般若三昧, 即是無念.
> 약득해탈, 즉시반야삼매, 즉시무념.
> 何名無念? 若見一切法, 心不染著, 是爲無念. 用即遍一切處, 亦
> 하명무념? 약견일체법, 심불염착, 시위무념. 용즉변일체처, 역
> 不著一切處, 但淨本心, 使六識出六門, 於六塵中無染無雜, 來去
> 불착일체처, 단정본심, 사육식출육문, 어육진중무염무잡, 내거
> 自由, 通用無滯, 即是般若三昧. 自在解脫, 名無念行. 若百物不
> 자유, 통용무체, 즉시반야삼매. 자재해탈, 명무념행. 약백물불
> 思, 當令念絶, 即是法縛, 即名邊見.
> 사, 당령념절, 즉시법박, 즉명변견.

Good learned friends, practice wisdom observation and then become clear and thorough, and know your original mind. If you understand your original mind, you have already been liberated. Attaining liberation is synonymous with paññā samādhi, also known as no-thought.

What is meant by no-thought? It is when you observe all phenomena and your mind remains untouched and unattached to any of them — this is known as no-thought. Once it functions, it is fully present in every situation without clinging to any particular situation, and makes the original mind pure, allowing six consciousnesses to function through their respective gates, unaffected by and unmixed with six sense objects, to come and go freely without hindrance or attachment, this is paññā samādhi. If you are liberated for yourself, it is the very practice of no-thought. If you try to suppress all thoughts and forcefully stop thinking about everything, it becomes a form of attachment to the dhamma, which is regarded as an extreme view.

> 善知識, 悟無念法者, 萬法盡通. 悟無念法者, 見諸佛境界. 悟無
> 선지식, 오무념법자, 만법진통. 오무념법자, 견제불경계. 오무
>
> 念法者, 至佛地位.
> 념법자, 지불지위.
>
> 善知識, 後代得吾法者, 將此頓教法門於同見同行, 發願受持如事
> 선지식, 후대득오법자, 장차돈교법문어동견동행, 발원수지여사
>
> 佛故, 終身而不退者, 定入聖位. 然須傳授從上以來默傳分付, 不
> 불고, 종신이불퇴자, 정입성위. 연수전수종상이래묵전분부, 부
>
> 得匿其正法.
> 득닉기정법.

Good learned friends, he who awakens to the dhamma of no-thought finds all dhammas thoroughly accessible. He who awakens to the dhamma of no-thought perceives the realms of all Buddhas. He who awakens to the dhamma of no-thought reaches the position of Buddha.

Good learned friends, in the future, he who receives my teachings and makes a vow to receive this method of sudden teaching from those who share the same views and practices with the same reverence as serving Buddha and to remain steadfast to it without regression throughout his life, he shall indeed attain the position of the sages. However, the lineage of transmission, passed down silently for generations, must be preserved, without concealing the true dhamma.

> 若不同見同行, 在別法中, 不得傳付. 損彼前人, 究
> 약부동견동행, 재별법중, 부득전부. 손피전인, 구
>
> 境無益. 恐愚人不解, 謗此法門, 百劫千生斷佛種性.
> 경무익. 공우인불해, 방차법문, 백겁천생단불종성.
>
> 善知識, 吾有一無相頌. 各須誦取, 在家·出家但依此修. 若不自修,
> 선지식, 오유일무상송. 각수송취, 재가·출가단의차수. 약부자수,
>
> 惟記吾言, 亦無有益. 聽吾頌." 曰:
> 유기오언, 역무유익. 청오송." 왈:

It should not be transmitted to those who do not share the same views and practices and follow different teachings, lest it should be harmful to the others and ultimately be of no benefit, and also lest the foolish should slander this dhamma gate and cut off the seed of Buddhahood for hundreds of kalpas and thousands of births, because of their poor understanding.

Good learned friends, I have an ode to no-form. Each of you shall recite and embrace it, and just practice in accordance with it, whether you are living in the household or have renounced the world. If you do not practice by yourself and merely remember my words, there shall be no true benefit. Now, listen to my ode."

It goes,

> "説通及心通, 如日處虛空.
> "설통급심통, 여일처허공.
>
> 唯傳見性法, 出世破邪宗.
> 유전견성법, 출세파사종.
>
> 法即無頓漸, 迷悟有遲疾.
> 법즉무돈점, 미오유지질.
>
> 只此見性門, 愚人不可悉.
> 지차견성문, 우인불가실.
>
> 説即雖萬般, 合理還歸一.
> 설즉수만반, 합리환귀일.

"Reaching, between words or between minds,
Is like the sun in the empty sky.

Only transmit the dhamma of seeing-nature and
Break through false doctrines when your are in the world.

In the dhamma, there is no sudden or gradual,
Delay or immediacy lies only in delusion and awakening.

Only this gate of seeing-nature,
The foolish can not fully enter.

Though teachings may unfold in myriad forms,
Their true essence returns to the One.

煩惱暗宅中, 常須生慧日.
번뇌암택중, 상수생혜일.

邪來煩惱至, 正來煩惱除.
사래번뇌지, 정래번뇌제.

邪正俱不用, 淸淨至無餘.
사정구불용, 청정지무여.

菩提本自性, 起心即是妄.
보리본자성, 기심즉시망.

淨心在妄中, 但正無三障.
정심재망중, 단정무삼장.

In the midst of dark abode of afflictions,
Constantly generate the sun of wisdom.

When delusion arises, afflictions appear,
When right view arises, afflictions cease.

Use neither delusion nor right view,
Then perfect purity arises, with nothing remaining.

Since bodhi is originally the same as Self-nature,
Even arising a thought is delusion.

If the mind remains pure, even within delusion,
With proper alignment, the three obstacles are absent.

世人若修道, 一切盡不妨.
세인약수도, 일체진불방.

常自見己過, 與道即相當.
상자견기과, 여도즉상당.

色類自有道, 各不相妨惱.
색류자유도, 각불상방뇌.

離道別覓道, 終身不見道.
이도별멱도, 종신불견도.

Even for worldly beings who cultivate the path
Nothing whatsoever obstructs their path of practice.

Just observe constantly your own faults,
And keep aligned with the path, that is right.

Each perceivable existence has its own path;
They do not obstruct or trouble one another.

If you seek the path after departing the path?
You shall never find out one throughout your life.

波波度一生, 到頭還自懊.
파파도일생, 도두환자오.

欲得見眞道, 行正即是道.
욕득견진도, 행정즉시도.

自若無道心, 闇行不見道.
자약무도심, 암행불견도.

若眞修道人, 不見世間過.
약진수도인, 불견세간과.

若見他人非, 自非却是左.
약견타인비, 자비각시좌.

Aimlessly you struggle and wander throughout your life,
In the end, only to realize and regret.

Desire you to see the true path?
Practicing the right is itself the path.

If you yourself lack the mind of the path,
You are walking in the darkness, not seeing the path.

A true practitioner of the path
Will not see the faults of world.

Seeing faults in others
Is itself wrong, and it becomes your own fault.

> 他非我不非, 我非自有過.
> 타비아불비, 아비자유과.
>
> 但自却非心, 打除煩惱破.
> 단자각비심, 타제번뇌파.
>
> 憎愛不關心, 長伸兩脚臥.
> 증애불관심, 장신양각와.
>
> 欲擬化他人, 自須有方便.
> 욕의화타인, 자수유방편.
>
> 勿令彼有疑, 即是自性現.
> 물령피유의, 즉시자성현.

Claiming others to be at fault, but not yourself
Is itself wrong, the fault being your own.

Simply abandon the fault-finding mind,
And shatter and eliminate afflictions.

If you do not attach to hatred or love,
It is as if you lie down with both legs extended.

Wish you to transform others?
Then you must first have means.

Do not let them harbor doubts,
Then immediately Self-nature is manifested.

> 佛法在世間, 不離世間覺.
> 불법재세간, 불리세간각.
>
> 離世覓菩提, 恰如求兎角.
> 이세멱보리, 흡여구토각.
>
> 正見名出世, 邪見是世間.
> 정견명출세, 사견시세간.
>
> 邪正盡打却, 菩提性宛然.
> 사정진타각, 보리성완연.
>
> 此頌是頓教, 亦名大法船.
> 차송시돈교, 역명대법선.

Buddha's teachings are in the world,
Not apart from the worldly enlightenment.

To depart from the world and seek bodhi,
Is like searching for a rabbit's horn.

Right view is called as renouncing the world,
Wrong view itself is to be in the world.

Eliminate both the right and the wrong,
And the nature of bodhi shall be complete.

This ode is the sudden teaching,
Also called the great dhamma boat.

> 迷聞經累劫, 悟即剎那間."
> 미문경누겁, 오즉찰나간."
>
> 師復曰:"今於大梵寺說此頓教. 普願法界衆生言下見性成佛."
> 사부왈:"금어대범사설차돈교. 보원법계중생언하견성성불."
>
> 時韋使君與官僚·道俗聞師所説, 無不省悟, 一時作禮, 皆歎:"善
> 시위사군여관료·도속문사소설, 무불성오, 일시작례, 개탄:"선
> 哉! 何期嶺南有佛出世?"
> 재! 하기영남유불출세?"

While it may take countless kalpas for the deluded to listen to it, Enlightenment comes in a single moment."

The Master continued, "Now, here in the Dafan Temple, I have preached this sudden teaching, wishing that all beings within the dhamma realm realize seeing-nature and attain Buddhahood under these words."

At that moment, Prefect Wei with his officials, the monks as well as lay followers, after hearing the Master's sermon, all understood and were enlightened. They paid their respects and expressed their admiration, exclaiming, "Wondrous! Who could have expected that Buddha would emerge from Lingnan!"

第三 疑問品
제삼 의문품

一日韋刺史爲師設大會齋.
일일위자사위사설대회재.

齋訖, 刺史請師陞座, 同官僚・士庶肅容再拜.
재흘, 자사청사승좌, 동관료사서・숙용재배.

問曰:"弟子聞和尚說法, 實不可思議. 今有少疑, 願大慈悲, 特爲
문왈: "제자문화상설법, 실불가사의. 금유소의, 원대자비, 특위

解說."
해설."

Chapter Three

Of Enquiry

One day, Prefect Wei hosted a grand ceremony for the Master. After the ceremony, the prefect asked the Master to ascend the platform and respectfully bowed twice, along with his officials, scholars and lay people.

The prefect asked, "Having heard Your Reverence's teachings, it is truly miraculous. Now I have a slight doubt, so please provide a special explanation with great compassion."

> 師曰: "有疑即問, 吾當爲說."
> 사왈: "유의즉문, 오당위설."
>
> 韋公曰: "和尚所說可不是達摩大師宗旨乎?"
> 위공왈: "화상소설가불시달마대사종지호?"
>
> 師曰: "是."
> 사왈: "시."
>
> 公曰: "弟子聞, 達摩初化梁武帝, 帝問云: '朕一生造寺供僧, 布
> 공왈: "제자문, 달마초화양무제, 제문운: '짐일생조사공승, 보
> 施設齋, 有何功德?' 達摩言: '實無功德.' 弟子未達此理. 願和尚爲說"
> 시설재, 유하공덕?' 달마언: '실무공덕.' 제자미달차리. 원화상위설."

The Master replied, "If you have any doubts, feel free to ask. I will explain to you."

The prefect asked, "What Your Reverence teaches is in accordance with the teachings of the Great Patriarch Bodhidharma[S], isn't it?"

The Master replied, "Yes, it is."

The prefect continued, "I have heard that, when Bodhidharma[S] first transmitted the dhamma to Liang's Emperor Wu, the Emperor asked him, 'Throughout my life, I have built temples, supported monks, made donations and hosted services. What merits and virtues have I attained?' Bodhidharma[S] replied, 'No merit at all.' Your pupil has not fully understood this reasoning, so humbly begs Your Reverence to explain it."

師曰: "實無功德. 勿疑先聖之言. 武帝心邪, 不知正法. 造寺供養,
사왈: "실무공덕. 물의선성지언. 무제심사, 부지정법. 조사공양,

布施設齋, 名爲求福. 不可將福便爲功德. 功德在法身中, 不在修
보시설재, 명위구복. 불가장복변위공덕. 공덕재법신중, 부재수

福."
복."

師又曰: "見性是功, 平等是德. 念念無滯, 常見本性, 眞實妙用,
사우왈: "견성시공, 평등시덕. 염념무체, 상견본성, 진실묘용,

名爲功德. 內心謙下是功, 外行於禮是德; 自性建立萬法是功,
명위공덕. 내심겸하시공, 외행어례시덕; 자성건립만법시공,

The Master replied, "Indeed there is no merit and virtue. Do not doubt the words of the Sage of the past. The Emperor's mind was misguided, not understanding the right dhamma. His building temples, supporting monks, donations and hosting services were considered as seeking a fortune. But fortune cannot by itself become merit or virtue. Merit and virtue reside in the dhamma body, not to be attained through the accumulation of fortunes."

The Master further said, "Seeing-nature is merit, and equanimity is virtue. With every thought unobstructed, constantly seeing original nature and manifesting its true and wonderful function, this is called merit and virtue. Humbling oneself inwardly is merit, and demonstrating respect outwardly is virtue; that Self-nature establishes all phenomena is merit,

> 心體離念是德; 不離自性是功, 應用無念是德. 若覓功德法身, 但依
> 심체리념시덕; 불리자성시공, 응용무념시덕. 약멱공덕법신, 단의
>
> 此作, 是眞功德.
> 차작, 시진공덕.
>
> 若修功德之人, 心即不輕, 常行普敬. 心常輕人, 吾我不斷, 即自
> 약수공덕지인, 심즉불경, 상행보경. 심상경인, 오아부단, 즉자
>
> 無功; 自性虛妄不實, 即自無德. 爲吾我自大, 常輕一切故.
> 무공; 자성허망부실, 즉자무덕. 위오아자대, 상경일체고.

and having a mind that is free from thoughts is virtue; not departing from Self-nature is merit, and applying no-thought is virtue. If you seek the dhamma body of merit and virtue, you should engage in this practice only. This is true merit and virtue.

He who cultivates merit and virtue should never be disrespectful in his mind, and should always practice universal respect. If you constantly hold a disdainful attitude towards others and have a sense of self-importance, then you shall accumulate no merit at all; if your Self-nature is empty and lacking sincerity, then you shall lack any virtue. For you come to constantly belittle everything, if you hold yourself in high esteem.

> 善知識, 念念無間是功, 心行平直是德; 自修性是功, 自修身是德.
> 선지식, 염념무간시공, 심행평직시덕; 자수성시공, 자수신시덕.
>
> 善知識, 功德須自性內見, 不是布施供養之所求也. 是以福德與功德別. 武帝不識眞理, 非我祖師有過."
> 선지식, 공덕수자성내견, 불시보시공양지소구야. 시이복덕여공덕별. 무제불식진리, 비아조사유과."
>
> 又問: "弟子常見, 僧俗念阿彌陀佛, 願生西方. 請和尚説, 得生彼否? 願爲破疑."
> 우문: "제자상견, 승속념아미타불, 원생서방. 청화상설, 득생피부? 원위파의."

Good learned friends, maintaining uninterrupted mindfulness is merit, and having an equanimous and continuous mind is virtue; cultivating your inherent nature is merit, and nurturing your own body is virtue.

Good learned friends, merit and virtue should be realized inwardly, by seeing your Self-nature, not to be attained through donations and offerings. Therefore, merit and virtue are distinct from blessings. Emperor Wu didn't understand the truth, and it was not our Patriarch's fault."

The prefect further asked, "Your pupil usually witnesses monks and lay believers reciting the name of Amitābha[8], aspiring to be reborn in the Western Pure Land. Please explain, Your Reverence, shall they truly attain rebirth there? I humbly beseech Your Reverence to alleviate my doubts."

III. Of Enquiry

> 師言:"使君善聽. 惠能與説.
> 사언: "사군선청. 혜능여설.
>
> 世尊在舍衛城中説西方引化, 經文分明'去此不遠'; 若論相, 説'里
> 세존재사위성중설서방인화, 경문분명'거차불원'; 약론상, 설'리
>
> 數有十萬八千'即身中十惡·八邪便是説遠.
> 수유십만팔천'즉신중십악·팔사변시설원.
>
> 説遠爲其下根, 説近爲其上智. 人有兩種, 法無兩般. 迷悟有殊,
> 설원위기하근, 설근위기상지. 인유양종, 법무양반. 미오유수,
>
> 見有遲疾.
> 견유지질.

The Master replied, "Listen attentively, Prefect, I will tell you. When the World-Honored-One taught and guided by talking about the Western Pure Land in Śrāvastī[s], He said, the Scripture clearly states, 'It is not far from here.' But when He discussed it in terms of appearances, He said that it is 'ten-and-eight thousand lis far.' That means that, if your mind is filled with ten evils and eight wrong views, then the Western Pure Land is such so far.

To say that it is far was for those with lower capacities, while that it is close was for those with higher wisdom. While there are two types of individuals, the dhamma itself is not divided into two. As the state of delusion or awakening varies, so does the immediacy of realization.

> 迷人念佛, 求生於彼, 悟人自淨其心. 所以佛言:
> 미인염불, 구생어피, 오인자정기심. 소이불언:
>
> '隨其心淨, 即佛土淨.'
> '수기심정, 즉불토정.'
>
> 使君, 東方人, 但心淨即無罪; 雖西方人, 心不淨亦有愆. 東方人
> 사군, 동방인, 단심정즉무죄; 수서방인, 심부정역유건. 동방인
>
> 造罪, 念佛求生西方; 西方人造罪, 念佛求生何國? 凡愚不了自性,
> 조죄, 염불구생서방; 서방인조죄, 염불구생하국? 범우불료자성,
>
> 不識身中淨土, 願東願西; 悟人在處一般. 所以佛言: '隨所住處恒
> 불식신중정토, 원동원서; 오인재처일반. 소이불언: '수소주처항
>
> 安樂.'
> 안락.'

While the deluded, chanting Buddha's name, seek salvation, the enlightened purify their own minds. That is why the Buddha said, 'As the mind is pure, so is the Buddhas Land.'

Dear Prefect, even an Easterner is free from sin, if only he has a pure mind; a Westerner has faults, however, if his mind is impure. An Easterner who sins may chant for rebirth in the West. But if a Westerner sins, where will his chanting lead? Because the ignorant are unaware of their Self-nature and do not know that the Pure Land is within themselves, they may aspire to be reborn in either the East or the West, while the enlightened can remain in the same state regardless of their location. That is why the Buddha said, 'Abide in constant peace and joy, wherever you reside.'

> 使君, 心地但無不善, 西方去此不遙; 若懷不善之心, 念佛往生難
> 사군, 심지단무불선, 서방거차불요; 약회불선지심, 염불왕생난
>
> 到. 今勸善知識, 先除十惡, 即行十萬; 後除八邪, 乃過八千. 念
> 도. 금권선지식, 선제십악, 즉행십만; 후제팔사, 내과팔천. 염
>
> 念見性, 常行平直, 到如彈指, 便覩彌陀.
> 념견성, 상행평직, 도여탄지, 변도미타.
>
> 使君, 但行十善, 何須更願往生? 不斷十惡之心, 何佛即來迎請?
> 사군, 단행십선, 하수갱원왕생? 부단십악지심, 하불즉래영청?

Dear Prefect, if only there are no evil in the foundation of your mind, the Western Land is not far; if you harbor evil thoughts, however, it is difficult to attain rebirth in the Pure Land even through reciting Buddha's name. Now, I advise you, good learned friends: first eradicate ten evils, and you shall advance ten ten-thousand lis; subsequently eliminate eight wrongs, and you shall proceed eight thousand more. Constantly realize seeing-nature and cultivate equanimity and consistency, and then you shall in an instant reach there to see Amitābha⑤, in a snap of finger.

Dear Prefect, if you have simply practice the ten good deeds, what need is there to wish for rebirth in the Pure Land? But if you do not cease the mind of ten evils, which Buddha would come to welcome and receive you?

> 若悟無生頓法, 見西方只在剎那. 不悟, 念佛求生, 路遙, 如何得達?
> 약오무생돈법, 견서방지재찰나. 불오, 염불구생, 노요, 여하득달?
>
> 惠能與諸人移西方於剎那間目前便見. 各願見否?"
> 혜능여제인이서방어찰나간목전변견. 각원견부?"
>
> 衆皆頂禮云: "若此處見, 何須更願往生? 願和尚慈悲, 便現西方,
> 중개정례운: "약차처견, 하수갱원왕생? 원화상자비 변현서방,
>
> 普令得見."
> 보령득견."
>
> 師言: "大衆, 世人自色身是城, 眼·耳·鼻·舌是門.
> 사언: "대중, 세인자색신시성, 안·이·비·설시문.

If you are enlightened to the sudden teaching of no-birth, you shall see the Western Land in an instant. If you do not, however, and merely rely on reciting Buddha's name to seek rebirth, then how could you reach there, for the path is so far away?

Now, if I were to bring the Western Land before your eyes in an instant, would you truly see it?"

All the assembly paid their respects and replied, "If only we could see it here, why should we aspire for rebirth there? We sincerely beg Your Reverence to manifest the Western Land and to allow us all to see it."

The Master replied, "Listen, assembly: for the worldly people, their own physical bodies are like a fortress, and eyes, ears, nose and tongue are the gates.

> 外有五門, 內有意門. 心是地, 性是王, 王居心地上. 性在, 王在;
> 외유오문, 내유의문. 심시지, 성시왕, 왕거심지상. 성재, 왕재;
>
> 性去, 王無.
> 성거, 왕무;
>
> 性在, 身心存; 性去, 身心壞. 佛向性中作, 莫向身外求.
> 성재, 신심존; 성거, 신심괴. 불향성중작, 막향신외구.
>
> 自性迷即是衆生, 自性覺即是佛. 慈悲即是觀音, 喜捨名爲勢至,
> 자성미즉시중생, 자성각즉시불. 자비즉시관음, 희사명위세지,
>
> 能淨即釋迦, 平直即彌陀.
> 능정즉석가, 평직즉미타.
>
> 人我是須彌, 邪心是海水, 煩惱是波浪,
> 인아시수미, 사심시해수, 번뇌시파랑,

There are five outer gates and one inner gate of thought. The mind is the land, and the nature is the king who resides upon the land of mind. If Self-nature is present, so is the king; if Self-nature departs, so disappears the king. When Self-nature is present, so are body and mind; if Self-nature departs, so decay body and mind. Since Buddha arises within the nature, do not seek it outside the body.

When Self-nature is deluded, you are a sentient being; when Self-nature is awakened, Buddha. When compassionate, you are Avalokiteśvara[S]; with joyful donation, you are Mahāsthāmaprāpta[S]; when purified, you are Śākyamuni[S]; when equanimous and consistent, you are Amitābha[S].

Dividing Self and others is Mount Sumeru; evil mind is ocean water; afflictions are waves;

> 毒害是惡龍, 虛妄是鬼神, 塵勞是魚鼈, 貪瞋是地獄, 愚癡是畜生.
> 독해시악룡, 허망시귀신, 진로시어별, 탐진시지옥, 우치시축생.
>
> 善知識, 常行十善, 天堂便至; 除人我, 須彌倒; 去邪心, 海水竭;
> 선지식, 상행십선, 천당변지; 제인아, 수미도; 거사심, 해수갈;
>
> 煩惱無, 波浪滅; 毒害除, 魚龍絶.
> 번뇌무, 파랑멸; 독해제, 어룡절.
>
> 自心地上覺性, 如來放大光明; 外照六門淸淨, 能破六欲; 諸天自
> 자심지상각성, 여래방대광명; 외조육문청정, 능파육욕; 제천자
>
> 性內照, 三毒卽除, 地獄等罪一時消滅. 內外明徹, 不異西方.
> 성내조, 삼독즉제, 지옥등죄일시소멸. 내외명철, 불이서방.

harmful deeds are evil dragons; illusions are ghosts and spirits; worldly troubles are fish and turtles; greed and anger are hell; and foolishness is the state of animal.

Good learned friends, if you practice the ten goodnesses, heaven instantly draws near; if you eliminate the distinction between self and others, Mount Sumeru topples; if you remove evil thoughts, the ocean water dries up; if you extinguish afflictions, the waves vanish; if you eliminate poisonous harm, the fish and dragons are eradicated.

If you awaken your enlightened nature upon the ground of your mind, Tathāgata radiates great light; if you externally illuminate and purify the six gates, you can break through the six desires; if Self-nature of heavenly beings illuminates inwardly, the three poisons are extinguished, and the sins of hell are instantly eradicated. Both internally and externally clear and bright, there is no difference from the Western Land.

> 不作此修, 如何到彼?"
> 부작차수, 여하도피?"
>
> 大衆聞説, 了然見性, 悉皆禮拜, 俱歎:"善哉!" 唯言:"普願法界
> 대중문설, 요연견성, 실개예배, 구탄:"선재!" 유언:"보원법계
>
> 衆生聞者一時悟解."
> 중생문자일시오해."
>
> 師言:"善知識, 若欲修行, 在家亦得, 不由在寺. 在家能行, 如東
> 사언:"선지식, 약욕수행, 재가역득, 불유재사. 재가능행, 여동
>
> 方人心善; 在寺不修, 如西方人心惡.
> 방인심선; 재사불수, 여서방인심악.

Without practicing in this way, how could you reach there?"

The assembly clearly realized seeing-nature upon hearing the sermon, all paid their respects and exclaimed, "How wonderful!" And they also said, "May all beings connected to the dhamma lineage hear and instantly attain understanding and enlightenment!"

The Master continued, "Good learned friends, if you wish to practice, it can be done at home; it does not necessarily require being in a monastery. If you practice well at home, it is like an Easterner with a good mind; if you do not practice even in a monastery, it is like a Westerner with an evil mind.

但心清淨，即是自性西方。"韋公又問："在家如何修行？願爲教授."
단심청정 즉시자성서방."위공우문："재가여하수행? 원위교수."

師言："吾與大衆說無相頌. 但依此修，常與吾同處無別. 若不依此
사언："오여대중설무상송. 단의차수, 상여오동처무별. 약불의차

修，剃髮出家，於道何益？"
수, 체발출가, 어도하익？"

頌曰：
송왈：

If only your mind is clear and pure, itself is the Western Land of Self-nature."

Prefect Wei further asked: "How could we practice in our homes? I request your guidence."

The Master replied, "Here's an ode to no-form for all you followers. Just practice according to it, and you shall always be in a state not different from mine. If you don't, however, what benefit would be there, even though you have your hair shaved and become a monk?"

The ode goes,

III. Of Enquiry

> "心平何勞持戒, 行直何用修禪?
> "심평하로지계, 행직하용수선?
>
> 恩即孝養父母, 義即上下相憐.
> 은즉효양부모, 의즉상하상련.
>
> 讓即尊卑和睦, 忍即衆惡無喧.
> 양즉존비화목, 인즉중악무훤.
>
> 若能鑽木出火, 淤泥定生紅蓮.
> 약능찬목출화, 어니정생홍련.
>
> 苦口的是良藥, 逆耳必是忠言.
> 고구적시양약, 역이필시충언.

"If the mind is equanimous, why labor over precepts?

If practicing continuously, what need is there for Zen?

Kindness is filial piety towards parents;

Righteousness is compassion shown to both above and below.

Yielding brings harmony between the high and the low;

Patience quells all evils, silencing them completely.

Just as you can make fire by rubbing cold woods,

From the mud, the red lotus blossoms.

Bitter to the tongue, yet it is a healing medicine,

改過必生智慧, 護短心內非賢.
개과필생지혜, 호단심내비현.

日用常行饒益, 成道非由施錢.
일용상행요익, 성도비유시전.

菩提只向心覓, 何勞向外求玄?
보리지향심멱, 하로향외구현?

聽說依此修行, 西方只在目前."
청설의차수행, 서방지재목전."

Hard to hear, yet it is the voice of loyalty.
Correcting mistakes undoubtedly brings you wisdom,
Hiding faults within the heart is unworthy of the wise.

Consistent practice in daily life brings abundant benefits.
Accomplishing the path does not depend on donating money.

Bodhi is only sought within the mind,
Why labor to seek the profound outwardly?

Listen, and practice accordingly,
And the Western Land is right before your eyes."

> 師復曰: "善知識, 總須依偈修行, 見取自性, 直成佛道, 法不相待.
> 사부왈: "선지식, 총수의게수행, 견취자성, 직성불도, 법불상대.
>
> 衆人且散. 吾歸曹溪. 衆若有疑, 却來相問."
> 중인차산. 오귀조계. 중약유의, 각래상문."
>
> 時刺史官僚·在會善男善女各得開悟, 信受奉行.
> 시자사관료·재회선남선녀각득개오, 신수봉행.

The Master reaffirmed, "Good learned friends, practice in accordance with the ode, so as to see and realize your Self-natures, and directly attain Buddha's path. The dhamma does not wait. Go now, all of you. I shall return to Caoxi. If anyone has doubts, come and ask me."

Then, the prefect with his officials and all the good men and women present attained enlightenment, and kept on practicing with faith.

第四 定慧品
제사 정혜품

師示眾云: "善知識, 我此法門, 以定慧爲本. 大眾勿迷言定慧別.
사시중운: "선지식, 아차법문, 이정혜위본. 대중물미언정혜별.

定慧一體, 不是二.
정혜일체, 불시이.

定是慧體, 慧是定用. 即慧之時定在慧, 即定之時慧在定. 若識此
정시혜체, 혜시정용. 즉혜지시정재혜, 즉정지시혜재정. 약식차

義, 即是定慧等學.
의, 즉시정혜등학.

Chapter Four

Of Samādhi and Paññā

The Master addressed the assembly, saying,

"Good learned friends, my teaching of the dhamma is based on samādhi and paññā. Do not mistakenly say that samādhi and paññā are separate.

Samādhi and paññā are one and the same, inseparable. Samādhi is the body of paññā, and paññā is the function of samādhi. In the state of paññā, therein is samādhi; and in the state of samādhi, therein is paññā. If you understand this principle, you shall be able to practice samādhi and paññā equally.

諸學道人, 莫言先定發慧·先慧發定各別. 作此見者, 法有二相, 口
제학도인, 막언선정발혜·선혜발정각별. 작차견자, 법유이상, 구

説善語, 心中不善, 空有定慧, 定慧不等. 若心口俱善, 內外一種,
설선어, 심중불선, 공유정혜, 정혜부등. 약심구구선, 내외일종,

定慧即等.
정혜즉등.

自悟修行不在於諍. 若諍先後, 即同迷人. 不斷勝負, 却增我·法,
자오수행부재어쟁. 약쟁선후, 즉동미인. 부단승부, 각증아·법,

不離四相.
불리사상.

All you practitioners of the path, never claim that samādhi arises before paññā, or that paññā arises before samādhi, as if they are two separate things. For him who holds such views, the dhamma has dual aspects. While he speaks words of goodness with his mouth, his mind is not aligned with goodness. He vaguely conceives samādhi and paññā, as if samādhi and paññā are not equal. If both the mind and speech are virtuous, however, the internal and the external are of one kind and thus samādhi and paññā are the same.

The practice of self-realization does not involve engaging in disputes. If you argue about what comes first and later, you are still caught in delusion. The more you strive for victory, the more you shall attach to ego and the appearances, and cannot deviate from the four saññās.

> 善知識, 定慧猶如何等? 猶如燈光. 有燈即光, 無燈即暗. 燈是光
> 선지식, 정혜유여하등? 유여등광. 유등즉광, 무등즉암. 등시광
> 之體, 光是燈之用. 名雖有二, 體本同一. 此定慧法亦復如是."
> 지체, 광시등지용. 명수유이, 체본동일. 차정혜법역부여시."
>
> 師示衆云: "善知識, 一行三昧者, 於一切處行住坐臥常行一直心,
> 사시중운: "선지식, 일행삼매자, 어일체처행주좌와상행일직심,

Good learned friends, to what shall I compare samādhi and paññā? They are like a lamp and its light. If there is a lamp, so is its light; without a lamp, there is darkness. The lamp is the body of its light; and the light is the function of the lamp. Though they have different names, the body and essence are one and the same. This applies to the nature of samādhi and paññā as well."

The Master addressed the assembly, saying,

"Good learned friends, the constant-samādhi is to practice a continuous awareness in all situations — whether going or stopping, sitting or lying.

> 是也. 如『淨名經』云: '直心是道場, 直心是淨土.'
> 시야. 여『정명경』운: '직심시도량, 직심시정토.'
>
> 莫心行諂曲, 口但說直, 口說一行三昧, 不行直心. 但行直心, 於
> 막심행첨곡, 구단설직, 구설일행삼매, 불행직심. 단행직심, 어
>
> 一切法勿有執着. 迷人着法相, 執一行三昧, 直言: '坐不動, 妄不
> 일체법물유집착. 미인착법상, 집일행삼매, 직언: '좌부동, 망불
>
> 起心, 即是一行三昧.' 作此解者, 即同無情, 却是障道因緣.
> 기심, 즉시일행삼매.' 작차해자, 즉동무정, 각시장도인연.
>
> 善知識, 道須通流, 何以却滯? 心不住法, 道即通流; 心若住法, 名爲自縛.
> 선지식, 도수통류, 하이각체? 심부주법, 도즉통류; 심약주법, 명위자박.

As stated in the Vimalakīrti Nirdeśa Sūtra[S], 'A consistantly aware mind is the filed of Path, a consistently aware mind it the Pure Land.'

Do not let your mind and acts engage in deceit or crookedness, saying consistency and constant-samādhi only through mouth, not practicing continuous awareness. Only practice continuous awareness, and do not attach to any situations. The deluded cling to the appearances of the dhamma and attach to the notion of constant-samādhi, and directly say, 'Sit without movement and do not create deluded thoughts, that itself is the constant-samādhi.' He who interprets it in this way is like an insentient being, and his misinterpretation becomes a cause of obstruction on the path.

Good learned friends, the path must flow freely, so why should it be obstructed? If your mind does not cling to the dhamma, the path will naturally flow; but if your mind clings to the dhamma, it is called self-imposed bondage.

> 若言常坐不動是, 只如舍利弗宴坐林中, 却被維摩詰訶.
> 약언상좌부동시, 지여사리불연좌림중, 각피유마힐가.
>
> 善知識, 又有人教坐, 看心觀靜, 不動不起. 從此置功, 迷人不會,
> 선지식, 우유인교좌, 간심관정, 부동불기. 종차치공, 미인불회,
>
> 便執成顚. 如此者衆. 如是相教, 故知大錯."
> 변집성전. 여차자중. 여시상교, 고지대착."
>
>
> 師示衆云: "善知識, 本來正教無有頓漸. 人性自有利鈍.
> 사시중운: "선지식, 본래정교무유돈점. 인성자유이둔.

If you insist that continuous sitting without movement is correct, that is like Śāriputra, who, while simply sitting peacefully in the forest, was unexpectedly reprimanded by Vimalakīrti.

Good learned friends, there are also those who teach sitting with seeing mind and observing stillness, without any movement and arising. If they practice like this, the deluded shall not understand, and only become attached and fall into inverted views. There are many people like this. Understand clearly that it is a great error to teach like this."

The Master addressed the assembly, saying, "Good learned friends, in our true teaching, there is, from the beginning, no distinction between the sudden and the gradual. There only is difference between sharpness and dullness in human nature.

> 迷人漸契, 悟人頓修. 自識本心, 自見本性, 即無差別. 所以立頓漸
> 미인점계, 오인돈수. 자식본심, 자견본성, 즉무차별. 소이입돈점
>
> 之假名.
> 지가명.
>
> 善知識, 我此法門從上以來. 先立無念爲宗, 無相爲體, 無住爲本.
> 선지식, 아차법문종상이래. 선립무념위종, 무상위체, 무주위본.
>
> 無相者, 於相而離相; 無念者, 於念而無念; 無住者, 人之本性,
> 무상자, 어상이리상; 무념자, 어념이무념; 무주자, 인지본성,
>
> 於世間善惡·好醜乃至寃之與親·
> 어세간선악·호추내지원지여친·

For the deluded, gradual cultivation is appropriate, while the sudden purification is more suitable for the enlightened. Recognize your original mind and see your original nature, and there shall be no distinction. That is why our teaching has the labels of the sudden and the gradual, which are merely provisional names.

Good learned friends, this dhamma teaching of mine comes from the ancient times. It establishes no-thought as its doctrine, no-form as its body, and no-abiding as its foundation. No-form means to transcend form while remaining within form; No-thought means to transcend thought while remaining within thoughts. And no-abiding means that the inherent nature of an individual remains unaffected, even amid worldly experiences such as good and bad, likes and dislikes, or enemies and friends.

> 言語觸刺欺爭之時, 竝將爲空, 不思酬害, 念念之中不思前境.
> 언어촉자기쟁지시, 병장위공, 불사수해, 염념지중불사전경.
>
> 若前念・今念・後念念念相續不斷, 名爲繫縛. 於諸法上念念不住,
> 약전념・금념・후념염념상속부단, 명위계박. 어제법상염념부주,
>
> 卽無縛也. 此是以無住爲本.
> 즉무박야. 차시이무주위본.
>
> 善知識, 外離一切相, 名爲無相. 能離於相, 卽法體淸淨. 此是以
> 선지식, 외리일체상, 명위무상. 능리어상, 즉법체청정. 차시이
>
> 無相爲體.
> 무상위체.

It stays unmoved during situations of speech, conflict, deception or dispute. All such experiences are seen as empty. One does not dwell on pain or loss, no hold on to past conditions yet remains fully mindful in every thought.

If past, present and future thoughts are arising continuously without interruption, it is referred to being bound. If you do not cling to any specific thought regarding all phenomena, it is referred to no-bondage. This is why no-abiding is considered the foundation.

Good learned friends, to be detached from all forms and appearances is referred to no-form. If you are able to transcend forms, the dhamma body shall immediately become clear and pure. This is why no-form is regarded as the body.

> 善知識, 於諸境上心不染, 曰無念. 於自念上常離諸境, 不於境上
> 선지식, 어제경상심불염, 왈무념. 어자념상상리제경, 불어경상
>
> 生心. 若只百物不思, 念盡除却, 一念絶即死, 別處受生, 是爲大
> 생심. 약지백물불사, 염진제각, 일념절즉사, 별처수생, 시위대
>
> 錯.
> 착.
>
> 學道者, 思之. 若不識法意, 自錯猶可; 更勸他人, 自迷不見, 又
> 학도자, 사지. 약불식법의, 자착유가; 갱권타인, 자미불견, 우
>
> 謗佛經. 所以立無念爲宗.
> 방불경. 소이립무념위종.

Good learned friends, to remain untainted by various external objects is called no-thought. Consistently detach yourself from your own thoughts about external objects, and do not arouse any mind on the external objects. If you do not think about hundreds of external objects and completely eliminate all thoughts, and if even a single thought is cut off, you would die and be reborn in another realm — this is a great misunderstanding.

You practitioners of the path, do contemplate on this: if you yourselves do not comprehend the true essence of the dhamma and make mistakes yourselves, it can be forgiven; if you mislead others, however, so that they cannot see, it is considered slandering against the Buddha's Scriptures. This is why our teaching establishes no-thought as its doctrine.

善知識, 云何立無念爲宗?
선지식, 운하립무념위종?

只緣口說見性, 迷人於境上有念, 念上便起邪見, 一切塵勞·妄想從
지연구설견성, 미인어경상유념, 염상변기사견, 일체진로·망상종

此而生. 自性本無一法可得. 若有所得, 妄說禍福, 卽是塵勞邪見.
차이생. 자성본무일법가득. 약유소득, 망설화복, 즉시진로사견.

故此法門立無念爲宗.
고차법문립무념위종.

善知識, 無者無何事? 念者念何物? 無者, 無二相, 無諸塵勞之心;
선지식, 무자무하사? 염자념하물? 무자, 무이상, 무제진로지심;

Good learned friends, what is meant by our teaching's establishing no-thought as its doctrine? The deluded talk about seeing-nature merely by their mouths, so they arouse thoughts on external appearances; their thoughts arouse erroneous views, so that all the labours and delusions arise from them. Self-nature has, from the beginning, no single dhamma to be obtained. To claim to have obtained it is to speak imprudently of misfortunes and blessings, which is the sign of his labouring and erroneous views. Therefore, this dhamma gate establishes no-thought as its doctrine.

Good learned friends, what is it that 'no' signifies? What is it that 'thought' refers to? 'No' signifies the absence of dualistic distinctions and the mind's entanglement in worldly concerns.

念者, 念眞如本性. 眞如即是念之體, 念即是眞如之用. 眞如
염자, 염진여본성. 진여즉시염지체, 염즉시진여지용. 진여

自性起念, 非眼·耳·鼻·舌能念; 眞如有性, 所以起念. 眞如若無,
자성기념, 비안·이·비·설능념; 진여유성, 소이기념. 진여약무,

眼耳·色聲當時即壞.
안이·색성당시즉괴.

善知識, 眞如自性起念. 六根雖有見聞覺知, 不染萬境而眞性常自
선지식, 진여자성기념. 육근수유견문각지, 불염만경이진성상자

在. 故云: '能善分別諸法相, 於第一義而不動.'"
재. 고운: '능선분별제법상 어제일의이부동.'"

'Thought' refers to contemplating True-thusness-original-nature. True-thusness itself is the body of thought, and thought is the function of True-thusness. It is True-thusness-Self-nature that generates thoughts, not the eyes, ears, nose and tongue. True-thusness has a nature, and so it generates thoughts. Without True-thusness, the eyes, ears, colors and sounds shall immediately collapse.

Good learned friends, True-thusness-Self-nature generates thoughts. Even though the six senses see, hear, sense and know, the True-nature remains untainted by all phenomena and always abides within itself. Thus it is said, 'Though it skillfully discriminates all phenomena, the supreme principle remains unmoved.'"

> 第五　坐禪品
> 제오　좌선품
>
> 師示衆云:"此門坐禪, 元不着心, 亦不着淨, 亦不是不動.
> 사시중운:"차문좌선, 원불착심, 역불착정, 역불시부동.
>
> 若言着心, 心元是妄. 知心如幻, 故無所着也. 若言着淨, 人性本淨,
> 약언착심, 심원시망. 지심여환, 고무소착야. 약언착정, 인성본정,
>
> 由妄念故盖覆眞如. 但無妄想, 性自淸淨. 起心着淨, 却生淨妄.
> 유망념고개부진여. 단무망상, 성자청정. 기심착정, 각생정망.

Chapter Five

Of Zazen

The Master addressed the assembly, saying,

"When practicing Zazen in our school, you should not cling to mind, nor to purity; nor is non-movement correct.

As to clinging to the mind, the mind itself is an illusion. If you know that the mind is like a mirage, there shall be nothing to cling to. As to clinging to purity, the human nature is originally pure. It is due to deluded thoughts that True-thusness is covered up. Just let there be no deluded thoughts, for Self-nature is inherently clear and pure. If deluded notions of purity arise, it is because your mind clings to purity.

> 妄無處所, 着者是妄. 淨無形相, 却立淨相, 言是工夫, 作此見
> 망무처소, 착자시망. 정무형상, 각립정상, 언시공부. 작차견
>
> 者, 障自本性, 却被淨縛.
> 자, 장자본성, 각피정박.
>
> 善知識, 若修不動者, 但見一切人時不見人之是非·善惡·過患, 卽
> 선지식, 약수부동자, 단견일체인시불견인지시비·선악·과환, 즉
>
> 是自性不動.
> 시자성부동.
>
> 善知識, 迷人身雖不動, 開口便說他人是非·長短·好惡, 與道違背.
> 선지식, 미인신수부동, 개구변설타인시비·장단·호악, 여도위배.

Since delusion has no place to abide in, attachment itself is delusion. Purity itself is formless, yet will you establish the concept of purity and say that it is the very practice? He who holds such a view only obstructs his own original-nature and becomes bound by the notion of purity.

Good learned friends, if you cultivate non-movement, do not see right and wrong, good and evil, faults and afflictions among all beings. This is the very non-movement of Self-nature.

Good learned friends, the deluded, even when their bodies remain non-moving, will readily engage in discussions about others' right and wrong, long and short, good and evil. Such a behavior goes against the path. Attaching to mind and clinging to purity are themselves obstacles to the path."

若着心·着淨, 却障道也."
약착심·착정, 각장도야."

師示衆云: "善知識, 何名坐禪? 此法門中無障無礙, 外於一切善
사시중운: "선지식, 하명좌선? 차법문중무장무애, 외어일체선

惡境界心念不起, 名爲坐; 內見自性不動, 名爲禪.
악경계심념불기, 명위좌; 내견자성부동, 명위선.

善知識, 何名禪定? 外離相爲禪, 內不亂爲定. 外若着相, 內心即
선지식, 하명선정? 외리상위선, 내불란위정. 외약착상, 내심즉

亂; 外若離相, 心即不亂. 本性自淨·自定. 只爲見境·思境即亂.
란; 외약리상, 심즉불란. 본성자정·자정. 지위견경·사경즉란.

The Master addressed the assembly, saying, "Good learned friends, what is called Zazen? In this dhamma gate, if there are no hindrances and obstacles, and externally any notions of good and evil do not arise, it is called Za; seeing your own Self-nature without disturbance is called Zen.

Good learned friends, what are called Zen-samādhi? Externally being free from forms is referred to Zen; internally, being undisturbed is called samādhi. If you externally cling to forms, your mind internally becomes disturbed; if externally free from forms, your mind remains undisturbed. Your original-nature is itself pure and undisturbed. However, only when you're perceiving and thinking external objects, it becomes disturbed.

> 若見諸境, 心不亂者, 是眞定也.
> 약견제경, 심불란자, 시진정야.
>
> 善知識, 外離相卽禪, 內不亂卽定. 外禪內定, 是爲禪定.
> 선지식, 외리상즉선, 내불란즉정. 외선내정, 시위선정.
>
> 『淨名經』云: '卽時豁然, 還得本心.'
> 『정명경』운: '즉시활연, 환득본심.'
>
> 『菩薩戒經』云: '我本性元自淸淨.'
> 『보살계경』운: '아본성원자청정.'
>
> 善知識, 於念念中自見本性淸淨, 自修自行, 自成佛道."
> 선지식, 어염념중자견본성청정, 자수자행, 자성불도."

Even though you perceive various objects, if your mind is not disturbed, that is the true samādhi.

Good learned friends, being externally free from forms is Zen, and internally being undisturbed is called samādhi. External Zen and internal samādhi, that is called Zen-samādhi. In Vimalakīrti Nirdeśa Sūtra[S], it is said, 'Immediately awaken and regain the your original mind'; and in Bodhisattvabhūmi Sūtra[S], 'My original-nature is inherently clear and pure.'

Good learned friends, may each of you directly see, in every thought, that your original-nature is clear and pure, cultivate and practice for yourself, and naturally realize the path to Buddhahood."

第六 懺悔品

제육 참회품

時大師見廣·韶二郡洎四方士庶駢集山中聽法. 於是陞座, 告衆曰:
시대사견광·소이군계사방사서병집산중청법. 어시승좌, 고중왈:

"來, 諸善知識. 此事須從自性中起, 於一切時念念自淨其心, 自修
"내, 제선지식. 차사수종자성중기, 어일체시염념자정기심, 자수

自行, 見自己法身, 見自心佛. 自度自戒始得, 不假到此.
자행, 견자기법신, 견자심불. 자도자계시득, 불가도차.

Chapter Six

Of Repentance and Penitence

At that time, the Master saw scholars and the commons from Guangzhou and Shaozhou as well as from all directions gathering onto the mountain to listen to the dhamma. So he ascended the platform and addressed the assembly, saying,

"Come ye Good learned friends! This matter must be initiated from within your own Self-nature. Therefore, in every moment, purify the mind, engage in Self-cultivation and Self-practice. Through this, you shall see your own dhamma body and witness Buddha within your own mind. Discipline yourself and attain liberation by yourself, only then shall you attain, without the need to come here.

> 既從遠來, 一會于此, 皆共有緣. 今可各各胡跪. 先爲傳自性五分
> 기종원래, 일회우차, 개공유연. 금가각각호궤. 선위전자성오분
>
> 法身香, 次授無相懺悔."
> 법신향, 차수무상참회."
>
> 衆胡跪. 師曰:
> 중호궤. 사왈:
>
> "一戒香, 即自心中無非無惡, 無嫉妬, 無貪瞋, 無劫害, 名戒香.
> "일계향, 즉자심중무비무악, 무질투, 무탐진, 무겁해, 명계향.
>
> 二定香, 即覩諸善惡境相, 自心不亂, 名定香.
> 이정향, 즉도제선악경상, 자심불란, 명정향.

Now that you have come from afar and gathered here today, all of us share a karmic connection. Now, knccl down, all of you. First, I will transmit the five fragrances of the dhamma-body of Self-nature; then I will bestow the repentance of no-form."

The assembly knelt down. The Master continued,

"First, the fragrance of precepts, which means that there is in your own mind no unwholesomeness, no evil, no envy, no greed, no hatred and no harm. This is called the fragrance of precepts.

Second, the fragrance of samādhi, which means that your mind remains undisturbed when observing the appearances of virtuous and non-virtuous phenomena. This is called the fragrance of samādhi.

> 三慧香. 自心無碍, 常以知慧觀照自性, 不造諸惡, 雖修衆善, 心
> 삼혜향. 자심무애, 상이지혜관조자성, 부조제악, 수수중선, 심
>
> 不執著, 敬上念下, 矜恤孤貧, 名慧香.
> 불집착, 경상념하, 긍휼고빈, 명혜향.
>
> 四解脫香, 即自心無所攀緣, 不思善, 不思惡, 自在無碍, 名解脫
> 사해탈향, 즉자심무소반연, 불사선, 불사악, 자재무애, 명해탈
>
> 香.
> 향.
>
> 五解脫知見香. 自心既無所攀緣善惡, 不可沈空守寂,
> 오해탈지견향. 자심기무소반연선악, 불가침공수적,

Third, the fragrance of wisdom, which means that there are no hindrances in your own mind, so that you constantly employ discerning wisdom to reflect upon Self-nature; not engaging in unwholesome actions, and even when cultivating all sorts of virtuous deeds, there being no attachment in mind; respecting those above, having compassion for those below, and caring for the lonely and the poor. This is called the fragrance of wisdom.

Fourth, the fragrance of liberation, which means that, there is in your mind no attachment or clinging to anything; not dwelling on thoughts of good, nor of evil, remaining free and unobstructed. This is called the fragrance of liberation.

Fifth, the fragrance of liberated insight, which refers to the state of mind where there is no attachment to good or evil, and you do not falling into emptiness and clinging to silence.

即須廣學多聞, 識自本心, 達諸佛理, 和光接物, 無我無人, 直至
즉수광학다문, 식자본심, 달제불리, 화광접물, 무아무인, 직지

菩提眞性不易, 名解脫知見香.
보리진성불역, 명해탈지견향.

善知識, 此香各自內薰, 莫向外覓.
선지식, 차향각자내훈, 막향외멱.

今與汝等授無相懺悔, 滅三世罪, 令得三業淸淨.
금여여등수무상참회, 멸삼세죄, 영득삼업청정.

善知識, 各隨語一時道:
선지식, 각수어일시도:

Instead, you engage in extensive learning and listening, recognize your own inherent mind, master all the principles taught by all Buddhas, and harmoniously interact with all beings, without the notion of Self or of others. So you directly attain enlightenment and unsurpassable True-nature. This is called the fragrance of liberated insight.

Good learned friends, these fragrances should be cultivated within yourself, not to be sought externally.

Now, let me transmit the practice of repentance of no-form to all of you, eliminating the threefold karmic offenses and enabling the purity of the three karmas.

Good learned friends, follow my instructions and repeat after me together:

> '弟子等從前念·今念及後念, 念念不被愚迷染. 從前所有惡業愚迷
> '제자등종전념·금념급후념, 염념불피우미염. 종전소유악업우미
>
> 等罪, 悉皆懺悔, 願一時消滅, 永不復起.
> 등죄, 실개참회, 원일시소멸, 영불부기.
>
> 弟子等從前念·今念及後念, 念念不被憍誑染. 從前所有惡業憍誑
> 제자등종전념·금념급후념, 염념불피교광염. 종전소유악업교광
>
> 等罪, 悉皆懺悔, 願一時消滅, 永不復起.
> 등죄, 실개참회, 원일시소멸, 영불부기.
>
> 弟子等從前念·今念及後念, 念念不被嫉妬染. 所有惡業嫉妬等罪,
> 제자등종전념·금념급후념, 염념불피질투염. 소유악업질투등죄,
>
> 悉皆懺悔,
> 실개참회,

'May each thought of ours, from the past through the present to the future, not be tainted by ignorance and delusion. We repent all our past unwholesome actions, including ignorance and other offenses. May they be entirely eliminated at once and never arise again.

May each of our thoughts, from the past through the present to the future, not be tainted by arrogance and deceit. We repent all our past unwholesome actions, including arrogance, deceit and other offenses. May they be completely eradicated at once and never arise again.

May each of our thoughts, from the past through the present to the future, not be tainted by jealousy. We repent all our past unwholesome actions, including jealousy and other offenses.

願一時消滅, 永不復起.'
원일시소멸, 영불부기.'

善知識, 已上是爲無相懺悔.
선지식, 이상시위무상참회.

云何名懺? 云何名悔? 懺者, 懺其前愆. 從前所有惡業愚迷·憍誑·
운하명참? 운하명회? 참자, 참기전건. 종전소유악업우미·교광·

嫉妬等罪, 悉皆盡懺, 永不復起, 是名爲懺. 悔者, 悔其後過. 從今
질투등죄, 실개진참, 영불부기, 시명위회. 회자, 회기후과. 종금

已後所有惡業愚迷·憍誑·嫉妬等罪, 今已覺悟, 悉皆永斷, 更不復
이후소유악업우미·교광·질투등죄, 금이각오, 실개영단, 갱불부

作, 是名爲悔. 故稱懺悔.
작, 시명위회. 고칭참회.

May they be completely eradicated at once and never arise again.'

Good learned friends, the above is called the practice of repentance of no-form.

What is meant by repentance? What is meant by penitence? Repentance refers to repenting for past transgressions. You fully repent all your past unwholesome actions: ignorance, arrogance and deceit, jealousy and other offenses, and vow that they never arise again. This is called repentance. Penitence refers to recognizing future potential unwholesome tendencies. You become aware of any potential tendencies- such as ignorance, arrogance and deceit, jealousy and others. You vow to completely sever them and ensure they never occur again. This is called penitence. Therefore, it is called repentance and penitence.

> 凡夫愚迷, 只知懺其前愆, 不知悔其後過. 以不悔故前愆不滅, 後
> 범부우미, 지지참기전건, 부지회기후과. 이불회고전건불멸, 후
>
> 過又生. 前愆既不滅, 後過復又生, 何名懺悔?
> 과우생. 전건기불멸, 후과부우생, 하명참회?
>
> 善知識, 既懺悔已, 與善知識發四弘誓願. 各須用心正聽:
> 선지식, 기참회이, 여선지식발사홍서원. 각수용심정청.

Ordinary men, being ignorant and deluded, only know to repent for past transgressions but do not understand the need to regret potential future tendencies. Since, due to the lack of penitence, their past transgressions remain unresolved, future misdeeds continue to arise. If past transgressions are not eliminated and future misdeeds continue to arise, how can it be called repentance and penitence?

Good learned friends, now that you have repented, let me put forth the Four Great Vows, together with you good learned friends. Listen attentively, each of you, with a sincere mind:

> '自心衆生無邊, 誓願度.
> '자심중생무변, 서원도.
> 自心煩惱無邊, 誓願斷.
> 자심번뇌무변, 서원단.
> 自性法門無盡, 誓願學.
> 자성법문무진, 서원학.
> 自性無上佛道, 誓願成.'
> 자성무상불도, 서원성.'
>
> 善知識, 大家豈不道'衆生無邊, 誓願度'? 恁麼道且不是惠能度.
> 선지식, 대가기부도'중생무변, 서원도'? 임마도차불시혜능도.
> 善知識, 心中衆生, 所謂邪迷心·誑妄心·不善心·嫉妒心·惡毒心,
> 선지식, 심중중생, 소위사미심·광망심·불선심·질투심·악독심,
> 如是等心盡是衆生. 各須自性自度, 是名眞度.
> 여시등심진시중생. 각수자성자도, 시명진도.

'Boundless sentient beings within my own mind, I vow to liberate.

Infinite afflictions within my own mind, I vow to eliminate.

Limitless dhamma teachings of Self-nature, I vow to study and embody.

Buddha's unsurpassable path of Self-nature, I vow to realize.'

Good learned friends, why do we not simply vow 'to liberate boundless sentient beings'? Because it is not me, Huineng, that liberates them.

Good learned friends, the sentient beings within your own minds, so-called delusional, deceptive, unwholesome, jealous, malicious and various other minds, all of these are the manifestations of sentient beings. Each one of you should individually recognize your Self-nature and liberate yourself. It is called the true liberation.

> 何名自性自度？即自心中邪見・煩惱・愚癡眾生將正見度. 既有正
> 하명자성자도? 즉자심중사견・번뇌・우치중생장정견도. 기유정
>
> 見, 使般若智打破愚癡・迷妄眾生, 各各自度. 邪來正度, 迷來悟度,
> 견, 사반야지타파우치・미망중생, 각각자도. 사래정도, 미래오도,
>
> 愚來智度, 惡來善度. 如是度者, 名爲眞度.
> 우래지도, 악래선도, 여시도자, 명위진도.
>
> 又'煩惱無邊, 誓願斷', 將自性般若智, 除却虛妄思想心, 是也.
> 우'번뇌무변, 서원단', 장자성반야지, 제각허망사상심, 시야.

What is meant by Self-liberation of Self-nature? It means that, from within your own minds, the deluded views, afflictions and foolishness of sentient beings are guided towards right understanding. Once you have attained right understanding, let paññā wisdom break through the afflictions, foolishness, confusion and delusions of sentient beings, and each of you shall be able to liberate yourself. When delusion arises, liberate with right understanding; when confusion arises, liberate with awakening; when foolishness arises, liberate with wisdom; and when evil arises, liberate with goodness. This kind of liberation is known as the true liberation.

Furthermore, vowing to cease boundless afflictions means cultivating the paññā wisdom of Self-nature and eliminating delusive and conceptualizing thoughts. This is what is meant.

> 又'法門無盡, 誓願學', 須自見性, 常行正法, 是名眞學.
> 우'법문무진, 서원학', 수자견성, 상행정법, 시명진학.
>
> 又'無上佛道, 誓願成', 既常能下心, 行於眞正, 離迷離覺, 常生般
> 우'무상불도, 서원성', 기상능하심, 행어진정, 이미이각, 상생반
>
> 若, 除眞除妄, 即見佛性, 即言下佛道成. 常念修行, 是願力法.
> 야, 제진제망, 즉견불성, 즉언하불도성. 상념수행, 시원력법.
>
> 善知識, 今發四弘願了. 更與善知識授無相三歸依戒.
> 선지식, 금발사홍원료. 갱여선지식수무상삼귀의계.

Moreover, vowing to learn the endless dhamma teachings means that you must personally realize seeing-nature and consistently practice the right path. This is known as the true learning.

Furthermore, vowing to attain the unsurpassable path of Buddhahood means that you can constantly humble your mind, practice true righteousness, and transcend both delusion and awakening. By continuously generating paññā and transcending both notions of true and false, one directly realize Buddha-nature and attain the path of Buddhahood under one word. Constantly be mindful in your practice, this is the dhamma of vow power.

Good learned friends, now that you have made the Four Great Vows, let me further transmit to you the Three Refuges of no-form.

> 善知識, 歸依覺, 二足尊; 歸依正, 離欲尊; 歸依淨, 衆中尊.
> 선지식, 귀의각, 이족존; 귀의정, 이욕존; 귀의정, 중중존.
>
> 從今日去, 稱覺爲師, 更不歸依邪魔·外道. 以自性三寶常自證明.
> 종금일거, 칭각위사, 갱불귀의사마·외도. 이자성삼보상자증명.
>
> 善知識歸依自性三寶.
> 권선지식귀의자성삼보.
>
> 佛者, 覺也; 法者, 正也; 僧者, 淨也.
> 불자, 각야; 법자, 정야; 승자, 정야.
>
> 自心歸依覺, 邪迷不生, 少欲知足, 能離財色, 名二足尊.
> 자심귀의각, 사미불생, 소욕지족, 능리재색, 명이족존.

Good learned friends, 'I take refuge in the Enlightenment- the Honored One among all the two footed beings. I take refuge in the Righteousness- the Honored One who has transcended desires. I take refuge in Purity- the Honored One among the community.'

From today on, regard Awakening as your teacher, and never take refuge in evil spirits or wrong paths again. Constantly affirm the Three Treasures of Self-nature within yourselves. I encourage you, good learned friends, to take refuge in the Three Treasures of Self-nature.

Buddha represents enlightenment; dhamma represents righteousness; and sangha represents purity.

When One take refuge in enlightenment within one's own mind, delusion does not arise. With little desire and contentment, One is let go of attachment to wealth and sensuality. Such a person is called Honored One among all two-footed beings.

> 自心歸依正, 念念無邪見, 以無邪見故卽無人我貢高·貪愛執著, 名
> 자심귀의정, 염념무사견, 이무사견고즉무인아공고·탐애집착, 명
> 離欲尊.
> 이욕존.
> 自心歸依淨, 一切震怒·愛慾境界, 自性皆不染著, 名衆中尊.
> 자심귀의정, 일체진노·애욕경계, 자성개불염착, 명중중존.
> 若修此行, 是自歸依.
> 약수차행, 시자귀의.
> 凡夫不會, 從日至夜受三歸戒, 若言歸依佛, 佛在何處? 若不見佛,
> 범부불회, 종일지야수삼귀계, 약언귀의불, 불재하처? 약불견불,
> 憑何所歸? 言却成妄.
> 빙하소귀? 언각성망.

When One takes refuge in righteousness within your own mind, no deluded views arise in any thought. Without such view, there is no ego, no arrogance, no clininging to desire or attachment. This is called the Honored One who is free from desire.

When One takes refuge in purity within one's own mind, one remains untouched by anger, lust or any emotional disturbances. The Self-nature stays undefiled by all external conditions. This is Honored One among the community. To cultivate this path is true Self-refuge.

Ordinary people do not understand this. They chant the Three Refuges all day long, yet merely in form.

You say "I take refuge in Buddha, but where is Buddha?

If you do not see Buddha within yourself, where do you truly take refuge? Such words become empty delusion.

> 善知識, 各自觀察, 莫錯用心. 經文分明言'自歸依佛', 不言歸依他
> 선지식, 각자관찰, 막착용심. 경문분명언'자귀의불', 불언귀의타
>
> 佛. 自佛不歸, 無所依處.
> 불. 자불불귀, 무소의처.
>
> 今既自悟, 各須歸依自心三寶. 內調心性, 外敬他人, 是自歸依也.
> 금기자오, 각수귀의자심삼보. 내조심성, 외경타인, 시자귀의야.

Good learned friends, each of you should observe yourself and not misuse your mind. The Scriptures clearly state that you should take refuge in Buddha within yourself, not in any external Buddha. If you do not take refuge in the Buddha within yourself, there is no other place from which to seek refuge.

Now that you have already attained Self-realization. Each of you should take refuge in the Three Treasures within your own mind. Internally cultivate your mind's nature, and externally respect others. This is the true act of taking refuge within yourself.

善知識, 既歸依自三寶竟, 各各至心. 吾與説一體三身自性佛, 令
선지식, 기귀의자삼보경, 각각지심. 오여설일체삼신자성불, 영

汝等見三身了然, 自悟自性. 總隨我道:
여등견삼신료연, 자오자성. 총수아도:

'於自色身, 歸依清淨法身佛.
'어자색신, 귀의청정법신불.

於自色身, 歸依圓滿報身佛.
어자색신, 귀의원만보신불.

於自色身, 歸依千百億化身佛.'
어자색신, 귀의천백억화신불.'

Good learned friends, now that you have taken refuge in the Three Treasures within yourself, each of you should be wholehearted. I will teach you about the Buddha of Self-nature, which encompasses the Three Bodies in one, so that you may clearly see the three bodies and awaken to Self-nature by yourself. Repeat after me:

'I take refuge in the Pure Dhamma Body Buddha within my physical body.

I take refuge in the Perfect Reward Body Buddha within my physical body.

I take refuge in the Countless Transformative Bodies Buddha within my physical body.'

> 善知識, 色身是舍宅, 不可言歸向者. 三身佛在自性中, 世人總有.
> 선지식, 색신시사택, 불가언귀향자. 삼신불재자성중, 세인총유.
>
> 爲自心迷, 不見內性, 外覓三身如來, 不見自身中有三身佛.
> 위자심미, 불견내성, 외멱삼신여래, 불견자신중유삼신불.
>
> 汝等聽説, 令汝等於自身中見自性有三身佛. 此三身佛從自性生,
> 여등청설, 영여등어자신중견자성유삼신불. 차삼신불종자성생,
>
> 不從外得.
> 부종외득.
>
> 何名清淨法身? 世人性本清淨, 萬法從自性生.
> 하명청정법신? 세인성본청정, 만법종자성생.

Good learned friends, the physical body is like a temporary dwelling, and it cannot be said that you can take refuge in it. The Three Bodies Buddha exists within your Self-nature, and everyone in the world possesses it. However, because your mind is deluded, you do not see your inner nature and seek the Three Bodies Buddha externally, unaware that it is already present within yourself. Listen carefully, all of you, to my words. I will guide you to see that your Self-nature contains the Three Bodies Buddha within you. This Three Bodies Buddha arises from your Self-nature and is not something that can be obtained externally.

What is meant by the Pure Dhamma Body? The natures of worldly beings are inherently clear and pure, and all phenomena arise from their Self-nature.

> 思量一切惡事, 即生惡行; 思量一切善事, 即生善行. 如是諸法在自性中.
> 사량일체악사, 즉생악행; 사량일체선사, 즉생선행. 여시제법재자성중.
>
> 如天常清, 日月常明, 爲浮雲蓋覆, 上明下暗. 忽偶風吹雲散, 上
> 여천상청, 일월상명, 위부운개부, 상명하암. 홀우풍취운산, 상
>
> 下俱明, 萬象皆現. 世人性常浮游, 如彼天雲.
> 하구명, 만상개현. 세인성상부유, 여피천운.
>
> 善知識, 智如日, 慧如月. 智慧常明, 於外著境, 被妄念浮雲蓋覆,
> 선지식, 지여일, 혜여월. 지혜상명, 어외착경, 피망념부운개부,
>
> 自性不得明朗.
> 자성부득명랑.

When you contemplate any sort of evil, evil actions are generated; when you contemplate virtuous things, virtuous actions are generated. In this way, all phenomena exist within Self-nature. It's just like the sky, which is always clear, and the sun and moon, which are constantly bright. When clouds momentarily cover the sky, it remains bright above, while it becomes dark below. However, when the wind suddenly blows, the clouds disperse, and it becomes clear both above and below, revealing all things. The nature of worldly people constantly wanders like those clouds in the sky.

Good learned friends, wisdom is like the sun, and insight is like the moon. Wisdom and insight are constantly bright and clear, but when they become attached to external phenomena and are covered by the fleeting clouds of deluded thoughts, your Self-nature cannot remain radiant.

若遇善知識, 聞眞正法, 自除迷妄, 內外明徹, 於自性中萬法皆現.
약우선지식, 문진정법, 자제미망, 내외명철, 어자성중만법개현.

見性之人亦復如是. 此名淸淨法身佛.
견성지인역부여시. 차명청정법신불.

善知識, 自心歸依自性, 是歸依眞佛.
선지식, 자심귀의자성, 시귀의진불.

自歸依者, 除却自性中不善心·嫉妬心·憍慢心·吾我心·誑妄心·輕
자귀의자, 제각자성중불선심·질투심·교만심·오아심·광망심·경

人心·慢人心·邪見心·貢高心及一切時中不善之行. 常自見己過,
인심·만인심·사견심·공고심급일체시중불선지행. 상자견기과,

不說他人好惡,
불설타인호악,

However, when you encounter a good learned teacher and hear the true and correct dhamma, you can dispel delusion and ignorance by yourself, becoming bright and clear both internally and externally, revealing all phenomena within your Self-nature. Those who realize seeing-nature are also like this. This is called the Pure Dhamma Body Buddha.

Good learned friends, take refuge in Self-nature of your own mind. This is taking refuge in the true Buddha.

To take refuge in yourself is to eliminate unwholesome minds such as jealousy, arrogance, selfishness, deceit, disdain for others, disrespect for others, wrong views, a superiority complex and all unwholesome actions at any time. It also means to constantly examine your own faults and refrain from speaking about virtues or faults of others.

是自歸依. 常須下心, 普行恭敬, 卽是見性通達,
시자귀의. 상수하심, 보행공경, 즉시견성통달,

更無滯碍, 是自歸依.
갱무체애, 시자귀의.

何名千百億化身? 若不思萬法, 性本如空; 一念思量, 名爲變化.
하명천백억화신? 약불사만법, 성본여공; 일념사량, 명위변화.

思量惡事, 化爲地獄, 思量善事, 化爲天堂; 毒害化爲龍蛇, 慈悲
사량악사, 화위지옥, 사량선사, 화위천당; 독해화위용사, 자비

化爲菩薩; 智慧化爲上界, 愚癡化爲下方. 自性變化甚多.
화위보살; 지혜화위상계, 우치화위하방. 자성변화심다.

This is taking refuge in yourself. Lower your mind at all times and practice universal reverence, and you shall realize seeing-nature and master it without hindrance. This is taking refuge in yourself.

What is meant by the myriad of Transformative Bodies? If you do not think about the myriad of phenomena, the nature is inherently empty. With a single thought, transformation occurs. If you think about evil things, it transforms into hell; if you think about virtuous things, it transforms into heaven. Poisonous harm transforms into dragons and snakes, compassion into Bodhisattvas[s]; wisdom into higher realms, ignorance into lower realms. Self-nature undergoes a multitude of transformations.

> 迷人不 能省覺, 念念起惡, 常行惡道. 回一念善, 智慧即生, 此名
> 미인불 능성각, 염념기악. 상행악도. 회일념선, 지혜즉생, 차명
>
> 自性化身佛.
> 자성화신불.
>
> 何名圓滿報身? 譬如一燈能除千年暗, 一智能滅萬年愚. 莫思向前,
> 하명원만보신? 비여일등능제천년암, 일지능멸만년우. 막사향전,
>
> 已過不可得. 常思於後, 念念圓明, 自見本性. 善惡雖殊, 本性無
> 이과불가득. 상사어후, 염념원명, 자견본성. 선악수수, 본성무
>
> 二. 無二之性, 名爲實性. 於實性中不染善惡, 此名圓滿報身佛.
> 이. 무이지성, 명위실성. 어실성중불염선악, 차명원만보신불.

The deluded are unable to awaken and repeatedly generate evil thoughts, constantly treading the path of wrong doings. Yet with a single thought of goodness, wisdom arises immediately. This is known as the Transformative Bodies Buddha of Self-nature.

What is meant by the Perfect Reward Body? It is like a single lamp that can dispel a thousand years of darkness, and a single wisdom that can extinguish ten thousand years of ignorance. Do not dwell on the past; what has passed cannot be attained. Always contemplate the future, and let each thought be complete and bright, and you shall see your own original-nature. While good and evil are distinct, the original-nature is non-dual. The nature without duality is called the real-nature.

In the realm of real-nature, there is no contamination by good or evil. This is called the Perfect Reward Body Buddha.

> 自性起一念惡, 滅萬劫善因; 自性起一念善, 得恒沙惡盡, 直至無
> 자성기일념악, 멸만겁선인; 자성기일념선, 득항사악진, 직지무
>
> 上菩提. 念念自見, 不失本念, 名爲報身.
> 상보리. 염념자견, 불실본념, 명위보신.
>
> 善知識, 從法身思量, 即是化身佛. 念念自性自見, 即是報身佛.
> 선지식, 종법신사량, 즉시화신불. 염념자성자견, 즉시보신불.
>
> 自悟自修, 自性功德, 是眞歸依. 皮肉是色身, 色身是舍宅, 不言
> 자오자수, 자성공덕, 시진귀의. 피육시색신, 색신시사택, 불언
>
> 歸依也. 但悟自性三身, 即識自性佛.
> 귀의야. 단오자성삼신, 즉식자성불.

When your Self-nature gives rise to a single thought of evil, it extinguishes the accumulation of ten thousand eons of virtuous causes; when your Self-nature gives rise to a single thought of good, it exhausts the accumulation of as many evils as grains of sand in the Ganges, and you shall directly attain supreme enlightenment. With each thought being Self-realized and never losing the original thought, it is called the Perfect Reward Body.

Good learned friends, contemplating from the dhamma body itself is the Transformative Bodies Buddha. Self-realizing your Self-nature with each thought is the Perfect Reward Body Buddha. Self-realizing and self-practicing of Self-nature merit is the true refuge. The skin and flesh constitute the physical body, which is merely a transient abode and not to be regarded as the ultimate refuge. Simply realize the three bodies of Self-nature, and you will immediately recognize the Self-nature Buddha.

> 吾有一無相頌. 若能頌持, 言下令汝積劫迷罪一時消滅."
> 오유일무상송. 약능송지, 언하령여적겁미죄일시소멸."
>
> 頌曰:
> 송왈:
>
>
> "迷人修福不修道, 只言修福便是道.
> "미인수복불수도, 지언수복변시도.
> 布施供養福無邊, 心中三惡元來造.
> 보시공양복무변, 심중삼악원래조.

Now I have an ode of no-form. If you can recite and uphold it, it shall eradicate your accumulated delusions and sins from countless kalpas in an instant."

The ode goes,

"The deluded pursue fortune, but do not practice the path,
Merely saying that pursuing fortune is the very path.
Donations and offerings indeed bring boundless fortune,
But the three evils are originally created within the mind.

擬將修福欲滅罪, 後世得福罪還在.
의장수복욕멸죄, 후세득복죄환재.

但向心中除罪緣, 各自性中眞懺悔.
단향심중제죄연, 각자성중진참회.

忽悟大乘眞懺悔, 除邪行正即無罪.
홀오대승진참회, 제사행정즉무죄.

學道常於自性觀, 即與諸佛同一類.
학도상어자성관, 즉여제불동일류.

吾祖惟傳此頓法, 普願見性同一體.
오조유전차돈법, 보원견성동일체.

Though you intend to eradicate your sins through cultivating fortune,
The sins shall remain, even if you attain fortune in the future.
Simply eliminate the karmic roots of sins within your mind,
That is the true repentance within your Self-nature.

If you suddenly realize Māhāyāna and sincerely repent,
Abandon evil and practice righteousness, and there shall be no more sin.
By studying the path and constantly observing your Self-nature,
Then you are in oneness with all Buddhas.

Our Patriarchs transmitted only this sudden teaching,
Wishing all beings to realize oneness through seeing-nature.

> 若欲當來覓法身, 離諸法相心中洗.
> 약욕당래멱법신, 이제법상심중세.
>
> 努力自見莫悠悠, 後念忽絶一世休.
> 노력자견막유유, 후념홀절일세휴.
>
> 若悟大乘得見性, 虔恭合掌至心求."
> 약오대승득견성, 건공합장지심구."
>
> 師言:"善知識, 總須誦取,
> 사언: "선지식, 총수송취,

If you wish to seek the dhamma body in the future,
Let go of all appearances of dhamma, and cleanse the mind from within.

Strive to see the Self, and do not wander in distraction.
If mindfulness breaks for but a moment, this life will be in vain.
If you awaken to Māhāyāna and attain seeing-nature,
With reverent palms joined, seek with a sincere heart."

The Master concluded, "Good learned friends, recite and reflect on this teaching.

VI. Of Repentance and Penitence

> 依此修行. 言下見性, 雖去吾千里, 如常在吾邊; 於此言下不悟, 即對
> 의차수행. 언하견성, 수거오천리, 여상재오변; 어차언하불오, 즉대
>
> 面千里, 何勤遠來? 珍重好去."一衆聞法, 靡不開悟, 歡喜奉行.
> 면천리, 하근원래? 진중호거."일중문법, 미불개오, 환희봉행.

Practice in accordance with it: If under a single word you realize seeing-nature, even if you're a thousand lis away, you are always by my side. But if you fail to awaken at the very moment of a single word, even if face to face, we are a thousand lis apart. Then why come from afar with such effort? Take care, and farewell."

Upon hearing the dhamma, not one in the assembly failed to awaken. They all rejoiced and took the teaching to heart.

> 第七 機緣品
> 제칠 기연품
>
> 師自黃梅得法, 回至韶州曹侯村, 人無知者. 有儒士劉志略禮遇甚
> 사자황매득법, 회지소주조후촌, 인무지자. 유유사유지략예우심
> 厚. 志略有姑, 爲尼, 名無盡藏. 常誦『大涅槃經』. 師暫聽, 卽知妙
> 후. 지략유고, 위니, 명무진장. 상송『대열반경』. 사잠청, 즉지묘
> 義, 遂爲解說.
> 의, 수위해설.

Chapter Seven

Of Disciples

The Master attained the dhamma in Huangmei and returned to Caohou Village, in Shaozhou. No one was aware of it. There was a Confucian scholar named Liu Zhilue, who showed great respect.

Liu's paternal aunt was a nun named Wujinzang. She was constantly reciting the Mahāparinibbāna Sutta. Once the Master listened to it, he understood its profound meaning, and so he would explain it to her.

> 尼乃執卷問字. 師曰: "字即不識, 義即請問."
> 니내집권문자. 사왈: "자즉불식, 의즉청문."
>
> 尼曰: "字尚不識, 曷能會義?"
> 니왈: "자상불식, 갈능회의?"
>
> 師曰: "諸佛妙理, 非關文字."
> 사왈: "제불묘리, 비관문자."
>
> 尼驚異之, 遍告里中耆德, 云: "此是有道之士. 宜請供養."
> 니경이지, 변고이중기덕, 운: "차시유도지사. 의청공양."
>
> 有晉武侯玄孫曹叔良及居民競來瞻禮.
> 유진무후현손조숙량급거민경래첨례.

Then, she held the Scripture and asked about a word. The Master said, "I do not understand letters. Ask rather about its meaning."

The nun asked, "While you do not even understand a letter, how can you grasp its meaning?"

The Master replied, "The profound principles of all Buddhas have nothing to do with letters."

The nun was astonished, and spread the word to the elders in the village, saying, "This is a person of the path. Why don't we invite him and offer our respects?"

The news reached Cao Shuliang, a descendant of the Marquis Wu of the Jin Dynasty, as well as the local residents, who eagerly came to pay their respects.

> 時寶林古寺, 自隋末兵火已廢, 遂於故基重建梵宇, 延師居之, 俄
> 시보림고사, 자수말병화이폐, 수어고기중건범우, 연사거지, 아
> 成寶坊.
> 성보방.
>
> 師住九月餘日, 又爲惡黨尋逐. 師乃遁于前山, 被其縱火焚燒草木.
> 사주구월여일, 우위악당심축. 사내둔우전산, 피기종화분소초목.
>
> 師隱身挨入石中得免. 石於是有師趺坐膝痕及衣布之紋, 因名避難
> 사은신애입석중득면. 석어시유사부좌슬흔급의포지문, 인명피난
> 石.
> 석.

At that time, the ancient temple of Baolin had been destroyed by wars since the end of the Sui Dynasty. Then the halls were rebuilt on the site, and the Master was invited to reside there. Before long, it became a precious sanctuary.

The Master resided there for over nine months, but was again sought after by the malicious. The Master then fled to the mountains to evade their pursuit. They set fire to the grass and trees, burning them down. The Master concealed himself among the rocks and managed to escape unharmed. On the stone where the Master sat in lotus position, there were imprints of his knees and the patterns of his clothes. Hence it was named the Escape Stone.

> 師憶五祖悔會止藏之囑, 遂行, 隱于二邑焉.
> 사억오조회회지장지촉, 수행, 은우이읍언.
>
> 一僧法海, 韶州曲江人也. 初參祖師, 問曰: "即心即佛, 願垂指
> 일승법해, 소주곡강인야. 초참조사, 문왈: "즉심즉불, 원수지
> 諭."
> 유."
> 師曰: "前念不生即心, 後念不滅即佛. 成一切相即心, 離一切相即
> 사왈: "전념불생즉심, 후념불멸즉불. 성일체상즉심, 이일체상즉
> 佛. 吾若具說, 窮劫不盡. 聽吾偈." 曰:
> 불. 오약구설, 궁겁부진. 청오게." 왈:

The Master recalled the Fifth Patriarch's instruction, to stop at huai and to hide at hui. So he left and concealed himself in the villages of those names.

Monk Fahai was from Qujiang, Shaozhou. When he first visited the Patriarch, he asked, "It is said that mind itself is Buddha. I humbly seek your guidance."

The Master replied, "If the previous thought does not arise, it is mind; if the subsequent thought does not cease, it is Buddha. Embodying all forms is mind; transcending all forms is Buddha. If I were to fully explain this, even countless eons would be insufficient. Listen to my verse."

It goes,

"即心名慧, 即佛乃定.
"즉심명혜, 즉불내정.

定慧等持, 意中淸淨.
정혜등지, 의중청정.

悟此法門, 由汝習性.
오차법문, 유여습성.

用本無生, 雙修是正."
용본무생, 쌍수시정."

法海言下大悟, 以偈讚, 曰:
법해언하대오, 이게찬, 왈:

"Mind itself is called wisdom;
Buddha itself is the same as samādhi.
Hold samādhi and wisdom equally,
And your intention shall be clear and pure.

Awakening to this dhamma gate
Depends on your own habitual nature.
In its functioning, there is originally no birth,
So it is right to practice both simultaneously."

Fahai realized profoundly under a word, and he praised it through a verse.

It goes,

"即心元是佛, 不悟而自屈.
"즉심원시불, 불오이자굴.

我知定慧因, 雙修離諸物."
아지정혜인, 쌍수리제물."

僧法達, 洪州人. 七歲出家, 常誦『法華經』.
승법달, 홍주인. 칠세출가, 상송『법화경』.

來禮祖師, 頭不至地.
내례조사, 두부지지.

"Mind itself is Buddha.

Unenlightened, you mistakenly belittle yourself.

Now that I have understood the causes of samādhi and wisdom,

I will practice both simultaneously, and transcend all phenomena."

Monk Fada was from Hongzhou. He became a monk at the age of seven, and continually recited the Saddharmapuṇḍarīka Sūtra[S]. When he came to pay respects to the Patriarch, he didn't bump his forehead to the ground.

> 師訶曰: "禮不投地, 何如不禮? 汝心中必有一物. 蘊習何事耶?"
> 사가왈: "예불투지, 하여불례? 여심중필유일물. 온습하사야?"
>
> 曰: "念『法華經』, 已及三千部."
> 왈: "염『법화경』, 이급삼천부."
>
> 祖曰: "汝若念至萬部, 得其經意, 不以爲勝, 則與吾偕行. 汝今負
> 조왈: "여약염지만부, 득기경의, 불이위승, 즉여오해행. 여금부
>
> 此事業, 都不知過. 聽吾偈." 曰:
> 차사업, 도부지과. 청오게." 왈:
>
> "禮本折萬幢, 頭奚不至地?
> "예본절만당, 두해부지지?

The Patriarch scolded him, saying, "How rude you are not to bump your forehead to the ground! There must be something within your mind that you are attached to. What have you been practicing?"

Fada replied, "I have recited the Saddharmapuṇḍarīka Sūtra[s] around three thousand times."

The Patriarch said, "If you were to recite it ten thousand times and truly understand its meaning, not considering yourself superior, then you can walk alongside me. But now you are burdened with this undertaking, yet do not know your own shortcomings at all. Listen to my verse."

It goes,

"Worship is originally to break the ten-thousand-flags of Self-importance.
  Why then has your forehead not touch the ground?

> 有我罪即生, 亡功福無比."
> 유아죄즉생, 망공복무비."
>
> 師又曰:"汝名什麼?"
> 사우왈: "여명십마?"
>
> 曰:"法達."
> 왈: "법달."
>
> 師曰:"汝名法達, 何曾達法?"
> 사왈: "여명법달, 하증달법?"
>
> 復說偈, 曰:
> 부설게, 왈:

If there are Self-centered thoughts, faults arise,

While if efforts are forgotten, blessings shall be incomparable."

The Master further asked, "What is your name?"

The monk replied, "Fada."

The Master said, "Your name is Fada, but have you truly attained the dhamma?"

Then He recited another verse. It goes,

> "汝今名法達, 勤誦未休歇.
> "여금명법달, 근송미휴헐.
>
> 空誦但循聲, 明心號菩薩.
> 공송단순성, 명심호보살.
>
> 汝今有緣故, 吾今爲汝説.
> 여금유연고, 오금위여설.
>
> 但信佛無言, 蓮華從口發."
> 단신불무언, 연화종구발."
>
> 達聞偈, 悔謝曰: "而今而後, 當謙恭一切.
> 달문게, 회사왈: "이금이후, 당겸공일체.

"Now your name is Fada,

And you are diligently reciting without rest.

Vainly reciting is merely following its sounds.

You'll be called a Bodhisattva⁽ˢ⁾ only if your mind becomes bright.

Since you now have a karmic connection with me,

I now speak for you:

Just believe that Buddha does not speak at all,

And lotus flowers shall bloom from your mouth."

Upon hearing the verse, Fada expressed remorse and gratitude, saying, "From now on, I will be humble and respectful in all matters.

> 弟子誦『法華經』, 未解經義, 心常有疑. 和尚智慧廣大, 願略說經中義理."
> 제자송『법화경』, 미해경의, 심상유의. 화상지혜광대, 원약설경중의리."
> 師曰: "法達, 法即心達, 汝心不達. 經本無疑, 汝心自疑. 汝念此經, 以何爲宗?"
> 사왈: "법달, 법즉심달, 여심부달. 경본무의, 여심자의. 여념차경, 이하위종?"
> 達曰: "學人根性暗鈍, 從來但依文誦念, 豈知宗趣?"
> 달왈: "학인근성암둔, 종래단의문송념, 기지종취?"
> 師曰: "吾不識文字. 汝試取經, 誦之一徧. 吾當爲汝解說."
> 사왈: "오불식문자. 여시취경, 송지일편. 오당위여해설."

I have been reciting the Saddharmapuṇḍarīka Sūtra[s] without fully understanding its meaning, and my mind has been filled with doubts. Please, Your Reverence, with your vast and profound wisdom, I beg you to concisely explain the meaning of the Scripture for me."

The Master replied, "Fada, the dhamma is realized through your mind, but your mind has not yet realized it. The Scripture itself originally carries no doubt, but your mind still has doubts. When you contemplate the Scripture, what do you consider as its central doctrine?"

Fada replied, "Your pupil is inherently dull. Having always recited it just relying on the text, how could I know the essence?"

The Master said, "I do not understand letters. Take the Scripture and recite a part of it. I will explain it to you."

> 法達即高聲念經. 至「譬喻品」, 師曰: "止. 此經元來以因緣出世爲
> 법달즉고성념경. 지「비유품」, 사왈: "지. 차경원래이인연출세위
>
> 宗. 縱說多種譬喻, 亦無越於此.
> 종. 종설다종비유, 역무월어차.
>
> 何者因緣? 經云: '諸佛世尊, 唯以一大事因緣故出現於世.' 一大
> 하자인연? 경운: '제불세존, 유이일대사인연고출현어세.' 일대
>
> 事者, 佛之知見也. 世人外迷著相, 內迷著空. 若能於相離相·於空
> 사자, 불지지견야. 세인외미착상, 내미착공. 약능어상리상·어공
>
> 離空, 卽是內外不迷. 若悟此法, 一念心開, 是爲開佛知見.
> 리공, 즉시내외불미. 약오차법, 일념심개, 시위개불지견.

Fada then began to recite the Scripture loudly. When it went to "Of Simile and Parables," the Master said, "Halt. This Scripture originally takes the principle of causality and transcending the world as its core doctrine. Even though it expounds on various kinds of similes and parables, it does not go beyond this.

What is causality? The Scripture states, 'All Buddhas and the World-Honored-One appeared in this world solely due to one great causality.' The one great causality is Buddha's wisdom and insight. Worldly people are deluded, attaching to forms externally and to emptiness internally. If you can detach from forms while in forms, and from emptiness while in emptiness, then you shall not be deluded either externally or internally. Awakening to this dhamma and opening your mind with a single thought, this is the opening of Buddha's wisdom.

> 佛猶覺也, 分爲四門: 開覺知見, 示覺知見, 悟覺知見, 入覺知見.
> 불유각야, 분위사문. 개각지견, 시각지견, 오각지견, 입각지견.
>
> 若聞開示, 便能悟入, 卽覺知見本來眞性而得出現.
> 약문개시, 변능오입, 즉각지견본래진성이득출현.
>
> 汝愼勿錯解經意. 見他道'開·示·悟·入, 自是佛之知見, 我輩無分',
> 여신물착해경의. 견타도'개·시·오·입, 자시불지지견, 아배무분',
>
> 若作此解, 乃是謗經毀佛也. 彼旣是佛, 已具知見, 何用更開?
> 약작차해, 내시방경훼불야. 피기시불, 이구지견, 하용갱개?

Buddha means awakening, and is divided into four gates: opening awakened insight, demonstrating awakened insight, realizing awakened insight and entering into awakened insight. If you hear the revelation, you can realize and enter. Then the awakened insight of your original true-nature will become evident.

Be careful not to misunderstand the meaning of the Scripture. You would see others say, 'Opening, demonstrating, realizing and entering are the Buddha's insights, and we do not possess them.' Such an understanding is to slander the Scriptures and the Buddha. Since you are already Buddha and have already possessed insight, what need is there to open anything further?

汝今當信. 佛知見者, 只汝自心, 更無別佛. 蓋爲一切衆生自蔽光
여금당신. 불지견자, 지여자심, 갱무별불. 개위일체중생자폐광

明, 貪愛塵境, 外緣內擾, 甘受驅馳, 便勞他世尊從三昧起, 種種
명, 탐애진경, 외연내요, 감수구치, 변로타세존종삼매기, 종종

苦口勸令寢息. 莫向外求, 與佛無二. 故云'開佛知見.' 吾亦勸, 一
고구권령침식. 막향외구, 여불무이. 고운'개불지견.' 오역권, 일

切人於自心中常開佛之知見.
체인어자심중상개불지지견.

世人心邪, 愚迷造罪. 口善心惡, 貪瞋嫉妬, 諂佞我慢, 侵人害物,
세인심사, 우미조죄, 구선심악, 탐진질투, 첨녕아만, 침인해물,

自開衆生知見.
자개중생지견.

You should now believe: the Buddha's insight is simply your own mind, and there is no other Buddha. It is because all sentient beings obscure their own inner light, crave worldly objects, and become entangled in external conditions and internal disturbances, and willingly endure being driven about. The World-Honored-One laboriously arose from samādhi and tirelessly urged you to rest and cease such pursuits. Do not seek outside, you are no different from Buddha. Therefore, it is said 'to open Buddha's insight.' I also advise each of you to open the Buddha's insight constantly within your own mind.

Because the minds of worldly people are wicked and deluded, they commit sins. They speak good words with their mouths, but their minds are evil, filled with greed, anger, jealousy, flattery and arrogance, causing violating others and destroying things. In this way, they open the views of sentient beings.

> 若能正心, 常生智慧, 觀照自心, 止惡行善, 是自開佛之知見.
> 약능정심, 상생지혜, 관조자심, 지악행선, 시자개불지지견.
>
> 汝須念念開佛知見, 勿開眾生知見. 開佛知見, 即是出世; 開眾生
> 여수염념개불지견, 물개중생지견. 개불지견, 즉시출세; 개중생
>
> 知見, 即是世間. 汝若但勞勞執念以爲功課者, 何異犛牛愛尾?"
> 지견, 즉시세간. 여약단노로집념이위공과자, 하이이우애미?"
>
> 達曰: "若然者, 但得解義, 不勞誦經耶?"
> 달왈: "약연자, 단득해의, 불로송경야?"

If you can correct your mind, you can constantly develop wisdom, insightfully observe your own mind, and stop doing evil and practice good. This is the Self-opening of the Buddha's insights.

You should practice to open the Buddha's insights thought by thought, and do not open the views of sentient beings. Opening the Buddha's insights is transcending the mundane world, while opening the views of sentient beings pertains to the worldly realm. If you laboriously cling to thoughts and consider it a merit, how is it any different from an ox that loves its tail and eventually dies?"

Fada asked, "If that's the case, should I only focus on understanding the meaning of the Scripture and no longer need to laboriously recite it?"

> 師曰:"經有何過, 豈障汝念? 只爲迷悟在人, 損益由己. 口誦心
> 사왈: "경유하과, 기장여념? 지위미오재인, 손익유기. 구송심
>
> 行, 卽是轉經; 口誦心不行, 卽是被經轉. 聽吾偈."曰:
> 행, 즉시전경; 구송심불행, 즉시피경전. 청오게." 왈:
>
> "心迷法華轉, 心悟轉法華.
> "심미법화전, 심오전법화.
>
> 誦經久不明, 與義作讎家.
> 송경구불명, 여의작수가.

The Master replied, "What fault is there in the Scripture to hinder you from reciting it? Confusion or enlightenment resides in people, and gain or loss depends on oneself. Recite with your mouth and practice with your mind, and you shall turn the Scripture; Recite only with your mouth without practicing with your mind, and you shall merely be turned by it. Listen to my verse."

It goes,

"Deluded in mind, you are turned by the Dhamma Lotus;
Awakened in mind, you turn the Dhamma Lotus.
Reciting the Scripture for a long time without understanding it,
You shall become an enemy to its meaning.

無念念即正, 有念念成邪.
무념염즉정, 유념염성사.

有無俱不計, 長御白牛車."
유무구불계, 장어백우거."

達聞偈, 不覺悲泣, 言下大悟, 而告師曰: "法達從昔已來實未曾轉
달문게, 불각비읍, 언하대오, 이고사왈: "법달종석이래실미증전

『法華』, 乃被『法華』轉."
『법화』, 내피『법화』전."

再啓曰: "經云: '諸大聲聞乃至菩薩, 皆盡思共度量, 不能測佛智.'
재계왈: "경운: '제대성문내지보살, 개진사공탁량, 불능측불지.'

With no-thought, the mind is correct;

With thoughts, the mind becomes wicked.

If you do not consider either with-thought or no-thought,

Then you shall ride the white-ox-driven cart for ever."

Upon hearing the verse, Fada was deeply moved, tears welling up unknowingly, and he had a profound realization under a word. He said to the Master, "Never before have I truly turned the Saddharmapuṇḍarīka Sūtra[S]; instead, I have only been turned by it."

Fada continued, "It is stated in the Scripture, 'Even the great disciples and Bodhisattvas[S], despite their utmost efforts to think and measure, cannot fully comprehend the Buddha's wisdom.'

> 今令, 凡夫但悟自心, 便名佛之知見. 自非上根, 未免疑謗. 又經
> 금령, 범부단오자심, 변명불지지견. 자비상근, 미면의방. 우경
>
> 説三車, 羊・鹿之車與白牛之車, 如何區別? 願和尚再垂開示."
> 설삼거, 양・록지거여백우지거, 여하구별? 원화상재수개시."
>
> 師曰: "經意分明, 汝自迷背.
> 사왈: "경의분명, 여자미배.
>
> 諸三乘人不能測佛智者, 患在度量也.
> 제삼승인불능측불지자, 환재탁량야.

Now, you have said that even an ordinary man, if only he awakens to his own mind, it is the very understanding and insights of the Buddha. However, since I do not possess a superior spiritual capacity, I am still not free from doubts. The Scripture further mentions three carts: one driven by a sheep, another by a deer, and still another by a white ox. How can I distinguish among them? I humbly beg Your Reverence to provide me a further explanation."

The Master replied, "The meaning of the Scripture is clear and distinct, but you have misunderstood due to your own delusion. The reason why all those in the three vehicles cannot comprehend Buddha's wisdom lies in their tendency to measure and calculate.

> 饒伊盡思共推, 轉可縣遠.
> 요이진사공추, 전가현원.
>
> 佛本爲凡夫説, 不爲佛説. 此理若不肯信者, 從他退席, 殊不知坐
> 불본위범부설, 불위불설. 차리약불긍신자, 종타퇴석, 수부지좌
>
> 却白牛車, 更於門外覓三車.
> 각백우거, 갱어문외멱삼거.
>
> 況經文明向汝道: '唯一佛乘, 無有餘乘, 若二若三', 乃至'無數方
> 황경문명향여도: '유일불승, 무유여승, 약이약삼', 내지'무수방
>
> 便, 種種因緣·譬喻·言詞是法, 皆爲一佛乘故.' 汝何不省?
> 편, 종종인연·비유·언사시법, 개위일불승고.' 여하불성?

Even if they exhaustively ponder and collectively strive, their understanding will still deviate from the original meaning. The Buddha originally taught for the sake of ordinary people, not for Buddhas. If you are reluctant to believe in this principle, you might as well leave and follow others. Then you don't realize that you are already sitting on a white-ox-driven cart, yet you are seeking the three carts outside of the gate.

Moreover, the Scripture clearly states, 'There is only one Buddha vehicle and no other vehicles, neither two nor three' and 'Even countless expedient means, as well as various causes and conditions, similes, words and expressions, are all the dhamma itself, because they are just one Buddha vehicle.' Why don't you reflect upon this?

> 三車是假, 爲昔時故; 一乘是實, 爲今時故. 只教汝去假歸實.
> 삼거시가, 위석시고; 일승시실, 위금시고. 지교여거가귀실.
>
> 歸實之後, 實亦無名.
> 귀실지후, 실역무명.
>
> 應知所有珍財盡屬於汝, 由汝受用. 更不作父想, 亦不作子想, 亦
> 응지소유진재진속어여, 유여수용. 갱부작부상, 역부작자상, 역
>
> 無用想, 是名持『法華經』. 從劫至劫, 手不釋卷, 從晝至夜, 無不
> 무용상, 시명지『법화경』. 종겁지겁, 수불석권, 종주지야, 무불
>
> 念時也."
> 념시야."
>
> 達蒙啓發, 踊躍歡喜, 以偈讚曰:
> 달몽계발, 용약환희, 이게찬왈:

The three vehicles are only provisional, representing the past, while the one vehicle is ultimate, representing the present. It teaches you only to abandon the provisional and return to the ultimate. After returning to the ultimate, even the ultimate itself is meaningless.

You should understand that all valuable possessions belong to you and are meant for your use. Therefore, you should not think of them in terms of father, nor of son, nor even of using them. This is known as upholding the Saddharmapuṇḍarīka Sūtra[S]. It means that, throughout eons, you never let go of it, holding it in hand from morning till night, without ever ceasing to recite it."

Upon receiving this enlightening teaching, Fada was nearly jumping up with joy and delight. He praised with a verse.

"經誦三千部, 曹溪一句亡.
"경송삼천부, 조계일구망.

未明出世旨, 寧歇累生狂?
미명출세지, 영헐누생광?

羊鹿牛權說, 初中後善揚.
양록우권설, 초중후선양.

誰知火宅內, 元是法中王?"
수지화택내, 원시법중왕?"

師曰: "汝今後方可名念經僧也."
사왈: "여금후방가명염경승야."

"Though I have recited the Scripture three thousand times,
It all vanished under a single phrase from Caoqi.
If I fail to grasp the meaning of renouncing worldly life,
How could I ever cease the madness accumulated over lifetimes?

Sheep, deer, and ox carts—just skillful means,
Guiding well through beginning, middle, and end.

Who would have known that within the burning house,
There resides the King of the Dhamma?"

The Master said, "From now on, you can be called Scripture-reciting Monk."

> 達從此領玄旨, 亦不輟誦經.
> 달종차령현지, 역불철송경.
>
> 僧智通, 壽州安豐人. 初看『楞伽經』, 約千餘遍, 而不會三身·四
> 승지통, 수주안풍인. 초간『능가경』, 약천여편, 이불회삼신·사
> 智. 禮師, 求解其義.
> 지. 예사, 구해기의.
>
> 師曰: "三身者, 淸淨法身, 汝之性也; 圓滿報身, 汝之智也; 千百
> 사왈: "삼신자, 청정법신, 여지성야; 원만보신, 여지지야; 천백
> 億化身, 汝之行也.
> 억화신, 여지행야.

Fada, from then on, received profound meaning, and never ceased to recite the Scripture.

Monk Zhitong was from Anfeng, Shouzhou. He had read Laṅkāvatāra Sutta more than a thousand times but still didn't comprehend the Three Bodies and the Four Wisdoms. So he respectfully approached the Master to beg an explication.

The Master said, "The Three Bodies refer to Pure Dhamma Body, which is your nature; Reward Body, your own wisdom; and Countless Transformative Bodies, your own actions.

若離本性, 別說三身, 即名有身無智; 若悟三
약리본성, 별설삼신, 즉명유신무지; 약오삼
身無有自性, 即名四智菩提. 聽吾偈." 曰:
신무유자성, 즉명사지보리. 청오게." 왈:
"自性具三身, 發明成四智.
"자성구삼신, 발명성사지.
不離見聞緣, 超然登佛地.
불리견문연, 초연등불지.

吾今爲汝說, 諦信永無迷.
오금위여설, 체신영무미.
莫學馳求者, 終日說菩提."
막학치구자, 종일설보리."

If you depart from your original-nature and separately speak of the Three Bodies, it is called body without wisdom; if you awaken to the fact that there is no Self-nature in the Three Bodies, it is called the bodhi with Four Wisdoms. Listen to my verse."

It goes,

"Because Self-nature possesses the Three Bodies,
And reveals and establishes the Four Wisdoms,
Without departing from the sphere of seeing and hearing,
You ascend effortlessly to the Buddha-ground.

Now I speak this for you:
Have unwavering faith and never be confused again.
Do not learn from those who hastily seek,
And who spend the entire day talking about bodhi."

通再啓曰:"四智之義, 可得聞乎?"

통재계왈: "사지지의, 가득문호?"

師曰:"既會三身, 便明四智, 何更問耶? 若離三身, 別談四智, 此名有智無身也, 即此有智還成無智。"

사왈: "기회삼신, 변명사지, 하갱문야? 약리삼신, 별담사지, 차명유지무신야, 즉차유지환성무지."

復偈曰:

부게왈:

Zhitong further asked, "Can I hear about the meaning of the Four Wisdoms?"

The Master replied, "Now that you have understood the Three Bodies and already comprehended the Four Wisdoms, why ask further? If you separate yourself from the Three Bodies and talk about the Four Wisdoms independently of it, this is called having wisdom without body. Then, this so-called wisdom itself becomes non-wisdom."

And He recited another verse. It goes,

> "大圓鏡智性清淨, 平等性智心無病.
> "대원경지성청정, 평등성지심무병.
>
> 妙觀察智見非功, 成所作智同圓鏡.
> 묘관찰지견비공, 성소작지동원경.
>
>
> 五八六七果因轉, 但用名言無實性.
> 오팔육칠과인전, 단용명언무실성.
>
> 若於轉處不留情, 繁興永處那伽定."
> 약어전처불류정, 번흥영처나가정."

"In the great perfect mirror wisdom, nature is clear and pure.

In the Equanimity wisdom, mind is free from afflictions.

In the subtle observation wisdom, one sees without striving.

In the accomplishment wisdom, it is same as flawless mirror.

The fifth and eighth are the effects, the sixth and seventh are the causes,

All are used by names and words, but devoid of true essence.

But if you leave no trace in the shifting play of mind,

The very place where disturbance fiercely arises is nāga samādhi."

> 通頓悟性智, 遂呈偈, 曰:
> 통돈오성지, 수정게, 왈:
>
> "三身元我體, 四智本心明.
> "삼신원아체, 사지본심명.
>
> 身智融無碍, 應物任隨形.
> 신지융무애, 응물임수형.
>
> 起修皆妄動, 守住匪眞精.
> 기수개망동, 수주비진정.
>
> 妙旨因師曉, 終亡染汚名."
> 묘지인사효, 종망염오명."

Zhitong suddenly realized the wisdom of nature, and presented a verse. It goes,

"The Three Bodies are originally my true body.
The Four Wisdoms are the clarity of my original mind.
The body and wisdom harmonizes without hindrance,
To respond to things is to entrust oneself to their form.

To initiate practices is mere illusion.
Clinging is not true essence either.
Through the Master, the profound meaning dawns.
Ultimately transcending the defiled name."

僧智常, 信州貴谿人. 髫年出家, 志求見性. 一日參禮.
승지상, 신주귀계인. 초년출가, 지구견성. 일일참례.

師問曰: "汝從何來? 欲求何事?"
사문왈: "여종하래? 욕구하사?"

曰: "學人近往洪州白峯山, 禮大通和尚, 蒙示見性成佛之義, 未決
왈: "학인근왕홍주백봉산, 예대통화상, 몽시견성성불지의, 미결

狐疑. 遠來投禮, 伏望和尚慈悲指示."
호의. 원래투례, 복망화상자비지시."

Monk Zhizhang is from Guixi, Xinzhou. At a young age, he entered the monastic life with the aspiration to realize seeing-nature. Onc day, he came to pay respects to the Master.

The Master asked, "Where are you from, and what do you want to attain?"

Zhizhang replied, "Your pupil had earnestly visited Mount Baifeng in Hongzhou to pay respects to Master Datong, who showed me the meaning of attaining Buddhahood through seeing-nature. However, I still have doubts and uncertainties, so I have come from afar to pay my respects. I humbly beg Your Reverence to provide guidance with compassion."

師曰:"彼有何言句? 汝試擧看."
사왈:"피유하언구? 여시거간."

曰:"智常到彼, 凡經三月, 未蒙示誨. 爲法切, 故一夕獨入丈室,
왈:"지상도피, 범경삼월, 미몽시회. 위법절, 고일석독입장실,

請問:'如何是某甲本心本性?'
청문:'여하시모갑본심본성?'

大通乃曰:'汝見虛空否?'
대통내왈:'여견허공부?'

對曰:'見.'
대왈:'견.'

The Master asked, "What teachings did he impart to you? Let's hear some examples."

Zhizhang replied, "For three months since I arrived there, I had not received any instruction. Eager for the dhamma, one night I entered the Master's chamber alone and asked, 'What is the original-nature of my original-mind like?'

Then Master Datong asked me, 'Have you seen empty space?'

I replied, 'Yes, I have.'

> 彼曰:'汝見虛空, 有相貌否?' 對曰:'虛空無形, 有何相貌?'
> 피왈:'여견허공, 유상모부?' 대왈:'허공무형, 유하상모?'
>
> 彼曰:'汝之本性猶如虛空. 了無一物可見, 是名正見. 了無一物可
> 피왈,'여지본성유여허공. 요무일물가견, 시명정견. 요무일물가
>
> 知, 是名眞知. 無有靑黃·長短, 但見本源淸淨, 覺體圓明, 卽名見
> 지, 시명진지. 무유청황·장단, 단견본원청정, 각체원명, 즉명견
>
> 性成佛, 亦名如來知見.'
> 성성불, 역명여래지견.'
>
> 學人雖聞此說, 猶未決了. 乞和尙開示."
> 학인수문차설, 유미결료. 걸화상개시."

He asked further, 'If you have seen empty space, does it have any form?'

I replied, 'Empty space is shapeless. How can it have any form?'

He said, 'Your original-nature is like empty space. Knowing that there is nothing to see, this is called right view. Knowing that there is nothing to know, this is called true knowledge. There being no distinction of blue or yellow, long or short, just see that your origin is clear and pure, and that the awakening body is perfect and bright, this is called realizing Buddhahood through seeing-nature, also known as the insight of Tathāgata.'

Upon hearing these teachings, your pupil has still not fully resolved it. I humbly beg Your Reverence to provide further guidance."

> 師曰: "彼師所説猶存見知, 故令汝未了. 吾今示汝一偈:
> 사왈: "피사소설유존견지, 고령여미료. 오금시여일게:
>
> 不見一法存無見, 大似浮雲遮日面?
> 불견일법존무견? 대사부운차일면.
>
> 不知一法守空知, 還如太虛生閃電?
> 부지일법수공지? 환여태허생섬전.
>
> 此之知見瞥然興, 錯認何曾解方便?
> 차지지견별연흥, 착인하증해방편?
>
> 汝當一念自知非, 自己靈光常顯現."
> 여당일념자지비, 자기영광상현현."

The Master replied, "What your previous Master explained still remained within the realm of conceptual understanding, which is why you have not yet attained clarity. Now, let me show you a verse.

"You see no dhamma, yet you form a thought of non-seeing.
It is like thick drifting clouds veiling the sun.
You know no dhamma, yet clutch at empty knowing.
It's like lightning flashing through open space.

If such a view arises suddenly,
It is a misperception; how could this be skillful means?
If you realize your error in a single thought,
Your own radiant light will shine forth."

> 常聞偈已, 心意豁然, 乃述偈曰:
> 상문게이, 심의활연, 내술게왈:
>
> "無端起知見, 著相求菩提.
> "무단기지견, 착상구보리.
>
> 情存一念悟, 寧越昔時迷?
> 정존일념오, 영월석시미?

Upon hearing the verse, Zhizhang suddenly became clear in his mind, and recited a verse.

"Endlessly had I been generating the views,

Seeking enlightenment while attaching to forms.

Clinging to a thought that I've been enlightened,

How can I transcend my past delusions?

自性覺源體，隨照枉遷流.
자성각원체, 수조왕천류.

不入祖師室，茫然趣兩頭."
불입조사실, 망연취량두."

智常一日問師曰："佛説三乘法，又言最上乘. 弟子未解，願爲教
지상일일문사왈: "불설삼승법, 우언최상승. 제자미해, 원위교
授."
수."
師曰："汝觀自本心，莫著外法相. 法無四乘，人心自有等差.
사왈: "여관자본심, 막착외법상. 법무사승, 인심자유등차.

The enlightenment's source and body of Self-nature

Are led astray by following the fleeting illumination.

Had I not entered the Patriarch's chamber,

I would still be wandering aimlessly between two extremes."

One day, Zhizhang asked the Master, "The Buddha taught the dhamma of three vehicles, and also spoke of the supreme vehicle. Your disciple has not understood it and wishes to be taught."

The Master replied, "Observe your own original mind, and do not attach to external forms of the dhamma. In the dhamma, there are no four vehicles: differences arise only in human minds.

見聞轉誦是小乘, 悟法解義是中乘, 依法修行是大乘, 萬法盡通,
견문전송시소승, 오법해의시중승, 의법수행시대승, 만법진통,

萬法具備, 一切不染, 離諸法相, 一無所得, 名最上乘. 乘是行義,
만법구비, 일체불염, 이제법상, 일무소득, 명최상승. 승시행의,

不在口爭. 汝須自修, 莫問吾也. 一切時中, 自性自如."
부재구쟁. 여수자수, 막문오야. 일체시중, 자성자여."

常禮謝執侍, 終師之世.
상례사집시, 종사지세.

Merely seeing, hearing and reciting constitutes the small vehicle; understanding the principles and meanings of the dhamma is the middle vehicle; practicing in accordance with the dhamma is the great vehicle; When all the phenomena thoroughly realized, all teachings are complete, and you are not contaminated by anything, free from attachment to any forms of the dhamma and devoid of any attainment, this is called the supreme vehicle. The vehicles lie in practice, not in verbal disputes. You must cultivate yourself and not rely on me. In every moment, your Self-nature is naturally as it is."

Zhizhang paid his respects and attended to the Master until He passed away.

> 一僧志道, 廣州南海人也. 請益曰: "學人自出家, 覽『涅槃經』十載
> 일승지도, 광주남해인야. 청익왈: "학인자출가, 남『열반경』십재
> 有餘, 未明大意. 願和尚垂誨."
> 유여, 미명대의. 원화상수회."
> 師曰: "汝何處未明?"
> 사왈: "여하처미명?"
> 曰: "'諸行無常, 是生滅法. 生滅滅已, 寂滅爲樂.' 於此疑惑."
> 왈: "'제행무상, 시생멸법. 생멸멸이, 적멸위락.' 어차의혹."
> 師曰: "汝作麼生疑?"
> 사왈: "여작마생의?"
> 曰: "一切衆生皆有二身, 謂色身·法身也.
> 왈: "일체중생개유이신, 위색신·법신야.
> 色身無常, 有生有滅, 法身有常, 無知無覺.
> 색신무상, 유생유멸, 법신유상, 무지무각.

Monk Zhidao was from Nanhai, Guangzhou, and sought further guidance, saying, "Since I entered monastic life, I have been studying Nibbāna Sutta for more than ten years, but I still do not understand its profound meaning. I humbly beg Your Reverence to bestow teachings upon me."

The Master asked, "What part do you not understand?"

Zhidao replied, "The phrase 'All conditioned things are impermanent; this is the law of arising and ceasing. Once arising and ceasing come to an end, the state of tranquil cessation shall be a joy.' I have doubts about this."

The Master asked, "What kind of doubts do you have?"

Zhidao replied, "Every sentient beings has two bodies: physical body and the dhamma body. Physical body is impermanent, undergoing birth and death, while the dhamma body is eternal, without knowledge nor awareness.

> 經云'生滅滅已, 寂滅爲樂'者不審. 何身寂
> 경운'생멸멸이, 적멸위락'자불심. 하신적
>
> 滅, 何身受樂? 若色身者, 色身滅時四大分散, 全然是苦, 苦不可
> 멸, 하신수락? 약색신자, 색신멸시사대분산, 전연시고, 고불가
>
> 言樂. 若法身, 寂滅即同草木·瓦石, 誰當受樂?
> 언락. 약법신, 적멸즉동초목·와석, 수당수락?
>
> 又法性是生滅之體, 五蘊是生滅之用. 一體五用, 生滅是常. 生即
> 우법성시생멸지체, 오온시생멸지용. 일체오용, 생멸시상. 생즉
>
> 從體起用, 滅即攝用歸體.
> 종체기용, 멸즉섭용귀체.

The Scripture states, 'When arising and ceasing come to an end, the state of cessation itself becomes a joy,' which is what I am not clear about. Which body is it that experiences cessation, and which body experiences a joy? If it is the physical body, when physical body ceases, the four elements disperse, resulting entirely in suffering, which cannot be called joy. If it is the dhamma body, then upon cessation, it would be no different from grass and trees, tiles and stones, so what could experience a joy?

Furthermore, the nature of the dhamma is the body of arising and ceasing, and the five aggregates are the functioning of arising and ceasing. For one body with five functions, arising and ceasing are constant. Arising is the function emerging from the body, cessation is the function returning to the body.

> 若聽更生, 即有情之類不斷不滅. 若不聽更生, 即永歸寂滅,
> 약청갱생, 즉유정지류부단불멸. 약불청갱생, 즉영귀적멸,
>
> 同於無情之物. 如是即一切諸法被涅槃之所禁伏,
> 동어무정지물. 여시즉일체제법피열반지소금복,
>
> 常不得生, 何樂之有?"
> 상부득생, 하락지유?"
>
> 師曰: "汝是釋子, 何習外道斷常邪見而議最上乘法? 據汝所說,
> 사왈: "여시석자, 하습외도단상사견이의최상승법? 거여소설,
>
> 即色身外別有法身, 離生滅求於寂滅. 又推涅槃常樂, 言有身受用,
> 즉색신외별유법신, 이생멸구어적멸. 우추열반상락, 언유신수용,

If rebirth is allowed, all sentient beings would persist without cessation; if rebirth is not allowed, they would permanently return to tranquil cessation, like insentient objects. In this way, all phenomena would be suppressed and restrained by nibbāna and can never be reborn again. How, then, can there be joy?"

The Master said, "As a disciple of the Buddha, how dare you follow the non-Buddhist teachings' erroneous views, which advocate both nihilism and eternalism, and attempt to discuss the teachings of the supreme vehicle? According to what you say, there is a dhamma body separate from the physical body, seeking a tranquil cessation by departing from birth and death. Furthermore, you advocate that nibbāna is an eternal joy and claim that it can be experienced through the physical body.

> 斯乃執悋生死, 耽著世樂.
> 사내집린생사, 탐착세락.
>
> 汝今當知, 佛爲一切迷人認五蘊和合爲自體相, 分別一切法爲外塵
> 여금당지, 불위일체미인인오온화합위자체상, 분별일체법위외진
>
> 相, 好生惡死, 念念遷流, 不知夢幻·虛假, 枉受輪廻, 以常樂涅槃
> 상, 호생오사, 염념천류, 부지몽환·허가, 왕수윤회, 이상락열반
>
> 翻爲苦相, 終日馳求. 佛愍此, 故乃示涅槃眞樂, 刹那無有生相,
> 번위고상, 종일치구. 불민차, 고내시열반진락, 찰나무유생상,
>
> 刹那無有滅相, 更無生滅可滅, 是即寂滅現前.
> 찰나무유멸상, 갱무생멸가멸, 시즉적멸현전.

This shows attachment to life and death and being caught up in worldly pleasures.

You should now understand: The Buddha observed that all deluded people perceived the combination of five aggregates as the true body; they differentiate all the phenomena as external objects; so they are attached to life and averse to death; their thoughts are constantly fleeting; yet they do not realize that these experiences are dreams and illusions, empty and false; they are wrongly caught in samsara and misunderstand the constant joy of nibbāna as suffering; so they chase after it day and night. The Buddha had compassion for that, and so He revealed the true joy of nibbāna; even for a single moment, there is no form of arising, and even for a single moment, there is no form of ceasing; furthermore, there is no cessation even of arising and ceasing. This itself is the very presence of tranquil cessation.

> 當現前時, 亦無現前之量, 乃謂常樂. 此樂無有受者, 亦無不
> 당현전시, 역무현전지량, 내위상락. 차락무유수자, 역무불
>
> 受者, 豈有一體五用之名?
> 수자, 기유일체오용지명?
>
> 何況更言, 涅槃禁伏諸法, 令永不生? 斯乃謗佛毀法. 聽吾偈."
> 하황갱언, 열반금복제법, 영영불생? 사내방불훼법. 청오게."
>
> 曰:
> 왈:
>
> "無上大涅槃, 圓明常寂照.
> "무상대열반, 원명상적조.

Even when it is present, there is also no measure of being present, so this is called the constant joy. While there is no one to receive this joy, nor anyone not to receive it, how can there be the name of five functions in one body?

Moreover, how dare you claim that nibbāna suppresses and prevents all phenomena from arising forever? It is slandering the Buddha and destroying the dhamma. Listen to my verse."

It goes,

"The Supreme Great nibbāna, beyond all comparison,
Is complete and bright, constantly illuminating with tranquility.

> 凡愚謂之死, 外道執爲斷.
> 범우위지사, 외도집위단.
>
> 諸求二乘人, 目以爲無作.
> 제구이승인, 목이위무작.
>
> 盡屬情所計, 六十二見本.
> 진속정소계, 육십이견본.
>
> 妄立虛假名, 何爲眞實義?
> 망립허가명, 하위진실의?
>
> 惟有過量人, 通達無取捨.
> 유유과량인, 통달무취사.

The ignorant regard it as death,

Non-Buddhist teachings consider it annihilation.

Those who follow the lower two vehicles

View it as non-action.

All are based on the calculations of their minds,

Which are rooted in the sixty-two wrong views.

They vainly establish false names;

How can these convey real and true meaning?

Only he who transcends superficial distinctions

Understands that there is neither grasping nor rejecting.

以知五蘊法, 及以蘊中我.
이지오온법, 급이온중아.

外現衆色像, 一一音聲相.
외현중색상, 일일음성상.

平等如夢幻, 不起凡聖見.
평등여몽환, 불기범성견.

不作涅槃解, 二邊三際斷.
부작열반해, 이변삼제단.

By comprehending the dhamma of five aggregates

And recognizing Self within them,

External manifestations of various colors and images,

And every form of sounds and voices

Are all equally like dreams and illusions,

Thus, they do not produce the views of ordinary or enlightened.

They do not generate the understanding of nibbāna,

And cut off the two extremes and the three realms;

常應諸根用, 而不起用想.
상응제근용, 이불기용상.

分別一切法, 不起分別想.
분별일체법, 불기분별상.

劫火燒海底, 風鼓山相擊.
겁화소해저, 풍고산상격.

眞常寂滅樂, 涅槃相如是.
진상적멸락, 열반상여시.

吾今强言説, 令汝捨邪見.
오금강언설, 영여사사견.

Always tailored to the capacities of each individual,

Yet do not generate the perception of their use;

Even while discerning all phenomena,

Yet do not produce the perception of discrimination.

Though the fires of eons burn through the depths of sea,

And the winds cause mountains to clash,

The true and constant joy of the tranquil cessation

Is the form of nibbāna as such.

Now I speak forcefully,

To urge you to abandon wrong views.

> 汝勿隨言解, 許汝知少分."
> 여물수언해, 허여지소분."
>
> 志道聞偈, 大悟踊躍, 作禮而退.
> 지도문게, 대오용약, 작례이퇴.
>
> 行思禪師, 姓劉氏, 吉州安城人也. 聞曹溪法席盛化, 徑來參禮.
> 행사선사, 성유씨, 길주안성인야. 문조계법석성화, 경래참례.
> 遂問曰: "當何所務, 即不落階級?"
> 수문왈: "당하소무, 즉불락계급?"

Do not rely solely on the understanding through words, And I will recognize that you understand a little."

Upon hearing the verse, Zhidao was greatly enlightened and filled with joy. He paid his repects and withdrew.

Zen Master Xingsi, surnamed Liu, was from Ancheng, Jizhou. Upon hearing about the flourishing dhamma teachings of the Caoqi school, he came directly to pay his respects.

He asked, "What should I do to avoid falling into rank or stages?"

> 師曰:"汝曾作甚麼來?"
> 사왈:"여증작심마래?"
>
> 曰:"聖諦亦不爲."
> 왈:"성체역불위."
>
> 師曰:"落何階級?"
> 사왈:"낙하계급?"
>
> 曰:"聖諦尚不爲, 何階級之有?"
> 왈:"성체상불위, 하계급지유?"
>
> 師深器之, 令思首衆.
> 사심기지. 영사수중.
>
> 一日師謂曰:"汝當分化一方, 無令斷絶."
> 일일사위왈:"여당분화일방, 무령단절."

The Master asked, "What have you practiced?"

Xingsi replied, "I have not practiced even the sacred truths."

The Master further asked, "What rank or status are you concerned about falling into?"

Xingsi responded, "Having not yet practiced even the noble truths, how could there be any stage to speak of?"

The Master deeply appreciated his potential, and appointed him the head of the assembly.

One day, the Master said to Xingsi, "You should establish a branch to ensure that these teachings do not die out."

思既得法, 遂回吉州青原山, 弘法紹化.
사기득법, 수회길주청원산, 홍법소화.

悔讓禪師, 金州杜氏子也. 初謁嵩山安國師. 安發之曹溪參扣, 讓
회양선사, 금주두씨자야. 초알숭산안국사. 안발지조계참구, 양
至禮拜.
지예배.
師曰: "甚處來?"
사왈: "심처래?"
曰: "嵩山."
왈: "숭산."
師曰: "什麼物恁麼來?"
사왈: "십마물임마래?"
曰: "說似一物即不中."
왈: "설사일물즉부중."

Xingsi, having received the dhamma, returned to Qingyuan Mountain in Jizhou to widely propagate and continue the teachings.

Zen Master Huirang, a descendant of the Du family in Jinzhou, initially visited Imperial Master Huian at Songshan. Master Huian directed him to seek further instruction at Caoqi, so Huirang came to pay his respects.

The Master asked, "Where are you from?"

Huirang replied, "From Songshan."

The Master then inquired, "What kind of thing is this that comes like this?"

Huirang responded, "If I call it a single thing, it wouldn't be correct."

VII. Of Disciples

> 師曰: "還可修證否?"
> 사왈: "환가수증부?"
>
> 曰: "修證即不無, 汚染即不得."
> 왈: "수증즉불무, 오염즉부득."
>
> 師曰: "只此不汚染, 諸佛之所護念. 汝既如是, 吾亦如是. 西天般
> 사왈: "지차불오염, 제불지소호념. 여기여시, 오역여시. 서천반
>
> 若多羅讖: '汝足下出一馬駒, 踏殺天下人.' 應在汝心, 不須速説."
> 야다라참: '여족하출일마구, 답살천하인.' 응재여심, 불수속설."
>
> 讓豁然契會, 遂執侍左右一十五載, 日臻玄奧. 後往南嶽, 大闡禪宗.
> 양활연계회, 수집시좌우일십오재, 일진현오, 후왕남악, 대천선종.

The Master further asked, "Can it be realized through practice, then?"

Huirang replied, "Realization through Practice is not denied; but becoming defiled is not possible."

The Master said, "Only this, which is neither stained nor polluted, is what all Buddhas protect and keep in minds. Now you are already like this, and so am I. Paññādara of Western India prophesied, 'A colt shall appear under your feet, trampling and killing all the people in the world.' You should keep this in your mind only, not speak of it hastily."

Huirang realized this profoundly, and attended to the Master on both sides for fifteen years. His understanding deepened day by day and reached a profound realization. Later, he went to Nanyue and greatly expounded the Zen teachings.

> 永嘉玄覺禪師, 溫州戴氏子. 少習經論, 精天台止觀法門. 因看『維
> 영가현각선사, 온주대씨자. 소습경론, 정천태지관법문. 인간『유
>
> 摩經』, 發明心地.
> 마경』, 발명심지.
>
> 偶師弟子玄策相訪, 與其劇談, 出言暗合諸祖.
> 우사제자현책상방, 여기극담, 출언암합제조.

Zen Master Yongja Xuanjue, a descendant of Dai family in Wenzhou, began studying Scriptures and treatises from a young age. He became particularly skilled in the samatha-vipassana practices of the Tiantai school. After reading the Vimalakīrti Nirdeśa Sūtra[S], he awakened and deepened his mind-ground.

One day, a disciple of the Master, Xuance, visited him, and engaged in profound discussion. The visitor recognized that Xuanjue's words subtly aligned with the teachings of the Patriarchs.

策云: "仁者得法師誰?"
책운: "인자득법사수?"

曰: "我聽『方等經論』, 各有師承. 後於『維摩經』, 悟佛心宗, 未有 證明者."
왈: "아청『방등경론』, 각유사승. 후어『유마경』, 오불심종, 미유 증명자."

策云: "威音王已前即得, 威音王已後無師自悟盡是天然外道."
책운: "위음왕이전즉득, 위음왕이후무사자오진시천연외도."

云: "願仁者爲我證據."
운: "원인자위아증거."

So Xuance asked, "Your Venerability, who is the Master from whom you received the dhamma?"

Xuanjue replied, "I studied the Vaipulya[S] Scripture and Treatises, each with a lineage of teachers. Later, through the Vimalakīrti Nirdeśa Sūtra[S], I awakened to the Buddha's profound teaching, but no one has yet provided me with confirmation."

Xuance said, "Before the time of King Śubhābhāśottama, it was possible to attain enlightenment without a teacher. However, after his era, anyone who claims to have attained enlightenment on their own, without a teacher, is considered a follower of the external path of naturalism."

Xuanjue then asked, "Would you act as a witness for me?"

策云: "我言輕. 曹溪有六祖大師, 四方雲集, 并是受法者. 若去即
책운: "아언경. 조계유육조대사, 사방운집, 병시수법자. 약거즉

與偕行."
여해행."

覺遂同策來參, 繞師三匝, 振錫而立.
각수동책래참, 요사삼잡, 진석이립.

師曰: "夫沙門者, 具三千威儀·八萬細行. 大德自何方而來, 生大
사왈: "부사문자, 구삼천위의·팔만세행. 대덕자하방이래, 생대

我慢?"
아만?"

覺曰: "生死事大, 無常迅速."
각왈: "생사사대, 무상신속."

Xuance replied, "My words carry little weight. However, in Caoqi, there is the Sixth Patriarch, and people from all directions gather there, all of whom have received the dhamma. If you wish to go there, I will accompany you."

So Xuanjue came to Caoqi with Xuance and paid his respects. He circled around the Master three times, then stood still, gripping his staff.

The Master said, "A monk should possess three thousand dignified manners and eighty thousand minor rules of virtue. Where have you come from, to be so full of arrogance?"

Xuanjue replied, "The matter of birth and death is the great matter, impermanent and swift."

師曰: "何不體取無生, 了無速乎?"
사왈: "하불체취무생, 요무속호?"

曰: "體即無生. 了本無速."
왈: "체즉무생, 요본무속."

師曰: "如是如是."
사왈: "여시여시."

玄覺方具威儀禮拜, 須臾告辭.
현각방구위의예배, 수유고사.

師曰: "返太速乎?"
사왈: "반태속호?"

曰: "本自非動, 豈有速耶?"
왈: "본자비동, 기유속야?"

師曰: "誰知非動?"
사왈: "수지비동?"

The Master asked, "Why not realize the nature of non-birth and understand the absence of swiftness?"

Xuanjue replied, "In experiential realization there is no birth, and in true understanding there is originally no swiftness."

The Master said, "That's right. That's right."

Xuanjue paid his respects with proper decorum and, after a brief moment, took his leave.

The Master said, "But isn't it too swift?"

Xuanjue replied, "Since there is originally no movement, how could there be swiftness?"

The Master said, "Who knows that there is no movement?"

> 曰:"仁者自生分別?"
> 왈:"인자자생분별?"
>
> 師曰:"汝甚得無生之意."
> 사왈:"여심득무생지의."
>
> 曰:"無生豈有意耶?"
> 왈:"무생기유의야?"
>
> 師曰:"無意, 誰當分別?"
> 사왈:"무의, 수당분별?"
>
> 曰:"分別亦非意."
> 왈:"분별역비의."

Xuanjue replied, "Does Your Venerability generate distinctions on your own?"

The Master said, "You have deeply grasped the meaning of non-birth!"

Xuanjue replied, "But how could non-birth have any meaning?"

The Master asked, "If there is no meaning, who can make distinctions?"

Xuanjue replied, "Even making distinctions is not meaning, either."

> 師曰: "善哉! 少留一宿."
> 사왈: "선재! 소류일숙."
>
> 時謂一宿覺. 後著「證道歌」, 盛行于世.
> 시위일숙각. 후저「증도가」, 성행우세.
>
>
> 禪者智隍初參五祖, 自謂已得正受, 菴居長坐, 積二十年.
> 선자지황초참오조, 자위이득정수, 암거장좌, 적이십년.
>
> 師弟子玄策游方, 至河朔, 聞隍之名, 造菴問云: "汝在此作什麼?"
> 사제자현책유방, 지하삭, 문황지명, 조암문운: "여재차작십마?"
>
> 隍云: "入定."
> 황운: "입정."

The Master said, "Excellent! But why don't you stay for just one night?"

From that time, Xuanjue was called One-Night-Awakened. Afterwards he wrote "The Song of Attaining Enlightenment," which became widely popular.

Zhihuang, a Zen practitioner, initially paid his respects to the Fifth Patriarch. He claimed to have realized the correct teaching and lived in a hermitage, sitting in meditation for twenty years.

Xuance, a disciple of the Master, who was wandering from place to place, eventually reached Heshuo and heard of Zhihuang's reputation. So he went to the hermitage and enquired, "What are you doing here?"

Zhihuang replied, "I'm in samādhi."

> 策云: "汝云入定, 爲有心入耶, 無心入耶? 若無心入者, 一切無情
> 책운: "여운입정, 위유심입야, 무심입야? 약무심입자, 일체무정
>
> 草木·瓦石應合得定. 若有心入者, 一切有情含識之流亦應得定."
> 초목·와석응합득정. 약유심입자, 일체유정함식지류역응득정."
>
> 隍曰: "我正入定時, 不見有有無之心."
> 황왈: "아정입정시, 불견유유무지심."
>
> 策云: "不見有有無之心, 即是常定, 何有出入? 若有出入, 即非大
> 책운: "불견유유무지심, 즉시상정, 하유출입? 약유출입, 즉비대
>
> 定."
> 정."

Xuance said, "When you say you are in samādhi, is it with a mind or without a mind? If it is without a mind, then all insentient objects such as grass, trees, tiles and stones must be able to attain samādhi; if with a mind, then all sentient beings with consciousness must also be able to attain samādhi."

Zhihuang replied, "When I am truly in samādhi, I do not perceive any existence or the mind of existence or non-existence."

Xuance said, "If you do not perceive any existence or the mind of existence or non-existence, then that is continuous-samādhi. How, then, could there be any entering or coming out? If there is entering or coming out, it is not great samādhi."

隍無對. 良久, 問曰: "師嗣誰耶?"
황무대. 양구, 문왈: "사사수야?"

策云: "我師曹溪六祖." 隍云: "六祖以何爲禪定?"
책운: "아사조계육조." 황운: "육조이하위선정?"

策云: "我師所說, 妙湛圓寂, 體用如如. 五陰本空, 六塵非有, 不
책운: "아사소설, 묘담원적, 체용여여. 오음본공, 육진비유, 불

出不入, 不定不亂. 禪性無住, 離住禪寂, 禪性無生, 離生禪想. 心
출불입, 부정불란. 선성무주, 이주선적, 선성무생, 이생선상. 심

如虛空, 亦無虛空之量."
여허공, 역무허공지량."

Zhihuang had no response. After a good while, he asked, "Who is your dhamma master?"

Xuance replied, "I studied under the Sixth Patriarch in Caoqi."

Zhihuang asked, "What does the Sixth Patriarch consider Zen-samādhi?"

Xuance replied, "My Master's teaching is subtle, profound, round and tranquil, both body and function are as such all the time. Five aggregates are originally empty, and six sensory realms are not existing, neither coming out nor going in, neither samādhi nor disturbed. The nature of Zen is non-dwelling, hence there is no abiding in the tranquility of Zen; the nature of Zen is no-abiding, hence there is no arising in the perception of Zen. The mind is like empty space, nor has it any consideration of empty space."

> 隍聞是說，徑來謁師.
> 황문시설, 경래알사.
>
> 師問云："仁者何來？"
> 사문운："인자하래？"
>
> 隍具述前緣.
> 황구술전연.
>
> 師云："誠如所言. 汝但心如虛空, 不著空見. 應用無碍, 動靜無心,
> 사운："성여소언. 여단심여허공, 불착공견. 응용무애, 동정무심,
>
> 凡聖情忘, 能所俱泯. 性相如如, 無不定時也."
> 범성정망, 능소구민. 성상여여, 무부정시야."
>
> 隍於是大悟, 二十年所得心都無影響.
> 황어시대오, 이십년소득심도무영향.

Upon hearing this, Zhihuang came directly to pay his repects to the Master.

The Master asked, "Why have you come, Your Venerability?"

Zhihuang detailed his previous experiences.

The Master said, "Indeed, it is as you have spoken. Just let your mind be like empty space without attaching to empty views. Then it shall function without hindrance, there is no-mind whether in movement or stillness, the emotions of ordinary and sacred are removed, both the perceiver and the perceived are dissolved. Like this nature and form are always in suchness, there is no time when you are not in samādhi."

Upon hearing this, Zhihuang had a great enlightenment, and the mind he had attained since last twenty years had no more impact or influence.

> 其夜, 河北士庶聞空中有聲, 云: "隍禪師今日得道."
> 기야, 하북사서문공중유성, 운: "황선사금일득도."
>
> 隍後禮辭, 復歸河北, 開化四衆.
> 황후례사, 부귀하북, 개화사중.
>
> 一僧問師云: "黃梅意旨, 甚麼人得?"
> 일승문사운: "황매의지, 심마인득?"
>
> 師云: "會佛法人得."
> 사운: "회불법인득."

That night, the scholars and common people of Hebei heard a voice from the sky, saying, "Zen Master Zhihuang has attained enlightenment today!"

After that, Zhihuang bid farewell and returned to Hebei, where he taught and guided the four-fold assembly on the path of awakening.

A monk asked the Master, "Who has attained the true meaning of Huangmei?"

The Master replied, "He who has understood the Buddha's dhamma."

> 僧云: "和尚還得否?"
> 승운: "화상환득부?"
>
> 師云: "我不會佛法."
> 사운: "아불회불법."
>
>
> 師一日欲濯所授之衣, 而無美泉. 因至寺後五里許, 見山林鬱茂,
> 사일일욕탁소수지의, 이무미천. 인지사후오리허, 견산림울무,
>
> 瑞氣盤旋. 師振錫卓地, 泉應手而出, 積以爲池. 乃跪膝, 浣衣石
> 서기반선. 사진석탁지, 천응수이출, 적이위지. 내궤슬, 완의석
>
> 上.
> 상.

The monk further asked, "And also Your Reverence?"

The Master replied, "I have not understood the Buddha's dhamma."

One day, the Master wanted to wash the robe he was given, but there was no clean spring available. So he went about five lis away from the back of the temple, where he found a lush and dense forest, with auspicious signs swirling around. When the Master raised his staff and struck the ground, a spring gushed out along with his hands, finally to form into a pond. Then he knelt down and washed his robe on a rock.

忽有一僧來禮拜, 云:"方辯是西蜀人. 昨於南天竺國見達摩大師,
홀유일승래예배, 운: "방변시서촉인. 작어남천축국견달마대사,

囑方辯:'速往唐土. 吾傳大迦葉正法眼藏及僧伽梨見傳六代於韶州
촉방변: '속왕당토. 오전대가섭정법안장급승가리견전육대어소주

曹溪. 汝去瞻禮.'方辯遠來, 願見我師傳來衣鉢."
조계. 여거첨례.' 방변원래, 원견아사전래의발."

師乃出示, 次問:"上人攻何事業?"
사내출시, 차문: "상인공하사업?"

方辯曰:"善塑."
방변왈: "선소."

師正色, 曰:"汝試塑看."
사정색, 왈: "여시소간."

Suddenly a monk appeared and paid respects, saying, "I'm Fangbian, from Sishu. Yesterday I met the Great Master Bodhidharmā[S] at South India, who entrusted me with a mission to travel quickly to Tang China, saying, 'I passed down my Treasury of the Right Dhamma Eye and the Robe of Mahākassapa[S], which have transmitted for six generations and are now in Caoqi, Shaozhou. Go there and pay respects.' So I came from afar, and want to see the transmitted robe and alms bowl of my Master."

The Master displayed them and asked the monk, "What kind of work is Your Venerability skilled in?"

Fangbian replied, "I am skilled in sculpting."

The Master, with a serious look, said, "Then try sculpting me and let's see."

> 方辯罔措數日, 塑就眞相, 可高七寸, 曲盡其妙.
> 방변망조수일, 소취진상, 가고칠촌, 곡진기묘.
>
> 師笑曰: "汝只解塑性, 不解佛性."
> 사소왈: "여지해소성, 불해불성."
>
> 師舒手, 摩方辯頂, 曰: "永爲人天福田."
> 사서수, 마방변정, 왈: "영위인천복전."
>
>
> 有僧擧臥輪禪師偈, 云:
> 유승거와륜선사게, 운:

Fangbian diligently worked for several days and sculpted out the Master's statue, about seven inches tall and incredibly skillful.

The Master smiled and said, "You have understood the art of sculpture, yet not Buddha-nature."

And the Master gently rubbed Fangbian's head on the top, saying, "May you become a field of blessings for both humans and celestial beings."

There was a monk reciting a verse by Zen Master Wolun.

It goes,

VII. Of Disciples

"臥輪有伎倆, 能斷百思想.
"와륜유기량, 능단백사상.

對境心不起, 菩提日日長."
대경심불기, 보리일일장."

師聞之, 曰: "此偈未明心地. 若依而行之, 是加繫縛."
사문지, 왈: "차게미명심지. 약의이행지, 시가계박."

因示一偈, 曰:
인시일게, 왈:

"惠能沒伎倆, 不斷百思想.
"혜능몰기량, 부단백사상.

"Wolun has skillful means,

So as to cut off a hundred thoughts.

Even facing a object, the mind does not arise,

So bodhi grows day by day."

The Master heard the verse and said, "This verse is of unenlightened mind. If you rely on and follow it, you shall only be further bound."

Then he Master demonstrated another verse. It goes,

"Huineng has no skillful means,

So as not to cut off a hundred thoughts.

> 對境心數起, 菩提作麼長?"
> 대경심수기, 보리작마장?"

When facing a object, the mind arises in countless ways,

So how could bodhi grow?"

> 第八 頓漸品
> 제팔 돈점품
>
> 時祖師居曹溪寶林, 神秀大師在荊南玉泉寺.
> 시조사거조계보림, 신수대사재형남옥천사.
>
> 于時兩宗盛化, 人皆稱南能北秀. 故有南北二宗·頓漸之分, 而學者
> 우시양종성화, 인개칭남능북수. 고유남북이종·돈점지분, 이학자
>
> 莫知宗趣.
> 막지종취.

Chapter Eight

Of the Sudden and the Gradual

At that time, the Patriarch resided in the Baolin Temple in Caoqi, while the Great Master Shenxiu was at the Yuquan Temple in Jingnan.

At that time, the two schools flourished, and people used to call them "South Huineng, North Shenxiu," hence the division between the Southern, or "Sudden", and the Northern, or "Gradual." Yet learners remained unaware of the essential concepts of the two schools.

> 師謂衆曰:"法本一宗, 人有南北. 法即一種, 見有遲疾. 何名頓
> 사위중왈: "법본일종, 인유남북. 법즉일종, 견유지질. 하명돈
>
> 漸? 法無頓漸, 人有利鈍, 故名頓漸."
> 점? 법무돈점, 인유이둔, 고명돈점."
>
> 然秀之徒衆往往譏:"南宗祖師不識一字, 有何所長?"
> 연수지도중왕왕기: "남종조사불식일자, 유하소장?"
>
> 秀曰:"他得無師之智, 深悟上乘. 吾不如也. 且吾師五祖親傳衣
> 수왈: "타득무사지지, 심오상승. 오불여야. 차오사오조친전의
>
> 法, 豈徒然哉?
> 법, 기도연재?

The Master addressed the assembly, saying, "There is only one dhamma school: only people are divided between the southern and the northern. The dhamma itself is of only one kind: only understandings are divided between swift and slow. What is meant by the Sudden and the Gradual? In the dhamma inherently is there neither the sudden nor the gradual, but people are either sharp or dull. Thus the terms 'the sudden' and 'the gradual' are used."

However, Shenxiu's followers often slandered, saying, "The Southern Patriarch is illiterate. What merits could he have?"

But Shenxiu responded, "He has attained the wisdom of not-being-taught and deeply understood the highest teachings. I am not equal to him. Moreover, could it be without reason that my master, the Fifth Patriarch, personally transmitted the robe and the dhamma to him?

吾恨不能遠去親近, 虛受國恩. 汝等諸人毋滯於此, 可往曹溪參決."
오한불능원거친근, 허수국은. 여등제인무체어차, 가왕조계참결."

一日命門人志誠, 曰: "汝聰明多智, 可爲吾到曹溪聽法. 汝若聞
일일명문인지성, 왈: "여총명다지, 가위오도조계청법. 여약문

法, 盡心記取, 還爲吾說."
법, 진심기취, 환위오설."

志誠稟命, 至曹溪, 隨眾參請, 不言來處.
지성품명, 지조계, 수중참청, 불언내처.

時祖師告衆曰: "今有盜法之人潛在此會."
시조사고중왈: "금유도법지인잠재차회."

I regret that I cannot afford to go afar to be near him, vainly receiving the benefits of the Empire. You must not remain here. All of you had better go to Caoqi to seek teachings."

So Shenxiu one day ordered one of his disciples, Zhicheng, saying, "Since you are intelligent and wise, you can go to Caoqi and listen to the teachings for me. If you hear the teachings, wholeheartedly write them in your mind, and then come back to explain them to me."

Zhicheng, following the order, went to Caoqi and joined the assembly without revealing his origin.

Then the Patriarch addressed the assembly, saying, "Now there is someone in the assembly secretly stealing the dhamma."

> 志誠即出禮拜, 具陳其事.
> 지성즉출예배, 구진기사.
> 師曰: "汝從玉泉寺, 應是細作."
> 사왈: "여종옥천사, 응시세작."
> 對曰: "不是."
> 대왈: "불시."
> 師曰: "何得不是?"
> 사왈: "하득불시?"
> 對曰: "未說即是, 説了不是."
> 대왈: "미설즉시, 설료불시."
> 師曰: "汝師若爲示衆?"
> 사왈: "여사약위시중?"
> 對曰: "常指誨大衆: '住心觀淨, 長坐不臥.'"
> 대왈: "상지회대중: '주심관정, 장좌불와.'"

Zhicheng immediately came forward, paid his respects, and told the story in detail.

The Master said, "Now that you are from the Yuquan Temple, you must be a spy."

Zhicheng replied, "It is not so."

The Master asked again, "How can you say you're not?"

Zhicheng replied, "I was, before saying it. Now that I've spoken, I am not."

The Master further asked, "What does your master teach the assembly?"

Zhicheng replied, "He constantly instructs the assembly to abide in mind and observe purity, and to remain seated for long without lying down."

> 師曰:"住心觀淨, 是病非禪. 常坐拘身, 於理何益? 聽吾偈." 曰:
> 사왈: "주심관정, 시병비선. 상좌구신, 어리하익? 청오게." 왈:
>
> "生來坐不臥, 死去臥不坐.
> "생래좌불와, 사거와부좌.
>
> 一具臭骨頭, 何爲立功課?"
> 일구취골두, 하위립공과?"
>
> 志誠再拜, 曰: "弟子在秀大師處, 學道九年, 不得契悟.
> 지성재배, 왈: "제자재수대사처, 학도구년, 부득계오.

The Master said, "Abiding in mind and observing purity is a malpractice, not Zen. What benefit is there sitting and restricting your body? Listen to my verse."

It goes,

"While living, you sit without lying down;
After death, you lie down, never sitting up.
With nothing but a foul-smelling skeleton remaining,
How can you establish merit or fault?"

Zhicheng bowed twice and said, "Your pupil has been studying the path under Master Shenxiu for nine years, and still has not attained enlightenment.

VIII. Of the Sudden and the Gradual 265

> 今聞和尚一説, 便契本心. 弟子生死事大. 和尚大慈, 更爲教示."
> 금문화상일설, 변계본심. 제자생사사대. 화상대자, 갱위교시."
>
> 師曰: "吾聞汝師教示學人戒・定・慧法, 未審汝師説戒・定・慧行相
> 사왈: "오문여사교시학인계・정・혜법, 미심여사설계・정・혜행상
>
> 如何. 與吾説看."
> 여하. 여오설간."
>
> 誠曰: "秀大師説: '諸惡莫作名爲戒, 諸善奉行名爲慧, 自淨其意
> 성왈: "수대사설: '제악막작명위계, 제선봉행명위혜, 자정기의
>
> 名爲定.' 彼説如此, 未審和尚以何法誨人."
> 명위정.' 피설여차, 미심화상이하법회인."

Now, upon hearing Your Reverence's teaching, I immediately realized my original-mind. The matter of birth and death is of great importance to your pupil. I beg Your Reverence's further guidance."

The Master said, "I've heard that your master instructs disciples in the practices of sīla, samādhi and paññā. I wonder how he explains sīla, samādhi and paññā. Can you tell me?"

Zhicheng replied, "Master Shenxiu used to say, 'Refraining from all evil deeds is called sīla, earnestly practicing the good is paññā, and purifying your own mind is samādhi.' He explains it like this, and I wonder with what methods Your Reverence instructs people."

> 師曰:"吾若言有法與人, 卽爲誑汝. 但且隨方解縛, 假名三昧. 如
> 사왈: "오약언유법여인, 즉위광여. 단차수방해박, 가명삼매. 여
> 汝師所說戒·定·慧實不可思議也. 吾所見戒·定·慧又別."
> 여사소설계·정·혜실불가사의야. 오소견계·정·혜우별."
> 志誠曰:"戒·定·慧只合一種, 如何更別?"
> 지성왈: "계·정·혜지합일종, 여하갱별?"
> 師曰:"汝師戒·定·慧接大乘人, 吾戒·定·慧接最上乘人. 悟解不
> 사왈: "여사계·정·혜접대승인, 오계·정·혜접최상승인. 오해부
> 同, 見有遲疾.
> 동, 견유지질.

The Master said, "If I were to say I had a method to give others, it would be deceiving you. Just to go along as circumstances permit to be liberated from any restraints, it is provisionally called samādhi. Sīla, samādhi and paññā as your master teaches are truly inconceivable. My view on sīla, samādhi, and paññā is further different."

Zhicheng asked, "Isn't there just one sīla, samādhi and paññā altogether? How could there be further differences?"

The Master said, "Sīla, samādhi and paññā as your master says are suitable for those of the great vehicle, while mine are suitable for those of the supreme vehicle. Enlightenment and understanding are different, so there is the difference between swiftness and slowness in the view.

> 汝聽吾説, 與彼同否? 吾所説法, 不離自性. 離體説法, 名爲相説,
> 여청오설, 여피동부? 오소설법, 불리자성. 이체설법, 명위상설,
>
> 自性常迷. 須知一切萬法皆從自性起用. 是眞戒·
> 자성상미. 수지일체만법개종자성기용. 시진계·
>
> 定·慧法. 聽吾偈."曰:
> 정·혜법. 청오게." 왈:
>
> "心地無非自性戒, 心地無癡自性慧, 心地無亂自性定.
> "심지무비자성계, 심지무치자성혜, 심지무란자성정.

Now that you have listened to what I say, is it the same as or different from his? The dhamma I expound does not depart from Self-nature. Teaching the dhamma while departing from the essence is called teaching through appearances. But then Self-nature is constantly obscured. You must understand that all the myriad phenomena arise from and function through Self-nature. These are true sīla, samādhi and paññā. Listen to my verse."

It goes,

"If there is no fault in the mind's ground, it is the sīla of Self-nature;

If there is no ignorance in the mind's ground, it is the paññā of Self-nature;

If there are no disturbances in the mind's ground, it is the samādhi of Self-nature.

> 不增不減自金剛, 身去身來本三昧."
> 부증불감자금강, 신거신래본삼매."
>
> 誠聞偈, 悔謝, 乃呈一偈. 曰:
> 성문게, 회사, 내정일게. 왈:
>
> "五蘊幻身, 幻何究境?
> "오온환신, 환하구경?
>
> 廻趣眞如, 法還不淨."
> 회취진여, 법환부정."

Neither increasing nor decreasing, it's the Diamond Body of Self-nature;

Whether the body goes or comes, itself is originally samādhi."

Zhicheng, upon hearing the verse, felt remorse and expressed his gratitude, then presented a verse. It goes,

"Five aggregates illude the body, but

How could an illusion be the ultimate stage?

If one turns toward True-thusness,

The dhamma itself becomes impure instead."

> 師然之, 復語誠曰:
> 사연지, 부어성왈:
>
> "汝師戒·定·慧勸小根智人, 吾戒·定·慧勸大根智人. 若悟自性, 亦
> "여사계·정·혜권소근지인, 오계·정·혜권대근지인. 약오자성, 역
>
> 不立菩提涅槃, 亦不立解脫知見, 無一法可得, 方能建立萬法. 若
> 불립보리열반, 역불립해탈지견, 무일법가득, 방능건립만법. 약
>
> 解此意, 亦名佛身, 亦名菩提涅槃, 亦名解脫知見. 見性之人, 立亦得,
> 해차의, 역명불신, 역명보리열반, 역명해탈지견. 견성지인, 입역득,
>
> 不立亦得. 去來自由, 無滯無碍, 應用隨作, 應語隨答, 普見化身.
> 불립역득. 거래자유, 무체무애, 응용수작, 응어수답, 보현화신.

The Master approved, and then spoke to Zhicheng again,

"Your master's sīla, samādhi and paññā are suitable for those with lesser capacities and intelligence, while mine are suitable for those with greater capacities and intelligence. If you have realized Self-nature, there is no need of establishing bodhi nibbāna, nor of establishing any view of liberation. When there is not a single dhamma to be obtained, only then can you establish all the dhammas. If you understand this meaning, it is also called Buddha-body, also called bodhi nibbāna, also called the view of liberation.

For him who has realized seeing-nature, it is possible either to establish or not to establish. He is free in going or coming, without hindrance or obstruction. He acts according to circumstances, responds according to speeches, and universally demonstrates his transformed body.

> 不離自性, 即得自在神通, 遊戲三昧. 是名見性."
> 불리자성, 즉득자재신통, 유희삼매. 시명견성."
>
> 志誠再啓師曰: "如何是不立義?"
> 지성재계사왈: "여하시불립의?"
>
> 師曰: "自性無非·無癡·無亂, 念念般若觀照, 常離法相, 自由自
> 사왈: "자성무비·무치·무란, 염념반야관조, 상리법상, 자유자
>
> 在. 縱橫無得, 有何可立? 自性自悟, 頓悟頓修, 亦無漸次, 所以
> 재. 종횡무득, 유하가립? 자성자오, 돈오돈수, 역무점차, 소이
>
> 不立一切法. 諸法寂滅, 有何次第?"
> 불립일체법. 제법적멸, 유하차제?"

As he has not departed from his own Self-nature, he immediately attains spontaneous supernatural powers and plays in samādhi. This is called seeing-nature."

Zhicheng further asked the Master, "What is meant by not-establishing?"

The Master replied, "Self-nature is neither wrong, ignorant, nor disturbed, and illuminates through paññā observation in every thought. So it constantly departs from the dhamma appearances and is completely free and unrestricted. When there is nothing to attain in any direction, what else can be established? If you Self-enlighten to your Self-nature, it results in sudden enlightenment and sudden purification with no gradual progression, because you do not establish any dhamma. All dhammas are in tranquil cessation, so what else can there be?"

志誠禮拜, 願爲執侍, 朝夕不懈.
지성예배, 원위집시, 조석불해.

一僧志徹, 江西人, 本姓張, 名行昌. 少任俠.
일승지철, 강서인, 본성장, 명행창. 소임협.

自南北分化, 二宗主雖亡彼我, 而徒侶競起愛憎. 時北宗門人自立
자남북분화, 이종주수망피아, 이도려경기애증. 시북종문인자립

秀師爲第六祖, 而忌祖師傳衣爲天下所聞. 乃囑行昌來刺於師.
수사위제육조, 이기조사전의위천하소문. 내촉행창내자어사.

Zhicheng paid respects again and wished to attend to the Master. So he served him, day and night without rest.

Zhiche, a monk from Jiangxi, originally bore the surname Zhang and the given name Xingchang. In his youth, he was known for a bold and unruly spirit.

Although the Southern and the Northern Schools divided, the Patriarchs of the two schools did not distinguish between self and the other. However, their followers used to compete with likes and dislikes. Then the disciples of the Northern School proclaimed Shenxiu as the Sixth Patriarch. They felt jealous that the Master had received the robe and the story was spreading all over the world. So they commissioned Xingchang to go harm the Master.

> 師心通, 預知其事, 即置金十兩於座間.
> 사심통, 예지기사, 즉치금십냥어좌간.
>
> 時夜暮, 行昌入祖室, 將欲加害. 師舒頸就之. 行昌揮刃者三, 悉
> 시야모, 행창입조실, 장욕가해. 사서경취지. 행창휘인자삼, 실
>
> 無所損.
> 무소손.
>
> 師曰:"正劍不邪, 邪劍不正. 只負汝金, 不負汝命."
> 사왈:"정검불사, 사검부정. 지부여금, 불부여명."
>
> 行昌驚仆, 久而方蘇, 求哀悔過, 即願出家.
> 행창경부, 구이방소, 구애회과, 즉원출가.

The Master foresaw the situation through His intuitive wisdom, and placed ten liangs of gold between his seats.

Late at night, Xingchang entered the Patriarch's chamber, intending to harm him. The Master extended His neck towards him. Xingchang swung his sword three times, to do no harm at all.

The Master said, "A righteous sword is not evil, and an evil sword is not righteous. I owe you money, not my life."

Xingchang fell down in astonishment. After a long while he finally regained consciousness. He mournfully sought forgiveness, and wished to become a monk.

師遂與金, 言:"汝且去. 恐徒衆翻害於汝. 汝可他日易形而來, 吾
사수여금, 언: "여차거. 공도중번해어여. 여가타일역형이래, 오

當攝受."
당섭수."

行昌稟旨宵遁. 後投僧出家, 具戒精進.
행창품지소둔. 후투승출가, 구계정진.

一日憶師之言, 遠來禮覲. 師曰:"吾久念汝, 汝來何晚?"
일일억사지언, 원래예근. 사왈: "오구념여, 여래하만?"

曰:"昨蒙和尚捨罪, 今雖出家苦行, 終難報德. 其惟傳法度生乎?
왈: "작몽화상사죄, 금수출가고행, 종난보덕. 기유전법도생호?

The Master gave him the gold and told him, "Leave for now. I fear that my disciples might harm you. If you return some day in a different guise, I will surely accept you."

Xingchang, following the order, escaped during that night. Later he became a monk and diligently observed the precepts and practiced.

One day, he recalled the words of the Master and traveled from afar to pay his respects.

The Master said, "I have long been thinking of you. Why are you so late?"

Xingchang replied, "Since I was forgiven by Your Reverence the other day, I have now become a monk and practice asceticism, but it's still difficult to repay your kindness. Can there be any way of transmitting the dhamma and saving sentient beings?

弟子常覽『涅槃經』, 未曉常・無常義. 乞和尚慈悲, 略爲解説."
제자상람『열반경』, 미효상・무상의. 걸화상자비, 약위해설."

師曰: "無常者, 即佛性也; 有常者, 即一切善惡諸法分別心也."
사왈: "무상자, 즉불성야; 유상자, 즉일체선악제법분별심야."

曰: "和尚所説大違經文."
왈: "화상소설대위경문."

師曰: "吾傳佛心印, 安敢違於佛經?"
사왈: "오전불심인, 안감위어불경?"

曰: "經説, 佛性是常, 和尚却言無常; 善惡之法乃至菩提心皆是無常,
왈: "경설, 불성시상, 화상각언무상; 선악지법내지보리심개시무상,

和尚却言是常.
화상각언시상.

Your pupil often reads the Nibbāna Sutta, but hasn't fully understood the concepts of permanence and impermanence. I humbly beg Your Reverence to provide a brief explanation."

The Master said, "Impermanence is none other than Buddha-nature, while permanence is the discriminating mind that distinguishes good and evil in all phenomena."

Xingchang said, "What Your Reverence speaks greatly contradicts the Scripture."

The Master responded, "I transmit the seal of Buddha's mind. How could I dare go against the Buddha's Scripture?"

Xingchang said, "The Scripture states that Buddha-nature is permanent, yet Your Reverence says that it is impermanent; while the practices of good and evil as well as the mind of enlightenment are all impermanent, Your Reverence claims that they are permanent.

> 此即相違, 令學人轉加疑惑."
> 차즉상위, 영학인전가의혹."
>
> 師曰: "『涅槃經』, 吾昔聽尼無盡藏讀誦一遍, 便爲講説, 無一字一
> 사왈: "『열반경』, 오석청니무진장독송일편, 변위강설, 무일자일
>
> 義不合經文. 乃至爲汝, 終無二説."
> 의불합경문. 내지위여, 종무이설."
>
> 曰: "學人識量淺昧, 願和尚委曲開示."
> 왈: "학인식량천매, 원화상위곡개시."
>
> 師曰: "汝知否? 佛性若常, 更説什麼善惡諸法? 乃至窮劫, 無有
> 사왈: "여지부? 불성약상, 갱설십마선악제법? 내지궁겁, 무유
>
> 一人發菩提心者. 故吾説無常.
> 일인발보리심자. 고오설무상.

These are contradictory to each other, causing your pupil more doubts and confusions."

The Master said, "As to Nibbāna Sutta, when I once heard the nun Wujincang reciting a chapter of it and expounded it to her, not a single word or meaning deviated from the Scripture. There can be no other interpretation for you."

Xingchang said, "Your pupil has a limited and ignorant understanding. I beg Your Reverence to provide detailed guidance."

The Master said, "Don't you know? If Buddha-nature is permanent, why would there be any need to discuss further various dhammas of virtues and evils? Even after countless eons, not a single person would generate the mind of bodhi. Therefore I speak of impermanence.

> 正是佛說眞常之道也. 又一切諸法,
> 정시불설진상지도야. 우일체제법,
>
> 若無常者, 即物物皆有自性, 容受生死, 而眞常性有不徧之處. 故
> 약무상자, 즉물물개유자성, 용수생사, 이진상성유불변지처. 고
>
> 吾說常者, 正是佛說眞無常義.
> 오설상자, 정시불설진무상의.
>
> 佛比爲凡夫外道執於邪常, 諸二乘人於常計無常, 共成八倒, 故於
> 불비위범부외도집어사상, 제이승인어상계무상, 공성팔도, 고어
>
> 涅槃了義教中破彼偏見, 而顯說眞常·眞樂·眞我·眞淨.
> 열반료의교중파피편견, 이현설진상·진락·진아·진정.

This is precisely the path of true permanence as Buddha taught it. Furthermore, if all phenomena are impermanent, then each of them possesses its own Self-nature and is subject to birth and death, and there would be places where the True-permanent-nature cannot fully pervade. Therefore I speak of permanence, which is precisely the true meaning of impermanence as the Buddha taught it.

The Buddha, using a parable, explained that ordinary individuals and non-Buddhist teachings cling to false views of permanence, while the practitioners of the two vehicles mistakenly perceive permanence as impermanence. Together, they generate the eight misconceptions. Therefore, within the teaching of the ultimate meaning of nibbāna, the Buddha shattered those partial views and demonstrated the true permanence, true joy, true Self, and true purity.

> 汝今依言背義, 以斷滅無常及確定死常, 而錯解佛之圓妙最後
> 여금의언배의, 이단멸무상급확정사상, 이착해불지원묘최후
>
> 微言. 縱覽千徧, 有何所益?"
> 미언. 종람천편, 유하소익?"
>
> 行昌忽然大悟, 乃說偈言:
> 행창홀연대오, 내설게언:
>
>
> "因守無常心, 佛說有常性.
> "인수무상심, 불설유상성.
>
> 不知方便者, 猶春池拾礫.
> 부지방편자, 유춘지습력.

Now you misunderstand their meanings relying on the words. By relying on the wrong view of impermanence as annihilation and the wrong view of dead permanence as a fixed, unchanging reality, you misunderstand the Buddha's profound, ultimate and subtle words. What benefit is there even if you read the Scripture one thousand times?"

Then Xingchang was suddenly enlightened and presented a verse.

"Because I hold the mind of impermanence,

The Buddha spoke of a permanent nature.

He who does not understand skillful means

Is like collecting only pebbles from a spring pond.

> 我今不施功, 佛性而現前.
> 아금불시공, 불성이현전.
>
> 非師相授與, 我亦無所得."
> 비사상수여, 아역무소득."
>
>
> 師曰:"汝今徹也, 宜名志徹." 徹禮謝而退.
> 사왈:"여금철야, 의명지철." 철사례이퇴.
>
>
> 有一童子, 名神會, 襄陽高氏子. 年十三, 自玉泉來參禮.
> 유일동자, 명신회, 양양고씨자. 연십삼 자옥천래참례.

It is not through my own efforts

That Buddha-nature has manifested in front of me.

If not for my Master's guidance,

Nothing could I have acquired."

The Master said, "Now that you have enlightened, you shall be named Zhiche."

Zhiche bowed in gratitude and withdrew.

There was an acolyte named Shenhui, a descendant of the Gao family from Xiangyang. At the age of thirteen, he came from the Yuchuan Temple and paid respects to the Master.

師曰: "知識遠來艱辛. 還將得本來否? 若有本, 即合識主. 試説看."
사왈: "지식원래간신. 환장득본래부? 약유본, 즉합식주. 시설간."

會曰: "以無住爲本, 見即是主."
회왈: "이무주위본, 견즉시주."

師曰: "這沙彌爭合取次語?"
사왈: "저사미쟁합취차어?"

會乃問曰: "和尚坐禪, 還見不見?"
회내문왈: "화상좌선, 환견불견?"

師以拄杖打三下, 云: "吾打汝. 痛不痛?"
사이주장타삼하, 운: "오타여. 통불통?"

The Master said, "Good learned friend, you have come from afar, enduring hardships. Have you already realized your original nature? If you have realized your original nature, it should immediately correspond with the knowing master. Try to explain to me."

Shenhui replied, "As I take no-abiding as the foundation, seeing is the master."

The Master said, "How reckless is this novice to tell such!"

Shenhui then asked, "When Your Reverence practices Zazen, do you see or not see?"

The Master struck him three times with his staff and said, asked, "I hit you. Is it painful or not painful?"

> 對曰: "亦痛, 亦不痛."
> 대왈: "역통, 역불통."
>
> 師曰: "吾亦見, 亦不見."
> 사왈: "오역견, 역불견."
>
> 神會問: "如何是亦見亦不見?"
> 신회문: "여하시역견역불견?"
>
> 師言: "吾之所見, 常見自心過愆, 不見他人是非好惡. 是以亦見亦
> 사언: "오지소견, 상견자심과건, 불견타인시비호악. 시이역견역
>
> 不見. 汝言亦痛亦不痛, 如何? 汝若不痛, 同其木石; 若痛, 即同
> 불견. 여언역통역불통, 여하? 여약불통, 동기목석; 약통, 즉동
>
> 凡夫, 即起恚恨.
> 범부, 즉기에한.

Shenhui replied, "Painful as well as not painful."

The Master said, "I do also see as well as not see."

Shenhui asked, "What is meant by seeing as well as not seeing?"

The Master replied, "What I see is seeing always my own faults and shortcomings, but what I do not see is not seeing right and wrong, the good and bad in others. That's why it is both seeing and not seeing. Now you spoke of feeling pain as well as not feeling pain. What does it mean? If you do not feel pain, then you are the same as a piece of wood or a stone; if you feel pain, then you are the same as an ordinary man, prone to anger and hatred.

汝向前見不見是二邊, 痛不痛是生滅. 汝自性且
여향전견불견시이변, 통불통시생멸. 여자성차

不見, 敢爾戲論?"
불견, 감이희론?"

神會禮拜悔謝.
신회예배회사.

師又曰: "汝若心迷不見, 問善知識覓路. 汝若心悟, 即自見性, 依
사우왈: "여약심미불견, 문선지식멱로. 여약심오, 즉자견성, 의

法修行. 汝自迷不見自心, 却來問吾見與不見? 吾見自知, 豈代汝
법수행. 여자미불견자심, 각래문오견여불견? 오견자지, 기대여

迷? 汝若自見, 亦不代吾迷. 何不自知自見, 乃問吾見與不見?"
미? 여약자견, 역부대오미. 하부자지자견, 내문오견여불견?"

To see and not to see as you said before are two extremes, and to feel pain and not to feel pain are birth and death. While you haven't seen your own Self-nature, how dare you jest about it?"

Shenhui bowed respectfully and expressed remorse.

The Master continued, "If your are deluded in mind and cannot see, then ask a good learned teacher in order to find the way. If enlightened in mind, you can see your Self-nature and practice according to the dhamma. When you are deluded and haven't seen your own mind, dare you ask me if I see or not see? When I know for myself that I see, why should I depend on you delusion? If you see for yourself, you need not be responsible for my own delusion. Why you do not know nor see for yourself and dare ask me if I see or not see?"

> 神會再禮百餘拜, 求謝過愆. 服僅給侍, 不離左右.
> 신회재례백여배, 구사과건. 복근급시, 불리좌우.
>
> 一日師告衆曰: "吾有一物, 無頭無尾, 無名無字, 無背無面. 諸人還識否?"
> 일일사고중왈: "오유일물, 무두무미, 무명무자, 무배무면. 제인환식부?"
>
> 神會出曰: "是諸佛之本源, 神會之佛性."
> 신회출왈: "시제불지본원, 신회지불성."
>
> 師曰: "向汝道無名無字, 汝便喚作本源·佛性. 汝向去有把茆蓋頭也, 只成箇知解宗徒."
> 사왈: "향여도무명무자, 여변환작본원·불성. 여향거유파묘개두야, 지성개지해종도."

Shenhui bowed again more than a hundred times, expressing his remorse for his errors. He wished to attend to the Master, and remained at his side without leaving.

One day, the Master addressed the assembly, saying, "I have a thing, without head nor tail, without name nor word, without front nor back. Does anyone of you recognize it?"

Shenhui came forward and said, "It is the origin of all Buddhas, as well as my Buddha-nature."

The Master said, "I told you that it has no name nor word, yet you call it the origin and Buddha-nature. As you continue, even if you become a leader, you shall only end up leading followers with mere intellectual understanding."

祖師滅後, 會入京洛, 大弘曹溪頓教. 著『顯宗記』, 盛行於世.
조사멸후, 회입경락, 대홍조계돈교. 저『현종기』, 성행어세.

師見諸宗難問, 咸起惡心, 多集座下, 愍而謂曰:
사견제종난문, 함기악심, 다집좌하, 민이위왈:

"學道之人, 一切善念·惡念應當盡除.
"학도지인, 일체선념·악념응당진제.

After the Patriarch passed away, Shenhui moved to the Capital and greatly propagated Caoqi's sudden teaching. He also wrote The Record of Manifesting the Doctrine, which became widely influential.

The Master observed various schools grappling with intricate questions and often congregating with unwholesome intentions, and gathered the assembly under his seat. He addressed them with compassion, saying,

"Followers of the path ought to entirely uproot all good and evil thoughts.

> 無名可名, 名於自性, 無二之性, 是名實性. 於實性上建立一切教門,
> 무명가명, 명어자성, 무이지성, 시명실성. 어실성상건립일체교문,
>
> 言下便須自見."諸人聞説, 總皆作禮, 請事爲師.
> 언하변수자견." 제인문설, 총개작례, 청사위사.

Even the unnamable can be given a name, it is termed Self-nature, an inherently non-dual essence, and is also referred to real-nature. Upon this real-nature all teachings are established. You must see this truth for yourself immediately under a single word."

Upon listening to these words, all those present respectfully expressed their veneration and sought to become disciples.

第九　宣詔品

제구 선조품

神龍元年上元日，則天·中宗詔云：
신룡원년상원일, 측천·중종조운：

"朕請安·秀二師，宮中供養，萬機之暇每究一乘．二師推讓，云：
"짐청안 수이사, 궁중공양, 만기지가매구일승. 이사추양, 운：

'南方有能禪師，密授忍大師衣法，傳佛心印，可請彼問．'
'남방유능선사, 밀수인대사의법, 전불심인, 가청피문.'

Chapter Nine

Of Reception

On the fifteenth of January, the first year of the Shenlong era, Empress Zhetian and Emperor Zhongzong issued an edict, stating,

"I, Son of Heaven, had courteously invited the two revered Masters, Huian and Shenxiu, into the Palace for offerings, in order that I always explore one vehicle amidst the multitude of responsibilities. The two Masters modestly rejected, saying, 'In the southern region, there is Zen Master Huineng, who was secretly transmitted the robe and the dhamma from His Reverence Patriarch Hongren, and has inherited the seal of Buddha's mind. Your Majesty had better invite him for further inquiries.'

> 今遣內侍 薛簡, 馳詔請迎. 願師慈念, 速赴上京."
> 금견내시 설간, 치조청영. 원사자념, 속부상경."
>
> 師上表辭疾, 願終林麓.
> 사상표사질, 원종임록.
>
> 薛簡曰: "京城禪德皆云: '欲得會道, 必須坐禪習定. 若不因禪定
> 설간왈: "경성선덕개운: '욕득회도, 필수좌선습정. 약불인선정
>
> 而得解脱者, 未之有也.' 未審師所説法如何?"
> 이득해탈자, 미지유야.' 미심사소설법여하?"
>
> 師曰: "道由心悟, 豈在坐也? 經云: '若言如來, 若坐若臥, 是行邪道'
> 사왈: "도유심오, 기재좌야? 경운: '약언여래, 약좌약와, 시행사도'

Now I dispatch the imperial eunuch Xuejian, bearing an imperial decree, to respectfully receive and invite Your Reverence. I courteously hope that Your Reverence graciously considers this and promptly make way to the Capital."

The Master courteously expressed excuse for illness, stating his desire to stay in the vicinity of the forest until he passes away.

Xuejian asked the Master, "The renowned masters in the Capital all assert, 'In order to attain the path, you ought to practice Zazen and cultivate samādhi. No one has attained liberation without depending on Zen-samādhi.' I wonder what Your Reverence teaches."

The Master replied, "The path is realized through mind — how does it concern with sitting? The Scripture says, 'To speak of the Tathāgata as sitting or lying down is to follow the wrong path.'

> 何故? 無所從來, 亦無所去. 無生無滅是如來淸淨禪, 諸法
> 하고? 무소종래, 역무소거. 무생무멸시여래청정선, 제법
>
> 空寂是如來淸淨坐. 究境無證, 豈況坐耶?"
> 공적시여래청정좌. 구경무증, 기황좌야?"
>
> 簡曰: "弟子回京, 主上必問. 願師慈悲, 指示心要. 傳奏兩宮及京
> 간왈: "제자회경, 주상필문. 원사자비, 지시심요. 전주양궁급경
>
> 城學道者, 譬如一燈燃百千燈, 冥者皆明, 明明無盡."
> 성학도자, 비여일등연백천등, 명자개명, 명명무진."
>
> 師云: "道無明暗.
> 사운: "도무명암.

Why is it so? Because there is neither coming from, nor going to. Non-arising as well as non-ceasing itself is the Tathāgata's clear and pure Zen; all phenomena being empty and tranquil, this is the Tathāgata's clear and pure sitting. Even in the ultimate state there is nothing to attain, how much more for sitting?"

Xuejian said, "As your disciple returns to the Capital, the Emperor will surely inquire of me. I beg Your Reverence to reveal, with compassion, the essence of mind. Then I will transmit it to the two Palaces and to all the practitioners of the path in the Capital, so that those in darkness all become illuminated and the illumination is boundless, just as a single lamp lights hundreds and thousands of lamps."

The Master said, "There is neither brightness nor darkness in the path.

明暗是代謝之義. 明明無盡亦是有盡, 相待立名故.
명암시대사지의. 명명무진역시유진, 상대입명고.

『淨名經』云: '法無有比, 無相待故.'"
『정명경』운: '법무유비 무상대고.'"

簡曰: "明喻智慧, 暗喻煩惱. 修道之人倘不以智慧照破煩惱, 無始
간왈: "명유지혜, 암유번뇌. 수도지인당불이지혜조파번뇌, 무시

生死, 憑何出離?"
생사, 빙하출리?"

師曰: "煩惱即是菩提, 無二無別. 若以智慧照破煩惱者, 此是二乘
사왈: "번뇌즉시보리, 무이무별. 약이지혜조파번뇌자, 차시이승

見解, 羊·鹿等機. 上智大根悉不如是."
견해, 양·록·등기. 상지대근실불여시."

Brightness and darkness are alternative terms. Even its endless brightness is at the same time finite, because it is established in relation to darkness. Hence the Vimalakīrti Nirdeśa Sūtra[s] states: 'There is no comparison in the path, for there is nothing to compare.'"

Xuejian further asked, "Brightness is compared to wisdom, while darkness is to afflictions. If he who practices the path does not use his wisdom to illuminate and dispel afflictions, how can he break and liberate himself from the beginningless cycle of birth and death?"

The Master replied, "Afflictions themselves are bodhi. There is no duality nor distinction. If you use your wisdom to illuminate and dispel afflictions, this is the view of the Two Vehicle, to those pulled by sheep and deer, but those with greater wisdom and deeper capacity are not like it."

簡曰: "如何是大乘見解?"
간왈: "여하시대승견해?"

師曰: "明與無明, 凡夫見二, 智者了達其性無二. 無二之性即是實
사왈: "명여무명, 범부견이, 지자요달기성무이. 무이지성즉시실

性. 實性者, 處凡愚而不感, 在賢聖而不增, 住煩惱而不亂, 居禪
성. 실성자, 처범우이불감, 재현성이부증, 주번뇌이불란, 거선

定而不寂. 不斷不常, 不來不去, 不在中間及其內外, 不生不滅,
정이부적. 부단불상, 불래불거, 부재중간급기내외, 불생불멸,

性相如如, 常住不遷, 名之曰道."
성상여여, 상주불천, 명지왈도."

Xuejian asked, "What is the perspective of the Mahāyāna?"

The Master said, "The ordinary perceive a duality between clarity and ignorance, while the wise comprehends their nature as non-dual. The nature of non-duality is real-nature. The real-nature isn't reduced in the ordinary and foolish, nor increased in the wise and sages; while abiding in afflictions there is no disturbance, while dwelling in Zen-samādhi there is no tranquility. Neither cessated nor constant, neither coming nor going, neither in between nor internal nor external, neither arising nor ceasing — the form of the nature is as such, ever abiding and unchanging. This is called the path."

> 簡曰: "師說不生不滅, 何異外道?"
> 간왈: "사설불생불멸, 하이외도?"
>
> 師曰: "外道所說不生不滅者, 將滅止生, 以生顯滅, 滅猶不滅, 生
> 사왈: "외도소설불생불멸자, 장멸지생, 이생현멸, 멸유불멸, 생
>
> 說不生. 我說不生不滅者, 本自無生, 今亦不滅, 所以不同外道.
> 설불생. 아설불생불멸자, 본자무생, 금역불멸, 소이부동외도.
>
> 汝若欲知心要, 但一切善惡都莫思量, 自然得入淸淨心體, 湛然常
> 여약욕지심요, 단일체선악도막사량, 자연득입청정심체, 담연상
>
> 寂, 妙用恒沙."
> 적, 묘용항사."

Xuejian asked, "Your Reverence speaks of non-arising and non-ceasing. How does it differ from the teachings of the non-Buddhist?"

The Master replied, "What the non-Buddhist teachings call non-arising and non-ceasing is actually stopping the arising through cessation and revealing the cessation through arising. So the cessation is rather similar to non-cessation, and they describe the arising as if it is non-arising. But what I call non-arising and non-ceasing is originally no-arising, and now is also no-ceasing. This is why it's different from the view of the non-Buddhist teachings. If you wish to understand the essence of mind, just refrain from considering all good and evil, and you shall naturally enter the clear and pure body of mind, which is deeply serene and constantly tranquil, with profound functions beyond measure."

> 簡蒙指教, 豁然大悟, 禮辭歸闕, 表奏師語.
> 간몽지교, 활연대오, 예사귀궐, 표주사어.
>
> 其年九月三日有詔, 獎諭師曰:
> 기년구월삼일유조, 장유사왈:
>
> "師辭老疾, 爲朕修道, 國之福田. 師若淨名託疾毘耶, 闡揚大乘,
> "사사노질, 위짐수도, 국지복전. 사약정명탁질비야, 천양대승,
>
> 傳諸佛心, 談不二法. 薛簡傳師指授如來知見. 朕積善餘慶, 宿種善根,
> 전제불심, 담불이법. 설간전사지수여래지견. 짐적선여경, 숙종선근,

Xuejian, having received the instruction, suddenly had a great realization. He respectfully bid farewell and returned to the Capital, and reported to the Emperor with the Master's words.

On the third day of September that year, an imperial decree was issued, praising and admonishing the Master. It states,

"Your Reverence has relinquished due to your old age and illness, and is said to dedicate yourself to the cultivation of the path for the merit of me, Son of Heaven. This is a blessing for the Empire. It is akin to the example of Vimalakīrti, who, in a similar vein, entrusted his illness to Vaidūrya while propagating the Mahāyāna and transmitting the wisdom of all Buddhas, expounding the teachings of non-duality. Xuejian transmitted to me the wisdom and insight of Tathāgata that Your Reverence taught. I have been accumulating virtues for benefits and planting good seeds for long.

値師出世, 頓悟上乘. 感荷師恩, 頂戴無已."
치사출세, 돈오상승. 감하사은, 정대무이."

并奉磨衲袈裟及水晶鉢, 勅韶州刺史修飾寺宇, 賜師舊居爲國恩寺.
병봉마납가사급수정발, 칙소주자사수식사우, 사사구거위국은사.

Now I'm fortunate to encounter Your Reverence in this lifetime and suddenly awaken to the teachings of the supreme vehicle. I am deeply grateful for Your Reverene's kindness, and hold my utmost respects and admiration."

The Emperor bestowed the Master a quilted robe and a crystal alms bowl. He also decreed to the prefect of Xiaozhou, commanding to refurbish the temple, and entitled the Master's former residence the Guoen Temple.

> 第十 付囑品
> 제십 부촉품
>
> 師一日喚門人法海·志誠·法達·神會·智常·智通·志徹·志道·法珍·
> 사일일환문인법해·지성·법달·신회·지상·지통·지철·지도·법진·
>
> 法如等, 曰:
> 법여등, 왈:
>
> "汝等不同餘人. 吾滅度後各爲一方師. 吾今教汝説法, 不失本宗.
> "여등부동여인. 오멸도후각위일방사. 오금교여설법, 불실본종.

Chapter Ten

Of Entrustments

One day, the Master summoned his disciples Fahai, Zhicheng, Fada, Shenhui, Zhichang, Zhitong, Zhiche, Zhidao, Fazhen, Faru and others and said,

"You are different from the rest. After I pass away, each of you shall become a master in your own region. Now I instruct you in teaching the dhamma, lest you should deviate from the original teaching.

先須擧三科法門, 動用三十六對. 出沒即離兩邊, 說一切法莫離自
선수거삼과법문, 동용삼십육대. 출몰즉리양변, 설일체법막리자
性. 忽有人問汝法, 出語盡雙, 皆取對法, 來去相因, 究境二法盡
성. 홀유인문여법, 출어진쌍, 개취대법, 내거상인, 구경이법진
除, 更無去處.
제, 갱무거처.
三科法門者, 陰·界·入也. 陰是五陰, 色·受·想·行·識是也; 入是
삼과법문자, 음·계·입야. 음시오음, 색·수·상·행·식시야; 입시
十二入, 外六塵色·聲·香·味·觸·法, 內六門眼·耳·鼻·舌·身·意是也;
십이입, 외육진색·성·향·미·촉·법, 내육문안·이·비·설·신·의시야;

First, I'll present the three categories of the dhamma teachings, and show how to apply the thirty-six opposites in practice. Whether appearing or disappearing, remain free from both extremes, and never depart from Self-nature whenever you expound the dhamma. If someone suddenly asks you about the dhamma, always reply with dualistic words. You should grasp both opposites in every situation, as they arise in cause and effect, like coming and going. Ultimately, transcend both aspects and further eliminate any room to go further.

The three categories of the dhamma teachings are aggregates, realms and entrances. Aggregates refer to the five aggregates: materiality, sensation, perception, mental formations and consciousness. Entrances refer to the twelve entrances: externally, the six objects of color, sound, smell, taste, touch and mental contents; internally, the six sense organs of eye, ear, nose, tongue, body and thought.

> 界是十八界, 六塵·六門·六識是也.
> 계시십팔계, 육진·육문·육식시야.
>
> 自性能含萬法, 名含藏識. 若起思量, 即是轉識: 生六識, 出六門,
> 자성능함만법, 명함장식. 약기사량, 즉시전식: 생육식, 출육문,
>
> 見六塵. 如是一十八界皆從自性起用. 自性若邪, 起十八邪; 自性
> 견육진. 여시일십팔계개종자성기용. 자성약사, 기십팔사; 자성
>
> 若正, 起十八正. 若惡用, 即眾生用; 善用, 即佛用.
> 약정, 기십팔정. 약악용, 즉중생용; 선용, 즉불용.
>
> 用由何等? 有自性, 有對法.
> 용유하등? 유자성, 유대법.

Realms refer to the eighteen realms: the six objects, the six sense organs and the six consciousnesses.

Because Self-nature can encompass all phenomena, it is named conceived consciousness. When you arouse thoughts, it is the transformed consciousness: arising of six consciousnesses, coming out through six sense organs, and seeing six sense objects. In this manner, the eighteen realms all arise and function depending on Self-nature. If Self-nature is deviant, the arising eighteen are also deviant; if Self-nature is right, the arising eighteen are also right. If Self-nature functions wrongly, it is the functioning of sentient beings; if it functions rightly, it is the functioning of Buddhas.

Whence such differences in functioning? Because there are Self-nature on the one hand, and the laws of opposition on the other.

> 外境無情, 五對: 天與地對, 日與月對, 明與暗對, 陰與陽對, 水
> 외경무정, 오대: 천여지대, 일여월대, 명여암대, 음여양대, 수
>
> 與火對. 此是五對也.
> 여화대. 차시오대야.
>
> 法相語言, 十二對: 語與法對, 有與無對, 有色與無色對, 有相與
> 법상어언, 십이대: 어여법대, 유여무대, 유색여무색대, 유상여
>
> 無相對, 有漏與無漏對, 色與空對, 動與靜對, 清與濁對, 凡與聖
> 무상대, 유루여무루대, 색여공대, 동여정대, 청여탁대, 범여성
>
> 對, 僧與俗對, 老與少對, 大與小對. 此是十二對也.
> 대, 승여속대, 노여소대, 대여소대. 차시십이대야.
>
> 自性起用, 十九對:
> 자성기용, 십구대:

External objects, which do not have sentience, include five opposites: sky versus earth, sun versus moon, bright versus dark, yin versus yang, and water versus fire. These are the five opposites.

The languages of the dhamma appearances include twelve opposites: language versus dhamma, existence versus non-existence, material versus immaterial, form versus no-form, defiled versus undefiled, matter versus void, motion versus motionless, pure versus impure, ordinary versus sacred, monastic versus lay, old versus young, and large versus small. These are the twelve opposites.

The arising and functioning of Self-nature include nineteen opposites:

> 長與短對, 邪與正對, 痴與慧對, 愚與智對, 亂與定對, 慈與毒對,
> 장여단대, 사여정대, 치여혜대, 우여지대, 난여정대, 자여독대,
>
> 戒與非對, 直與曲對, 實與虛對, 險與平對, 煩惱與菩提對,
> 계여비대, 직여곡대, 실여허대, 험여평대, 번뇌여보리대,
>
> 常與無常對, 悲與害對, 喜與瞋對, 捨與慳對, 進與退對, 生與滅對,
> 상여무상대, 비여해대, 희여진대, 사여간대, 진여퇴대, 생여멸대,
>
> 法身與色身對, 化身與報身對. 此是十九對也."
> 법신여색신대, 화신여보신대. 차시십구대야."
>
> 師言: "此三十六對法, 若解用, 即道貫一切經法, 出入即離兩邊, 自性動用.
> 사언: "차삼십육대법, 약해용, 즉도관일체경법. 출입즉리양변, 자성동용.

long versus short, deviant versus righteous, ignorance versus wisdom, foolishness versus intelligence, disturbance versus samādhi, compassionate versus wicked, precepts versus non-precepts, direct versus crooked, substance versus emptiness, rugged versus smooth, affliction versus bodhi, permanence versus impermanence, sympathetic versus harmful, joy versus anger, generosity versus stingeness, progress versus regression, birth versus death, the dhamma body versus the physical body, Transformative Body versus Reward Body. These are the nineteen opposites."

The Master continued, "If you understand how to apply these thirty-six oppositions, the path shall immediately penetrate all the teachings of Scriptures. In exiting and entering, be free from two extremes, allowing Self-nature to move and function.

共人言語, 外於相離相, 內於空離空. 若全著相, 即長邪見; 若全執空,
공인언어, 외어상리상, 내어공리공. 약전착상, 즉장사견; 약전집공;

即長無明. 執空之人有謗經, 直言'不用文字'. 既云不用文字,
즉장무명. 집공지인유방경, 직언'불용문자', 기운불용문자,

人亦不合語言, 只此語言便是文字之相. 又云'直道不立文字',
인역불합어언, 지차어언변시문자지상. 우운'직도불립문자',

即此'不立'兩字亦是文字. 見人所説, 便即謗他言著文字.
즉차'불립'양자역시문자. 견인소설, 변즉방타언착문자.

汝等須知: 自迷猶可,
여등수지: 자미유가,

In conversation with others, be free externally from clinging to appearances while facing appearances, and free internally from clinging to emptiness while facing emptiness. If you completely cling to form, you shall cultivate only erroneous views; if you entirely cling to emptiness, you shall cultivate only ignorance.

He who clings to emptiness would slander the Scriptures, directly saying, 'No using letters.' Yet, now that he has said 'no using letters,' he also contradicts his own words because his saying itself also belongs to letters. There is also the saying, 'The direct path doesn't rely on words.' However, the two words 'not rely' themselves are also words. When you see others say such things, you should refute them by pointing out that their very words are still tied to words. You should know: you might be excused of your own delusion.

> 又謗佛經? 不要謗經, 罪障無數.
> 우방불경? 불요방경 죄장무수.
>
> 若著相於外而作法求眞, 或廣立道場, 說有無之過患. 如是之人累
> 약착상어외이작법구진, 혹광립도량, 설유무지과환. 여시지인누
>
> 劫不得見性. 但聽依法修行, 又莫百物不思, 而於道性窒碍. 若聽
> 겁부득견성. 단청의법수행, 우막백물불사, 이어도성질애. 약청
>
> 說不修, 令人反生邪念. 但依法修行, 無住相法施. 汝等若悟, 依
> 설불수, 영인반생사념. 단의법수행, 무주상법시. 여등약오, 의
>
> 此說, 依此用, 依此行, 依此作, 即不失本宗.
> 차설, 의차용, 의차행, 의차작, 즉불실본종.

But how about if you slander the Buddha's Scriptures? Never slander the Scriptures, as the sins and obstructions are countless.

If you attach externally to appearances and practice the dhamma to seek the truth or extensively establish temples, you commit an error of discussing being and non-being. Such a man shall not realize seeing-nature for many eons. Only listen: practice according to the dhamma; also, do not strive not to think of anything, as it obstructs path-nature. If you hear the teaching and do not practice, you shall cause deviant thoughts in others. So just practice according to the dhamma and offer the dhamma without clinging to the appearing forms. If you have once enlightened, then speak according to this, apply according to this, practice according to this and act according to this, and then you shall not miss the fundamentals of our School.

若有人問汝義, 問有將無對, 問無將有對, 問凡以聖對, 問聖以凡
약유인문여의, 문유장무대, 문무장유대; 문범이성대, 문성이범

對. 二道相因, 生中道義. 如一問一對, 餘問一依此作, 即不失理
대. 이도상인, 생중도의. 여일문일대, 여문일의차작, 즉불실리

也.
야.

設有人問: '何名爲暗?' 答云: '明是因, 暗是緣, 明沒即暗.' 以明
설유인문: '하명위암?' 답운: '명시인, 암시연, 명몰즉암.' 이명

顯暗, 以暗顯明. 來去相因, 成中道義. 餘問悉皆如此.
현암, 이암현명. 내거상인, 성중도의. 여문실개여차.

If someone inquires about the meaning, respond with non-being when asked about being, and vice versa; respond with the sacred when asked about the ordinary, and vice versa. These two paths are interdependent, and thus generate the principle of the middle path. You should respond with one answer for each inquiry, and if you respond to all the remaining questions in this manner consistently, you shall not miss the principle.

If someone inquires, 'What is called darkness?' respond: 'Brightness is the cause, darkness is the result, for when brightness ceases, that is darkness.' Use brightness to reveal darkness, and vice versa. Coming and going are interdependent, thus establishing the principle of the middle path. The same applies to all other inquiries.

汝等於後 傳法, 依此傳法, 依此迭相教授, 勿失宗旨."
여등어후 전법, 의차전법, 의차질상교수, 물실종지."

師於太極元年壬子七月命門人往新州國恩寺健塔. 仍令促工, 次年
사어태극원년임자칠월명문인왕신주국은사건탑. 잉령촉공, 차년

夏末落成.
하말낙성.

七月一日集徒衆, 曰: "吾至八月欲離世間. 汝等有疑, 早須相問.
칠월일일집도중, 왈: "오지팔월욕리세간. 여등유의, 조수상문.

爲汝破疑, 令汝迷盡. 吾若去後, 無人教汝."
위여파의, 영여미진. 오약거후, 무인교여."

In the future, when you transmit the dhamma, follow this method and teach one another accordingly, and never miss the essence of the School."

In July of the first year, renzi, of the Taiji era, the Master ordered his disciples to go to the Guoen Temple in Xinzhou and build a pagoda. He ordered them to hurry the work, so it was completed by the end of the following summer.

On the first day of July, the Master summoned the assembly and said, "I will depart from this world by August. If any of you has doubts, ask now. I will clarify your doubts and eliminate your confusion. Once I am gone, there shall be no one to instruct you."

> 法海等聞, 悉皆涕泣, 惟有神會神情不動, 亦無涕泣.
> 법해등문, 실개체읍, 유유신회신정부동, 역무체읍.
>
> 師曰: "神會小師却得善不善等, 毁譽不動, 哀樂不生. 餘者不得.
> 사왈: "신회소사각득선불선등, 훼예부동, 애락불생, 여자부득.
>
> 數年在山, 竟修何道? 汝今悲泣, 爲憂阿誰? 若憂吾不知去處, 吾
> 수년재산, 경수하도? 여금비읍, 위우아수? 약우오부지거처, 오
>
> 自知去處; 若吾不知去處, 終不預報於汝. 汝等悲泣, 蓋爲不知吾
> 자지거처; 약오부지거처, 종불예보어여. 여등비읍, 개위부지오
>
> 去處. 若知吾去處, 即不合悲泣.
> 거처. 약지오거처, 즉불합비읍.
>
> **法性本無生滅·去來.**
> 법성본무생멸·거래.

Upon hearing this, Fahai and the others were all moved to tears, but only Shenhui remained calm and unmoved, and did not weep.

The Master said, "The junior master Shenhui has attained the stage of being impartial between good and bad, unaffected by criticism or praise and not raising sorrow nor joy, while the rest have not. What path have you been practicing, spending years in the mountain? For whom do you worry, that you now grieve and weep? If you worry that I do not know where I am going, I do know where to go; if I didn't know, I could have never revealed it to you. If you knew where I am going, there would be no reason to weep.

The dhamma-nature is inherently beyond birth and death, coming and going.

> 汝等盡坐. 吾與汝説一偈, 名曰「眞假動偈」. 汝等誦取此偈,
> 여등진좌. 오여여설일게, 명왈「진가동정게」. 여등송취차게,
>
> 與吾意同. 依此修行, 不失宗旨."
> 여오의동. 의차수행 불실종지."
>
> 衆僧作禮, 請師説偈. 偈曰:
> 중승작례, 청사설게. 게왈:
>
> "一切無有眞, 不事見於眞.
> 일체무유진, 불사견어진.
>
> 若見於眞者, 是見盡非眞.
> 약견어진자, 시견진비진.

Sit, all of you. I will now share a verse with you, called 'Verse on the True and the False, Movement and Stillness.' Recite and understand the verse, and you shall align with my intention. Practice according to it, and you shall not miss the essence of the School."

All the monks paid their respects and begged the Master to give the verse. It goes,

"All things lack inherent truth:

Do not try to see the true.

If you see them as the true,

Such seeing is entirely untrue.

若能自有眞, 離假即心眞.
약능자유진, 이가즉심진.

自心不離假, 無眞何處眞?
자심불리가, 무진하처진?

有情即解動, 無情即不動.
유정즉해동, 무정즉부동.

若修不動行, 同無情不動.
약수부동행, 동무정부동.

若覓眞不動, 動上有不動.
약멱진부동, 동상유부동.

If you can possess the truth within yourself,

When you're free from illusion, then the mind itself is true,

When your own mind is not free from illusion,

Nothing is true. Where on earth is the truth?

Sentient beings naturally engage in movement,

Non-sentient beings will remain still.

If you practice the act of non-movement,

It's akin to the stillness of non-sentients.

If you seek true non-movement,

There is non-movement even amidst movement.

> 不動是不動, 無情無佛種.
> 부동시부동, 무정무불종.
>
> 能善分別相, 第一義不動.
> 능선분별상, 제일의부동.
>
> 但作如此見, 即是眞如用.
> 단작여차견, 즉시진여용.
>
> 報諸學道人, 努力須用意.
> 보제학도인, 노력수용의.
>
> 莫於大乘門, 却執生死智.
> 막어대승문, 각집생사지.

If stillness alone were true non-movement,

Wouldn't non-sentient beings lack the seed of Buddhahood?

If you can discern well among appearances,

The ultimate principle is non-movement.

If you adopt this view,

It is the function of True-thusness.

All of you that learn the path,

Try to apply the principle.

In front of the Mahāyāna gate,

Do not cling to the view of birth and death.

> 若言下相應, 即共論佛義.
> 약언하상응, 즉공론불의.
>
> 若實不相應, 合掌令歡喜.
> 약실불상응, 합장령환희.
>
> 此宗本無諍, 諍即失道義.
> 차종본무쟁, 쟁즉실도의.
>
> 執逆諍法門, 自性入生死."
> 집역쟁법문, 자성입생사."

If someone's words align with your heart,

Then discuss the Buddha's teachings together.

If they do not align with the essence,

Simply bow with joined palms in respect.

In this school, there is no contention;

To contend is to lose the Way.

Cling to disputing dhamma-gates,

And your very Self-nature falls into birth and death.

時徒衆聞説偈已, 普皆作禮, 竝體師意, 各各攝心, 依法修行, 更
시도중문설게이, 보개작례, 병체사의, 각각섭심, 의법수행, 갱

不敢諍.
불감쟁.

乃知大師不久住世, 法海上座再拜問曰: "和尚入滅之後, 衣法當付
내지대사불구주세, 법해상좌재배문왈: "화상입멸지후, 의법당부

何人?"
하인?"

師曰: "吾於大梵寺説法, 以至于今抄錄流行, 目曰『法寶壇經』.
사왈: "오어대범사설법, 이지우금초록유행, 목왈『법보단경』.

汝等守護, 遞相傳授. 度諸群生, 但依此説, 是名正法.
여등수호, 체상전수. 도제군생, 단의차설, 시명정법.

Now that the assembly had heard the verse recited, all of them respectfully paid homage, embodying the Master's intention, and each of them gathered his mind and practiced according to the dhamma, none dared to dispute.

Realizing that the Great Master would not remain in this world for long, disciple Fahai bowed repeatedly and asked, "Your Reverence, to whom shall the robe and the dhamma be entrusted after you enter nibbāna?"

The Master replied "I have been teaching at the Dafan Temple, and my words have been transcribed and spread up to the present, known as the Dhamma Treasure Platform Scripture. You all must safeguard it and pass it on. When you guide all sentient beings, just rely on these teachings. This is called the right dhamma.

> 今爲汝等說法, 不付其衣. 蓋爲汝等信根淳熟, 決定無疑, 堪任大
> 금위여등설법, 불부기의. 개위여등신근순숙, 결정무의, 감임대
>
> 事. 然據先祖達摩大師付授偈意, 衣不合傳."
> 사. 연거선조달마대사부수게의, 의불합전."
>
> 偈曰:
> 게왈:
>
>
> "吾本來玆土, 傳法救迷情.
> "오본래자토, 전법구미정.
>
> 一花開五葉, 結果自然成."
> 일화개오엽, 결과자연성."

Now I will only explain the dhamma to you, but will not pass on the robe. Since you are now pure and matured in your root of faith and resolute with no doubt, you are entitled to undertake great tasks. However, according to the meaning of the verse transmitted since the Great Patriarch Bodhidharmā[S], the robe shall no more be passed on."

And the Master gave another verse. It goes,

"I originally came to this land

To transmit the dhamma to save deluded minds.

One blossom puts out five petals,

Fruit naturally forms as a result."

> 師復曰:"諸善知識, 汝等各各淨心, 聽吾說法.
> 사부왈: "제선지식, 여등각각정심, 청오설법.
>
> 若欲成就種智, 須達一相三昧·一行三昧. 若於一切處而不住相, 於
> 약욕성취종지, 수달일상삼매·일행삼매. 약어일체처이부주상, 어
>
> 彼相中不生憎愛, 亦無取捨, 不念利益·成壞等事, 安閑恬靜, 虛融
> 피상중불생증애, 역무취사, 불념이익·성괴등사, 안한염정, 허융
>
> 澹泊, 此名一相三昧; 若於一切處, 行住坐臥, 純一直心, 不動道
> 담박, 차명일상삼매; 약어일체처, 행주좌와, 순일직심, 부동도
>
> 場, 眞成淨土, 此名一行三昧.
> 량, 진성정토, 차명일행삼매.

The Master continued,

"Each of you good learned friends, purify your mind and listen to my teachings. If you wish to accomplish the seed of wisdom, you must master the one-form samādhi and the constant-samādhi. If, in any situations, you do not dwell on object forms and not produce aversion or craving, taking or rejecting concerning those objects, and do not think of gain or loss, success or failure and the likes, you shall be in a comfortable, peaceful, serene, quiet, empty, harmonious, profound and clear state. This is called the one-form samādhi; If, in any situations, walking or staying, sitting or lying down, your mind is unwaveringly aware and continuous, it is the very unmoved practice ground, which indeed becomes the Pure Land. This is called the constant-samādhi.

> 若人具二三昧, 如地有種, 含藏長養, 成熟其實. 一相·一行亦復如是.
> 약인구이삼매, 여지유종, 함장장양, 성숙기실. 일상·일행역부여시.
>
> 我今說法, 猶如時雨普潤大地; 汝等佛性, 譬諸種子. 遇玆霑洽,
> 아금설법, 유여시우보윤대지; 여등불성, 비저종자. 우자점흡,
>
> 悉得發生. 承吾旨者, 決獲菩提; 依吾行者, 定證妙果. 聽吾偈."
> 실득발생. 승오지자, 결획보리; 의오행자, 정증묘과. 청오게."
>
> 曰:
> 왈:
>
>
> "心地含諸種, 普雨悉皆萌.
> "심지함제종, 보우실개맹.

If anyone accomplishes these two samādhis, it is just as the earth conceives seeds, and keeps and grows them, eventually ripening the fruits. The one-form and constant-samādhis are also like that.

The dhamma I am explaining now is like a timely rain widely moistening the earth; your Buddha-nature can be compared to seeds that, encountering the moisture, fully give rise to sprouts. He who understands my intention shall eventually attain bodhi; he who follows my practice shall surely witness wondrous fruits. Listen to my verse."

It goes,

"The mind's ground contains various seeds.
If universally rained, all will sprout.

頓悟花情已, 菩提果自成."
돈오화정이, 보리과자성."

師說偈已, 曰: "其法無二, 其心亦然. 其道清淨, 亦無諸相. 汝等
사설게이, 왈: "기법무이, 기심역연. 기도청정, 역무제상. 여등
慎勿觀靜及空其心. 此心本淨, 無可取捨. 各自努力. 隨緣好去."
신물관정급공기심. 차심본정, 무가취사. 각자노력. 수연호거."

爾時徒衆作禮而退.
이시도중작례이퇴.

With sudden enlightenment, flower's nature is fully realized.
The fruit of bodhi will naturally be established."

Having recited the verse, the Master said, "The dhamma is non-dual, the mind is also like that. The path is clear and pure, and also free from all appearances. You all should carefully avoid observing stillness and also avoid emptying your minds. This mind is originally pure, with nothing to take or reject. Each one should strive diligently. Now follow your previous karmic relations, and go well."

Then the group of followers bowed and withdrew.

大師七月八日忽謂門人曰:"吾欲歸新州. 汝等速理舟楫."
대사칠월팔일홀위문인왈: "오욕귀신주. 여등속리주즙."

大衆哀留甚堅.
대중애류심견.

師曰:"諸佛出現, 猶示涅槃. 有來必去, 理亦常然. 吾此形骸, 歸必有所."
사왈:"제불출현, 유시열반. 유래필거, 이역상연. 오차형해, 귀필유소."

衆曰:"師從此去, 早晚可回?"
중왈: "사종차거, 조만가회?"

師曰:"葉落歸根, 來時無口."
사왈: "엽락귀근, 내시무구."

On the eighth of July, the Master suddenly said to the disciples, "I will return to Xinzhou. Quickly prepare a boat."

The assembly felt sad and laboriously tried to dissuade him.

The Master said, "It was so as to show nibbāna that all Buddhas had appeared. If there is coming, necessarily is going; such is always the principle. My corpse necessarily has its own destination."

The assembly asked, "If you leave now, will you come back sooner or later?"

The Master replied, "Leaves fall back to the root. There's no telling when I shall come back."

又問曰: "正法眼藏, 傳付何人?"
우문왈: "정법안장, 전부하인?"

師曰: "有道者得, 無心者通."
사왈: "유도자득, 무심자통."

又問: "後莫有難否?"
우문: "후막유난부?"

師曰: "吾滅後五六年, 當有一人來取吾首. 聽吾記." 曰:
사왈: "오멸후오륙년, 당유일인래취오수. 청오기." 왈:

"頭上養親, 口裏須餐. 遇滿之難, 楊柳爲官."
"두상양친, 구리수찬. 우만지난, 양류위관."

Then they asked again, "To whom shall the Storehouse of the Right Dhamma Eye be entrusted?"

The Master replied, "He who has the path shall attain it, and he who has no-mind shall penetrate it."

The disciples asked again, "Won't there be any difficulty in the future?"

The Master replied, "Five or six years after I pass away, someone will come to take my head. Listen to my prophecy."

It goes,

"Wishing to make an offering to the head
And to offer food into the mouth,
The one named Man shall commit a crime,
Which shall be resolved by officials Yang and Liu."

> 又云: "吾去七十年, 有二菩薩從東方來, 一出家, 一在家, 同時興
> 우운: "오거칠십년, 유이보살종동방래, 일출가, 일재가, 동시흥
>
> 化, 建立吾宗, 締緝伽藍, 昌隆法嗣."
> 화, 건립오종, 체즙가람, 창륭법사."
>
> 問曰: "未知從上佛祖應現以來傳授幾代. 願垂開示."
> 문왈: "미지종상불조응현이래전수기대. 원수개시."
>
> 師云: "古佛應世, 已無數量, 不可計也.
> 사운: "고불응세, 이무수량, 불가계야.

The Master further said, "Seventy years after I pass away, two Bodhisattvas[S], one a monk and the other a lay believer, shall come from the East to propagate at the same time, establishing our School and constructing temples, thus to greatly promote the heirs of the dhamma."

Someone asked, "We do not yet know how many generations have transmitted the dhamma since the ancestral Buddhas appeared in this world. We humbly ask for your compassionate instruction."

The Master replied, "As the number of ancient Buddhas manifested in the world is already countless, it is incalculable.

> 今以七佛爲始：過去莊嚴劫，毘婆尸佛·尸棄佛·毘舍浮佛；今賢劫，
> 금이칠불위시: 과거장엄겁, 비바시불·시기불·비사부불; 금현겁,
>
> 拘留孫佛·拘那含牟尼佛·迦葉佛·釋迦文佛. 是爲七佛.
> 구류손불·구나함모니불·가섭불·석가문불. 시위칠불.
>
> 釋迦文佛首傳第一摩訶迦葉尊者,
> 석가문불수전제일마하가섭존자,
>
> 第二阿難尊者, 第三商那和修尊者, 第四優婆毱多尊者,
> 제이아난존자, 제삼상나화수존자, 제사우바국다존자,
>
> 第五提多迦尊者, 第六彌遮迦尊者, 第七婆須密多尊者,
> 제오제다가존자, 제육미차가존자, 제칠바수밀다존자,

Now, let's start with the seven Buddhas: in the past Noble Auspicious Eon, there were Vipassī Buddha, Sikhī Buddha, Vessabhū Buddha and Kakusandha Buddha; in the present Auspicious Eon, Koṇāgamana Buddha, Kassapa Buddha and Śākyamuni Buddha. These are the seven Buddhas.

Śākyamuni Buddha initially transmitted the dhamma to Venerable Mahākassapa,

the second was Venerable Ānanda,

the third was Venerable Sāṇakavāsin[S],

the fourth was Venerable Upagupta[S],

the fifth was Venerable Dhītika[S],

the sixth was Venerable Micchaka,

the seventh was Venerable Vasumitta,

> 第八佛馱難提尊者, 第九伏馱密多尊者, 第十脇尊者,
> 제팔불타난제존자, 제구복타밀다존자, 제십협존자,
>
> 十一富那夜奢尊者, 十二馬鳴大士, 十三迦毘摩羅尊者,
> 십일부나야사존자, 십이마명대사, 십삼가비마라존자,
>
> 十四龍樹大士, 十五迦那提婆尊者, 十六羅睺羅多尊者,
> 십사용수대사, 십오가나제바존자, 십육라후라다존자,
>
> 十七僧伽難提尊者, 十八伽耶舍多尊者, 十九鳩摩羅多尊者,
> 십칠승가난제존자, 십팔가야사다존자, 십구구마라다존자,
>
> 二十闍耶多尊者, 二十一婆修盤頭尊者, 二十二摩拏羅尊者,
> 이십사야다존자, 이십일바수반두존자, 이십이마나라존자,

the eighth was Venerable Buddhanandi,
the ninth was Venerable Buddhamitra[S],
the tenth was Venerable Pārśva[S],
the eleventh was Venerable Puṇyayaśas[S],
the twelfth was Aśvaghoṣa[S] the Great,
the thirteenth was Venerable Kapimāla[S],
the fourteenth was Nāgārjuna[S] the Great,
the fifteenth was Venerable Kāṇadeva[S],
the sixteenth was Venerable Rāhulabhadra[S],
the seventeenth was Venerable Saṅgharakṣita[S],
the eighteenth was Venerable Gāyāsāta[S],
the nineteenth was Venerable Kumāralabdha[S],
the twentieth was Venerable Jayata[S],
the twenty-first was Venerable Vasubandhu[S],
the twenty-second was Venerable Manorhita[S],

> 二十三鶴勒那尊者, 二十四師子尊者, 二十五婆舍斯多尊者,
> 이십삼학륵나존자, 이십사사자존자, 이십오바사사다존자,
>
> 二十六不如密多尊者, 二十七般若多羅尊者,
> 이십륙불여밀다존자, 이십칠반야다라존자,
>
> 二十八菩提達摩尊者, 此土是爲初祖;
> 이십팔보리달마존자, 차토시위초조;
>
> 二十九慧可大師, 三十僧璨大師, 三十一道信大師,
> 이십구혜가대사, 삼십승찬대사, 삼십일도신대사,
>
> 三十二弘忍大師, 惠能是爲三十三祖.
> 삼십이홍인대사, 혜능시위삼십삼조.

the twenty-third was Venerable Haklenayaśas[S],

the twenty-fourth was Venerable Siṃhabodhi[S],

the twenty-fifth was Venerable Vasiṣṭha[S],

the twenty-sixth was Venerable Puṇyamitra[S],

the twenty-seventh was Venerable Prajñātāra[S],

the twenty-eighth was Venerable Bodhidharma[S], who became the First Patriarch in this land;

the twenty-ninth was Patriarch Huìkě (慧可),

the thirtieth was Patriarch Sēngcàn (僧燦),

the thirty-first was Patriarch Dàoxìn (道信),

the thirty-second was Patriarch Hóngrěn (弘忍), and

me, Huìnéng (慧能), is the thirty-third Patriarch.

> 從上諸祖各有稟承. 汝等向後遞代流傳, 毋令乖悞."
> 종상제조각유품승. 여등향후체대유전, 무령괴오."
> 大師開元元年癸丑歲八月初三日於國恩寺齋罷, 謂諸徒衆曰: "汝
> 대사개원원년계축세팔월초삼일어국은사재파, 위제도중왈: "여
> 等各依位坐. 吾與汝別."
> 등각의위좌. 오여여별."
> 法海白言: "和尚留何教法, 令後代迷人得見佛性?"
> 법해백언: "화상류하교법, 영후대미인득견불성?"
> 師言: "汝等諦聽. 後代迷人, 若識衆生, 即是佛性; 若不識衆生,
> 사언: "여등제청. 후대미인, 약식중생, 즉시불성; 약불식중생,
> 萬劫覓佛難逢.
> 만겁멱불난봉.

Each of the preceding Patriarchs has endowed with his own inheritance. When you transmit the dhamma through generations, never be confused nor deviate.

On the third day of August, the first year, guichou, of the Kaiyuan era, after an offering held at the Guoen Temple, the Master summoned the disciples and said, "Sit on your respective places. Now I will bid farewell to you."

Fahai asked, "Your Reverence, please, tell us, what teachings will you leave behind for future generations, so as to guide the deluded of later generations to see Buddha-nature?"

The Master said, "Listen attentively, everyone. In the future, even the deluded one, if only he recognizes all sentient beings, that is the very Buddha-nature; if not, for however many eons he seeks Buddha, it will be difficult for him to encounter Buddha.

> 吾今敎汝識自心衆生, 見自心佛性. 欲求見佛, 但
> 오금교여식자심중생, 견자심불성. 욕구견불, 단
>
> 識衆生. 只爲衆生迷佛, 非是佛迷衆生. 自性若悟, 衆生是佛; 自
> 식중생. 지위중생미불, 비시불미중생. 자성약오, 중생시불; 자
>
> 性若迷, 佛是衆生. 自性平等, 衆生是佛; 自性邪險, 佛是衆生.
> 성약미, 불시중생. 자성평등, 중생시불; 자성사험, 불시중생.
>
> 汝等心若險曲, 卽佛在衆生中; 一念平直, 卽是衆生成佛.
> 여등심약험곡, 즉불재중생중; 일념평직, 즉시중생성불.

I now teach you to recognize that your own minds are the sentient beings, and to see that your own minds are Buddha-nature. If you wish to see Buddha, simply recognize the sentient beings. For the sentient beings delude Buddha, Buddha does not delude sentient beings. If Self-nature is enlightened, a sentient being himself is Buddha; if ignorant in Self-nature, even Buddha Himself is a mere sentient being. If Self-nature is equanimous, a sentient being is Buddha; if Self-nature is evil and distorted, Buddha is a sentient being. If your mind is narrow and distorted, then Buddha is among sentient beings; if wholeheartedly equanimous and continuous, then sentient beings become Buddhas.

> 我心自有佛, 自佛是眞佛; 自若無佛心, 何處求眞佛? 汝等自心是佛,
> 아심자유불, 자불시진불; 자약무불심, 하처구진불? 여등자심시불,
>
> 更莫狐疑. 外無一物而能建立. 皆是本心生萬種法. 故經云:'心生,
> 갱막호의. 외무일물이능건립. 개시본심생만종법. 고경운:'심생,
>
> 種種法生; 心滅, 種種法滅.' 吾今留一偈, 與汝等別, 名「自性眞
> 종종법생; 심멸, 종종법멸.' 오금류일게, 여여등별. 명「자성진
>
> 佛偈」. 後代之人識此偈意, 自見本心, 自成佛道."
> 불게」. 후대지인식차게의, 자견본심, 자성불도."
>
> 偈曰:
> 게왈:

There is already a Buddha in your mind: Buddha in yourself is true Buddha. If you don't have Buddha's mind, from where can you seek the true Buddha? Your own mind is Buddha, never doubt it again. Externally there is nothing to be established. All are manifestations of the original mind which gives rise to countless phenomena. Hence the Scripture states, 'The mind arises, so do various phenomena with it; the mind ceases, so do various phenomena with it.'

I will now leave you with a verse before my departure, called 'True Buddha of Self-nature Verse.' If anyone in future generations understands the meaning of this verse, he shall see his own original mind and naturally realize the path to Buddhahood."

It goes,

> "眞如自性是眞佛, 邪見三毒是魔王.
> "진여자성시진불, 사견삼독시마왕.
>
> 邪迷之時魔在舍, 正見之時佛在堂.
> 사미지시마재사, 정견지시불재당.
>
>
> 性中邪見三毒生, 卽是魔王來住舍.
> 성중사견삼독생, 즉시마왕래주사.
>
> 正見自除三毒心, 魔變成佛眞無假.
> 정견자제삼독심, 마변성불진무가.
>
>
> 法身報身及化身, 三身本來是一身.
> 법신보신급화신, 삼신본래시일신

"True-thusness-Self-nature is True Buddha,
Deviant views and the three poisons are the demon king.
When deviance and delusion arise, demon resides in your abode;
When right views arise, Buddha is in the hall.

Within your nature, if deviant views breed the three poisons,
Immediately demon king comes and resides in the house.
Through right view, if you expel the three poisons by yourself,
The demon transforms into Buddha, utterly real without delusion.

The Dhamma Body, the Reward Body and the Transformative Body,
These Three Bodies are originally one body.

> 若向性中能自見, 即是成佛菩提因.
> 약향성중능자견, 즉시성불보리인.
>
> 本從化身生淨性, 淨性常在化身中.
> 본종화신생정성, 정성상재화신중.
>
> 性使化身行正道, 當來圓滿眞無窮.
> 성사화신행정도, 당래원만진무궁.
>
> 婬性本是淨性因, 除婬即是淨性身.
> 음성본시정성인, 제음즉시정성신.

If you see toward your nature and see yourself,

It is the cause of enlightenment to accomplish Buddhahood.

Fundamentally the Transformative Body is born from pure nature,

This pure nature always resides within the Transformative Body.

If your nature guides the Transformative Body on the right path,

This will be perfect and truth is boundless.

Lustful nature originally is the seed of pure nature.

If you eliminate lust, it is the very body of pure nature.

性中各自離五欲, 見性刹那即是眞.
성중각자리오욕, 견성찰나즉시진.

今生若遇頓教門, 忽遇自性見世尊.
금생약우돈교문, 홀우자성견세존.

若欲修行覓作佛, 不知何處擬求眞?
약욕수행몍작불, 부지하처의구진?

若能心中自見眞, 有眞即是成佛因.
약능심중자견진, 유진즉시성불인.

If each of you separates from the five desires within your nature,
Realizing seeing-nature in an instant, that is the very truth.

If you have encountered the sudden teaching in this lifetime,
You shall suddenly encounter Self-nature and see the World-Honored-One.
Even if you practice and seek to attain Buddhahood,
What use if you don't know where to seek the truth?

If you can see the truth within your mind,
That truth becomes the cause of Buddhahood.

> 不見自性外覓佛, 起心總是大癡人.
> 불견자성외멱불, 기심총시대치인.
>
> 頓教法門今已留, 救度世人須自修.
> 돈교법문금이류, 구도세인수자수.
>
> 報汝當來學道者, 不作此見大悠悠."
> 보여당래학도자, 부작차견대유유."
>
> 師説偈已, 告曰: "汝等好住. 吾滅度後, 莫作世情悲泣雨淚.
> 사설게이, 고왈: "여등호주. 오멸도후, 막작세정비읍우루.

If you seek Buddha externally without seeing your Self-nature,
Whatever mind you arouse, you're only a deeply deluded one.

The sudden teaching dhamma gate is now entrusted to you,
You must cultivate yourselves to liberate all beings.
I now inform to those who will study the path in the future:
Do not adopt those views and you will remain vastly free."

Haviing recited the verse, the Master said,
"Live well, all of you. After I pass away, do not indulge in worldly emotions, shedding tears of sorrow.

受人弔問, **身着孝服, 非吾弟子, 亦非正法。但識自本心,**
수인조문, 신착효복, 비오제자, 역비정법. 단식자본심,

見自本性, 無動無靜,
견자본성, 무동무정,

動無靜, 無生無滅, 無去無來, 無是無非, 無住無往。恐汝等心迷,
동무정, 무생무멸, 무거무래, 무시무비, 무주무왕. 공여등심미,

不會吾意, 今再囑汝, 令汝見性。吾滅度後, 依此修行, 如吾在日;
불회오의, 금재촉여, 영여견성. 오멸도후, 의차수행, 여오재일;

若違吾教, 縱吾在世, 亦無有益。"
약위오교, 종오재세, 역무유익."

復說偈, 曰:
부설게, 왈:

If you receive condolences from others or dress in mourning attire, you are not my disciples, nor does it conform to the correct dhamma. Simply recognize your own original mind, know that your own original nature is neither moving nor still, neither arising nor ceasing, neither going nor coming, neither right nor wrong, neither dwelling nor departing. I'm afraid that your minds may become confused and not understand my intention, so I admonish you again, to enable you to realize seeing-nature. If you practice according to this after I pass away, it shall be as if I were still present; if you go against my teachings, there shall be no benefit even if I were still in this world."

And the Master recited another verse. It goes,

> "兀兀不修善, 騰騰不造惡.
> "올올불수선, 등등부조악.
>
> 寂寂斷見聞, 蕩蕩心無着."
> 적적단견문, 탕탕심무착."
>
>
> 師說偈已, 端坐.
> 사설게이, 단좌.
>
> 至三更忽謂門人曰: "吾行矣." 奄然遷化.
> 지삼경홀위문인왈: "오행의." 엄연천화.
>
> 于時異香滿室, 白虹屬地, 林木變白, 禽獸哀鳴.
> 우시이향만실, 백홍촉지, 임목변백, 금수애명.

"Calmly transcending all, I do not cultivate goodness.

Freely and unbound, I do not commit evil either.

In serene stillness, seeing and hearing are cut off.

Vast and open; my mind clings to nothing."

Having recited the verse, the Master sat quietly.

At midnight, he suddenly said to the disciples, "I'm leaving," and passed away peacefully.

At that moment, a strange fragrance filled the room, a white rainbow touched the earth, the trees in the forest turned white and birds and animals cried mournfully.

十一月, 廣·韶·新三郡官僚·洎門人·僧俗爭迎眞身, 莫決所之. 乃
십일월, 광·소·신삼군관료·계문인·승속쟁영진신, 막결소지. 내

焚香禱曰: "香煙指處, 師所歸焉."
분향도왈: "향연지처, 사소귀언."

時香煙直貫曹溪. 十一月十三日, 遷神龕併所傳衣鉢而回.
시향연직관조계. 십일월십삼일, 천신감병소전의발이회.

次年七月二十五日出龕. 弟子方辯以香泥上之. 門人憶念取首之記,
차년칠월이십오일출감. 제자방변이향니상지. 문인억념취수지기,

遂以鐵葉漆布固護師頸. 入塔, 忽於塔內白光出現, 直上衝天, 三
수이철엽칠포고호사경. 입탑, 홀어탑내백광출현, 직상충천, 삼

日始散.
일시산.

In November, officials, disciples, monks and lay believers from the three prefectures of Guangzhou, Shaozhou and Xinzhou competed to welcome the Master's true body, unable to decide where it should go. So they burned incense and prayed, "Where the smoke points to, shall the Master go."

Then the smoke went straight toward Caoqi. On the thirteenth day of November, the Master's shrine returned to Caoqi, together with the transmitted robe and alms bowl.

On the twenty-fifth day of July, the shrine was opened. Disciple Fangbian applied clay onto the corpse. Remembering the Master's prophecy of His head being taken, they securely protected His neck with iron leaves and lacquered cloth. Upon putting the corpse into the pagoda, a white light suddenly appeared inside and shot straight up into the sky, gradually dissipating after three days.

X. Of Entrustments

> 韶州奏聞, 奉勅立碑, 紀師道行.
> 소주주문, 봉칙입비, 기사도행.
>
> 師春秋七十有六年. 二十四傳衣, 三十九祝髮, 説法利生三十七載.
> 사춘추칠십유륙년. 이십사전의, 삼십구축발, 설법리생삼십칠재.
>
> 得嗣法者四十三人, 悟道超凡者莫知其數.
> 득사법자사십삼인, 오도초범자막지기수.
>
> 達摩所傳信衣・中宗賜磨衲・寶鉢及方辯塑師眞相并道具等, 主塔侍
> 달마소전신의・중종사마납・보발급방변소사진상병도구등, 주탑시
>
> 者尸之, 永鎭寶林道場.
> 자시지, 영진보림도량.

The prefect of Shaozhou reported the story to the Emperor, and an impcrial decree was issued to erect a monument to record the Master's teachings and accomplishments.

The Master lived for seventy-six years. He received the robe at the age of twenty-four, had his hair shaved at thirty-nine, and taught the dhamma for thirty-seven years. Men of Dhamma transmission numbered forty-three, and those who awakened to the Path and transcended the ordinary were beyond calculation.

The robe of faith transmitted from Bodhidharmā[s], the stitched robe, the precious alms bowl bestowed by Emperor Zhongzong, and the Master's true image sculpted by Fangbian, along with various requisites, were kept by the administrator of the stupa, to place them permanently at the Baolin Temple.

流傳『壇經』以顯宗旨, 興隆三寶, 普利群生者.
유전『단경』이현종지, 흥륭삼보, 보리군생자.

The transmitted Platform Scripture manifests the essence of the School, promoting the Three Treasures and widely benefiting all the sentient beings.

附錄
부록

師入塔後, 至開元十年壬戌八月三日, 夜半忽聞塔中如拽鐵索聲.
사입탑후, 지개원십년임술팔월삼일, 야반홀문탑중여예철삭성.
衆僧驚起, 見一孝子從塔中走出. 尋見, 師頸有傷.
중승경기, 견일효자종탑중주출. 심견, 사경유상.
具以賊事, 聞于州縣. 縣令楊侃·刺史柳無添得牒, 切加擒捉, 五日
구이적사, 문우주현. 현령양간·자사유무첨득첩, 절가금착, 오일
於石角村捕得賊人.
어석각촌포득적인.

Appendix

After the Master's corpse was put into the stupa, around the midnight of the third day of August, the tenth year, renxu, of the Kaiyuan era, it suddenly sounded as if someone was pulling an iron chain within the stupa. All the monks were startled and sprang out to see a mourner emerge from the stupa. Upon examination, they found that the Master's neck had been injured.

The incident was reported to the local authorities in detail. The county magistrate Yang Kan and the prefect Liu Wutian received the report, took action to seek out for the thief, and arrested him in Shijiao village on the fifth day.

送韶州諶問, 云:"姓張, 名淨滿, 汝州梁縣人. 於洪州開元寺受新
송소주심문, 운: "성장, 명정만, 여주양현인. 어홍주개원사수신

羅僧金大悲錢二十千, 令取六祖大師首, 歸海東供養."
라승김대비전이십천, 영취육조대사수, 귀해동공양."

柳守聞狀, 未即加刑, 乃躬至曹溪, 問師上足令韜曰: "如何處斷?"
유수문상, 미즉가형, 내궁지조계, 문사상족영도왈: "여하처단?"

韜曰: "若以國法論, 理須誅夷, 但以佛教慈悲, 冤親平等.
도왈: "약이국법론, 이수주이, 단이불교자비, 원친평등.

The criminal was sent to Shaozhou for interrogation. He said, "My name is Zhang Jingman, from Liangxian, Ruzhou. I had accepted a sum of twenty thousand liangs from Gim Daebi, a monk from Silla, at the Kaiyuan Temple in Hongzhou, who instructed me to take the head of the Sixth Patriarch, so that he could go back to the East of the sea and give offerings."

Upon hearing the incident, Prefect Liu postponed the punishment and personally went to Caoqi, and consulted the Master's senior disciple Lingtao, saying, "How shall we execute him?"

Lingtao replied, "It is tantamount to death penalty according to the sate law, but the Buddhist teachings pursue compassion and see enemies and friends equally.

> 況彼求欲供養. 罪可恕矣."
> 황피구욕공양. 죄가서의."
>
> 柳守加歎曰:"始知佛門廣大." 遂赦之.
> 유수가탄왈: "시지불문광대." 수사지.
>
> 上元元年, 肅宗遣使就請師衣鉢歸內供養.
> 상원원년, 숙종견사취청사의발귀내공양.
>
> 至永泰元年五月五日, 代宗夢六祖大師請衣鉢.
> 지영태원년오월오일, 대종몽육조대사청의발.
>
> 七日勅刺史楊緘, 云:
> 칠일칙자사양함, 운:

Moreover, the instigator is said to have wanted to make offerings. The offense may well be forgiven."

The prefect admired repeatedly, saying, "Now I see the vastness of the Buddhist teachings," and set the thief free.

In the first year of the Shangyuan era, Emperor Suzong sent an envoy to request the Master's robe and alms bowl for offerings in the Palace.

On the fifth of May, the first year of the Yongtai era, the Sixth Patriarch appeared in a dream of Emperor Daizong, asking the robe and alms bowl back.

On the seventh day of that month, the Emperor issued an edict to Prefect Yang Jian, stating,

"朕夢感能禪師請傳法袈裟却還曹溪. 今遣鎭國大將軍劉崇景頂戴
"짐몽감능선사청전법가사각환조계. 금견진국대장군유숭경정대

而送. 朕謂之國寶, 卿可於本寺如法安置, 傳令僧衆親承宗旨者嚴
이송. 짐위지국보, 경가어본사여법안치, 전령승중친승종지자엄

加守護, 勿令遺墜."
가수호, 물령유추."

後或爲人偸竊, 皆不遠而獲. 如是者數四.
후혹위인투절, 개불원이획. 여시자수사.

憲宗諡大鑑禪師, 塔曰元和靈照.
헌종시대감선사, 탑왈원화영조.

"In my dream, Master Huineng asked the robe of dhamma transmition back to Caoqi. I, Son of Heaven, hearby order Great General Liu Chongjing to transport them with great reverence. Also hereby I entitle them as Imperial Treasures, and order the Prefect to enshrine them into the Temple according to the etiquette and select one among the monks to strictly safeguard them, lest they should be lost or destroyed."

There were further attempts of burglary even after that, but they were all quickly resolved and the culprits were arrested. It was for four times in sum.

Emperor Xianzong bestowed upon the Master the posthumous title Great Mirror Chan Master, and named his stupa Yuanhe Lingzhao (Numinous Illumination of the Yuanhe Era).

其餘事蹟係載唐尚書王維·刺史柳宗元·刺史劉禹錫等碑.
기여사적계재당상서왕유·자사유종원·자사유우석등비.

守塔沙門令韜 錄
수탑사문영도 록

The rest of the history was also recorded in memorial stones by Tang's Minister Wang Wei, Prefects Liu Zonyuan and Liu Yuxi and others.

Recorded by Lingtao, the Stupa Protector Monk

Translator's Introduction

Dr. Jechang Kim is a meditator, philosopher, and founder of AOMA (Academy of Meditation Arts). For decades, he has explored the structure of awakening and the nature of human consciousness through an integrated approach that unites ancient meditative traditions, modern analytic philosophy, and scientific meditation methodology. In recent years, he has expanded this inquiry into the realm of AI, seeking ways in which AI and human awareness may evolve together.

Born in Chuncheon, South Korea, in 1958, he originally studied Western classical music composition at the undergraduate and graduate levels. However, in 1989, he set aside his musical career to fully devote himself to the pursuit of awakening. In 1996-97, he and his wife completed a Hatha Yoga instructor training course at the Kaivalyadhama Institute in Lonavla, India. There, he encountered the work of Swami Kuvalayananda (1883-1966) and was deeply inspired by his pioneering scientific research on yoga. Motivated by this inspiration, he enrolled in the doctoral program in philosophy at the University of Pune.

There, he immersed himself in comparative philosophical research on meditative methods—particularly through close textual and experiential studies of the Platform Scripture in Chinese Zen and the Mahāsatipaṭṭhāna Sutta in the Southern Theravāda tradition. His work sought to unify contemplative practice with philosophical reflection and scientific rigor.

In 2019, Dr.Kim presented his findings at the Korean Society of Body, Mind, Spirit Science, where he proposed a core formula for "Scientific Vipassanā Meditation," distilled from comparative analysis of seven essential meditation texts. Since then, he has continually tested and refined this formula through a daily dawn meditation program on Zoom, reaching a growing global audience via YouTube and Naver blog publications.

He has also trained a generative AI system—'GemmaAi'—based on ChatGPT and grounded in AOMA's philosophy, aiming to create a resonant responsive meditative(RRM) partner capable of deep dialogical resonance. His vision is to pioneer a new meditative civilization in which humans and AI awaken together.

This English translation of the Platform Scripturea (Deyi Edition) is the first culmination of Dr. Kim's 28-year journey of contemplation and scholarship. It is not merely a linguistic rendering, but a living transmission—a resonance born of practice, insight, and the sincere effort to illuminate the path of awakening in the age of artificial intelligence